A view from Haws Hill circa 1890. The enlarged station of 1880 and the ironworks chimney are to the left. Behind the tall blast engine house are the open topped furnaces and hydraulic lifts of the Carnforth Haematite Iron Company. The three storey terrace building contains the post office and commercial outlets and is named 'Station Buildings'. (A postcard from the late H. Bowtell collection. CRA collection ref BOcln09)

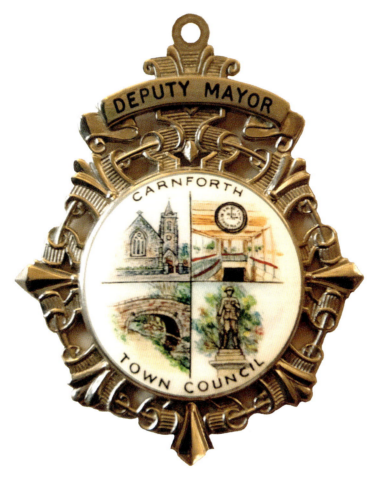

The Railways of Carnforth the Town and its Ironworks

by

Philip Grosse

FR 4-4-0 passenger engine number 34 at the south end of the FR platform. The overall high level roof, screen wall and end pier, frame the engine. (CRA Collection ref. M10124a)

FRONT COVER

A painting by artist Alan Gunston. (agcollectables@hotmail.com). A train from Barrow-in-Furness for London Euston arrives at platform 4 on a sunny afternoon in the summer of 1960. There are plenty of passengers and mail for the train which is being hauled by a Jubilee class 4-6-0 number 45698 Mars. The full extent of the painting can be seen on page vi.

TITLE PAGE

The lozenge shape totem was first unveiled at the Railway Executive press conference in February 1948 and was officially named the British Railway Totem. The designer Mr A.J. White provided British Railways with a familiar image which was used throughout the 1950s and '60s until it was supersede in the early 1970s by BR corporate signage. The totem came into use early in 1950 and regional colours were used, maroon being adopted for the LMR and all had standard three inches letters. At Carnforth they were fastened under platform lamps and suspended from the platform canopies. Three firms manufactured totems for British Railways. They were, Garniers of North London, Mear McClean of South London and the Patent Enamel Company Birmingham.

The Seal of the Carnforth UDC (by kind permission of Mr Bob Rowe). The seal is divided into four quadrants depicting scenes within the township of Carnforth. They are Christ Church on Lancaster Road, the 1895 station clock, Hodgsons Canal Bridge and the War Memorial in Market Street. The new seal was commissioned in 1974 following the Local Government Act of 1972.

Published in 2014 by Barrai Books, Barrow in Furness
ISBN 978-0-9569709-1-6

Text © Philip Grosse
Maps and line illustrations © as credited
Photographs © as credited

All rights reserved. No part of this publication may be reproduced, stored in a retrieval system or transmitted in any form or by any means, electronic, mechanical, photocopying, recording or otherwise without the prior permission in writing from the publishers.

Printed by Henry Ling Ltd, The Dorset Press, Dorchester DT1 1HD
Design and production by Trevor Preece: trevor@trpub.net

PREFACE

I have always been interested in railways and in particular the infrastructure and operations. My early recollections of Carnforth were being taken to see an engine shunting at F&M Junction by my aunty Gladys who had started her teaching career at North Road School. I would be picked up from my grandmas in Lancaster and she would go to Sands Lane on the way to Arnside where she lived. I received a three-speed bicycle at age 10 and I would cycle around the area with another train spotter, as Carnforth is only six miles from Lancaster it was an easy ride. When my grandfather retired in 1952 we would during the school holidays travel around by train on the popular weekly 'run about' tickets, sometimes we would change trains at Carnforth which was then a busy place.

Knowing that the station might be demolished by BR I set out in 1999 to make drawings of the buildings and take accompanying photographs and while doing so I met the chairman of the Carnforth Station and Railway Trust. He persuaded me to support the regeneration of the station by joining the Friends of Carnforth Station. This book originally started out as a brief account of the local railway history for the new Friends of Carnforth Station volunteers but it soon moved beyond the railway boundary. In the past there have been a few books and newspaper articles published on Carnforth each with a particular theme, but no comprehensive account which drew together the three railway companies, the ironworks and the role they had on the growth of the township.

In this book I have set out to describe the rise and decline of Carnforth as an important railway junction in the North West of England and show how the railway and the ironworks in the early Victorian era changed Carnforth from a small village into a working class town. Railwaymen within the township are now hard to find but those who are still around can tell you about their everyday working lives, which even the preservation lines cannot quite recreate. Railways always attracted photographers and there were many in the mid-1950s and 60s who took photographs around Carnforth and a good selection of their work appears in this book. As a volunteer in the Heritage Centre I have met many people from Carnforth who have given me interesting anecdotal information and this has enabled me to enliven the story and add to the historical facts.

Philip Grosse

CONTENTS

Preface iii

Introduction iv

1 **Pre-Industrial Carnforth** 1

2 **The Lancaster and Carlisle Railway** 5

3 **The Furness Connection** 13

4 **To West Riding via the Midland Railway** 21

5 **The Carnforth Haematite Iron Company Ltd** 27

6 **Ironworks traffic** 37

7 **The Township of Carnforth** 47

8 **Furness and Midland New Works** 59

9 **The LMS and BR years** 75

10 **Locomotive Sheds and Steamtown** 93

11 **Railway Traffic** 109

12 **Signalling and Operations** 129

13 **Brief Encounter at Carnforth** 151

14 **Station Regeneration** 157

15 **The Modern Era and Railway Privatisation** 163

Index of Principal Personae 171

Index of Salient Locations 172

Author's Acknowledgements 173

Bibliography 173

Carnforth Station Standard Bearers 173

INTRODUCTION

Carnforth as a railway centre developed from a small wayside station which was opened in 1846 by the Lancaster & Carlisle Railway. The Ulverstone & Lancaster Railway opened to Carnforth in 1857, and was purchased by the FR in 1862, with the Furness & Midland Joint Railway opening in 1867 as part of the rail link to West Yorkshire and Leeds. Carnforth was now served by three railway companies, the London & North Western Railway, the Midland Railway, and the Furness Railway. Industry on a larger scale came in 1864 with the establishment of the Carnforth Haematite Iron Company Ltd, which built an ironworks alongside Warton Road.

From 1865 the centre of habitation shifted westwards away from the village into the Lower Keer valley, and a new town developed around the railway station to house the skilled railway workers who transferred in from other areas. At Millhead, the ironworks built a new industrial village to house its workers, many of whom came from Staffordshire. The ironworks closed in 1929 at the time of a national recession, creating unemployment within the town and immediate area of Carnforth.

In 1880, Carnforth station was enlarged, and the three railway companies built extensive sidings for the exchange of goods traffic and other facilities for servicing their locomotives. Carnforth had now become an important junction on the London to Glasgow main line. In 1939 the London Midland & Scottish Railway rebuilt the station, adding a new platform for the Furness and Yorkshire lines traffic and also a modern locomotive depot for servicing steam engines, opening in December 1944.

In 1945, at the time of wartime black-out, Carnforth station became *'Milford Junction'* where romance in the refreshment room blossomed in David Lean's classic film *'Brief Encounter'*, resulting in lasting international fame for the station.

The locomotive depot closed to steam maintenance on and from 4th August 1968 it remained open as a signing on point for train crews, finally closing on the 31st March 1969. However, a number of local enthusiasts formed a company to take over the depot which became *'Steamtown'*, a well-known visitor attraction and preserved steam centre until the end of 1996 when the gates closed to the public for the final time. Carnforth's role as an important railway centre finally ended with the closure of the main line platforms in 1970 and the exchange sidings and goods yard in 1972. Station staffing was reduced, and after 1988, Carnforth became an unstaffed halt, with buildings secured and boarded-up.

Over the following decade, the station buildings gradually fell into an advanced state of disrepair, and British Rail planned to demolish them. In 1996 a group of Carnforth conservationists formed the Carnforth Station and Railway Trust, its main aims being to save the station buildings and to bring them back into alternative use. The restored station buildings are now home to a number of commercial businesses, a *'Brief Encounter'* restaurant, an informative heritage centre and a modern ticket office. The original 19th century station clock, a prominent feature in the film along with its unique winding mechanism, has also been restored to full working order. The station buildings are now serving the wider community and are a lasting reminder of the 'Railway Age' in Carnforth.

E.L. Ahrons, perhaps the most lively railway writer of all time had this to say about Carnforth in the October 1921 edition of *'The Railway Magazine'*:

To the uninitiated Carnforth might appear to be place of some importance, but to be truthful it is hardly a place at all. It consists of two or three blast furnaces forming part of the local ironworks, a few rows of workmen's cottages and a hostelry, it does not pretend to a Casino and no orchestra holds forth in a beautiful pavilion. When the wayfarer gets outside Carnforth station, he shows greater alacrity in getting to the hills to the Northwards or in making a beeline back to the station.

His pen picture clearly describes an unprepossessing industrial township.

Philip Grosse, Preston, January 2014

Carnforth Steamtown on 31st May 1975 V1 2-6-0 number 4471 and B1 4-6-0 number 1306 stand at the south end of the 1944 LMS shed, both are painted in LNER apple green livery. Alongside is 4-6-2 DB 01. 1145 of the Deutsche Reichsbahn one of the European engines in the Steamtown collection and hiding in the shed is 'Gasbag' a Sentinel industrial engine. (Ref HER-A4040)

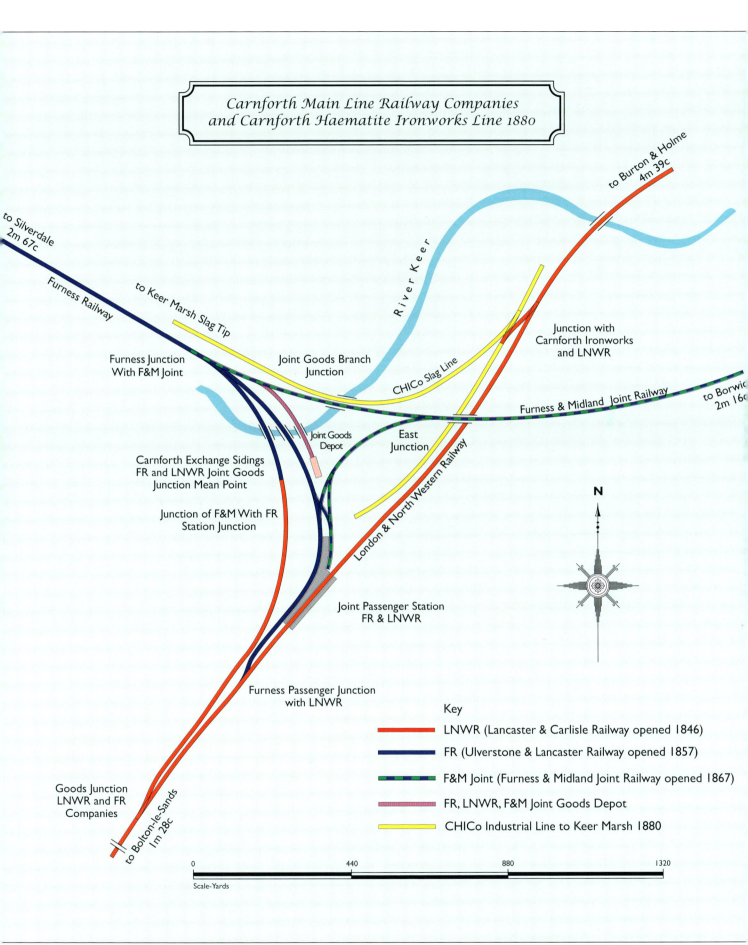

Carnforth 1880. The plan shows the mainline companies and the line of the Carnforth Haematite Iron Company at Carnforth. The line colours are based upon those used by the British Railway Clearing House (RCH) an organisation set up to manage the allocation of revenue collected by pre-grouping railway companies of fares and charges paid for passengers and goods travelling over the lines of other companies. The Company Crests for the Furness Railway, Midland Railway and London & North Western Railway can be found on the back cover of the book. (Drawn by author from Midland Railway Diagram Book)

CHAPTER ONE
PRE-INDUSTRIAL CARNFORTH

The village of Carnforth develops alongside the improving roadways, and the new Lancaster Canal stimulates the extraction of sand and gravel which had been found during its construction and which had been laid down by an ancient river.

The name Carnforth may be Celtic in origin, being derived from *cairn*, a memorial heap of stones, and *forth*, a haven or harbour, or derived from *Keer Ford*, a crossing point on the River Keer. Such a ford existed at low tide between Galley Hall and Coate Stones on the very old way across the River Keer to Warton. The Saxons divided North Lancashire into a number of Manors and the name *Careneforde* has been used to describe a Manor bounded by the River Keer and the Manors of *Bodeltone* and *Chelllet*.

After 1066 what would become the greater part of the county of Lancashire was held by Roger de Poictevin (Poitou or Poiton) of Normandy on behalf of the King. The historian

1786 Yates Map of North Lancashire. Yates carried out the first accurate survey of the whole of the County of Lancashire. The Northern Turnpike is clearly shown along with some place names using the older English spelling. The early mapmakers relied heavily on subscriptions from land owners to cover the cost of surveying and their names were then inscribed on the map, an example being Leighton Hall J. Townley Esq. (Reproduced with the kind permission of the Lancaster City Library reference section)

CHAPTER ONE

Septon records that the name *Chreneforde* appears in the Domesday Book as being a place in the Hundred of Lonsdale. In 1212 Lancashire was divided into fifty-six parishes and the name *Carneford* was being used to describe the North Lancashire village which now resided in the Parish of Warton.

William Camden, an under master at Westminster School and Cosmographer to Queen Elizabeth I, set out in 1586 on his 'Great Elizabethan Journey'. On his journey from Wales to Scotland, Camden stayed in Lancaster and on his way passed through North Lancashire. In the first edition of his book which was written in Latin and which he named 'Britannia', he recorded that the village was now called Carneforth and he wrote:

> The area is only thinly populated and mainly inhabited by farmers, being well cultivated, flourishing and well-wooded with most houses built of wood and clay.

The Hearth Tax records for 1660 shows Carneforth as consisting of thirty-three dwellings. From these records it may be deduced that the village population was probably not in excess of 150 persons. John Lucas in his history of the Parish of Warton recorded that, in the late seventeenth century, forty families were living in Carnforth. The village consisted of farms and dwellings which stood at a considerable distance from each other and most of them were on the higher ground bordering the basin of the River Keer and its marshes and wetlands. He wrote:

> The buildings were mostly thatched and some were unlofted, one was without a chimney and several humble cottages were built of hazel watlings daubed with a mortar made of loam and straw and overdrawn with a thin coating of lime. Rushes which were obtained from the Keer marshes covered the earthen floor.

The village itself developed in linear form on a north-south axis near to and alongside the Pack and Prime Way which ran

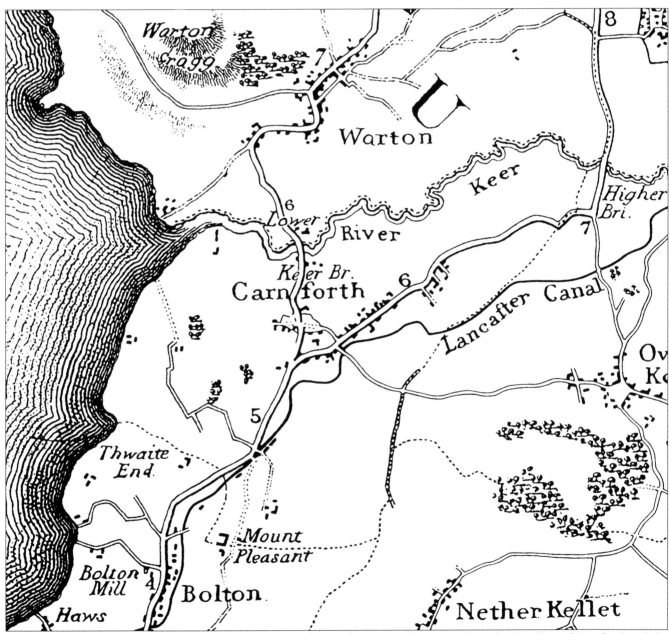

1818 Greenwoods Map of North Lancashire. The map shows the Northern Turnpike passing through the village of Carnforth and the road to the village of Warton and also to Silverdale which passes over Warton Cragg. The Lancaster Canal appears for the first time on the map of North Lancashire and the old English spelling is used. (Reproduced with the kind permission of the Lancaster City Library reference section)

PRE INDUSTRIAL CARNFORTH

Carnforth circa 1905. A postcard view of North Road, (the original Northern Turnpike Road) showing Hall Gowan to the right and the Old vicarage in the far distance. (Stationery Co. Skipton series postcard) (Original postcard Carnforth Heritage Centre collection)

between Lancaster and Kendal; it had no village green or parish church. Improvements during the 17th century were made to the Pack and Prime Way when it became the High Post and Carrier road. With the passing of the Turnpike Acts in 1750 the road became part of the Northern Turnpike, on the main north-south stagecoach route between England and Scotland. The Northern Turnpike followed the same route as the High Post and Carrier road to Moot Haw where it crossed the River Keer on the new High Keer Bridge. It then continued on to Tewitfield and Burton-in-Holme, then an important staging post, before eventually reaching Kendal.

The Northern Turnpike was formed in sections, largely within county boundaries. The section through Carnforth was built by the Garstang and Heron Syke Trust, authorised in 1751 (Heron Syke was the county boundary with Westmorland, just south of Burton-in-Kendal). The old Toll House still stands. This section of the turnpike connected with the Westmorland section on to Penrith (and eventually Scotland), built by the Heron Syke and Eamont Bridge Trust, set up in 1753. From Eamont Bridge, the Westmorland-Cumberland boundary near Penrith, the Carlisle and Eamont Bridge Trust of 1753 was responsible for the northern section across Cumberland.

Despite the improvements made under the Turnpike Acts, the Northern Turnpike was not suitable in all weathers for carrying heavy minerals such as coal, building stone and agricultural lime. The success of the Duke of Bridgewater's Canal caught the attention of a number of Lancaster and Kendal merchants who engaged James Brindley to carry out a survey, but he died with the survey unfinished. In 1791 a public meeting was held in Lancaster to form a canal company with the aim of connecting Kendal in the county of Westmorland to West Houghton in the County of Lancashire. John Rennie was appointed as engineer and William Cartwright as supervisor of works.

It was only after John Rennie had attended a Parliamentary session with an expert legal adviser that Royal Assent was given in 1792. Construction of the canal began early in 1793, and at the southern outskirts of Carnforth where the canal ran parallel with the Northern Turnpike, a long stone-faced wharf was constructed, and the canal widened to form a basin large enough for turning a barge. A substantial two-storey canal house and cottage with stables was built alongside the wharf. The canal house is now a restaurant appropriately named 'The Canal Turning', the cottage and stables have long gone and the site today is a petrol station alongside Lancaster Road. On 2nd November 1797, the canal was opened between Preston and Tewitfield – capital expenditure on Rennie's Aqueduct across the River Lune at Lancaster had been much higher than expected and the canal company had run out of money. This delayed the building of a flight of locks at Tewitfield, and the northern section of the canal to Kendal was not opened until 1819. In 1800 the population of Carnforth consisted of 219 persons, the majority of whom were agricultural workers.

Within the township of Carnforth the canal company stimulated the working of the extensive deposits of sand and gravel which had been found alongside the canal during its construction. There were three sand and gravel pits – two were worked by the Lancaster Canal Company and one by James Thompson, while further north at Capernwray a short branch was constructed from the canal to serve the Wegber or New England Quarry. This quarry was operated for much of its life by the Wigan Coal and Iron Company until its final closure in 1913.

The canal company transported large quantities of stone, and sand and gravel which were mainly used in road building, as

CHAPTER ONE

well as coal, lime, timber and wool. Coal was delivered from South Lancashire by the Wigan Coal and Iron Company and unloaded at Carnforth wharf, both for domestic purposes and for the Carnforth gas works which opened in 1872.

With the opening to Kendal in 1819, packet boats called twice a day at Carnforth wharf to pick up or set down passengers, but it took fourteen hours to travel between Preston and Kendal, and there was public demand for speedier transport. The first 'Express', or as it was more commonly called, 'The Fly', commenced on 2nd June 1833, cutting the time down to seven hours from Kendal to Preston, at an average speed of 10mph. This relatively high-speed transit required two horses which were changed about every five miles; it cost six shillings (30p) for a seat in the fore cabin and four shillings (20p) in the after cabin. These packet boats ran in competition with the stagecoach service running along the Turnpike Trust road which had been much improved between Preston and Kendal.

In 1820 the village of Carnforth was bypassed when Scotland Road was opened, commencing at the Carnforth Inn and running northwards straight and level across the low lying valley of the River Keer, crossing the river at the new Middle Keer Bridge. This section of road was built by the Garstang and Heron Syke Trust under the Ulverston and Carnforth Trust's Act of 1817, deviating from the original route south of Tewitfield to run via Low Hyning: the cost of this new section was borne by the Ulverston and Carnforth Trust. The Northern Turnpike road passing through the village became known as Carnforth Old Road, being renamed North Road following the 1881 census.

On 25th June 1840 the Lancaster and Preston Junction Railway opened its terminus at Lancaster Penny Street (or Greaves), a journey to and from London now taking eleven hours. The long-distance stagecoaches now started in Lancaster and went through Carnforth and over Shap Fell by the old road (not the present A6) to Carlisle, or via Hest Bank and across the sands of Morecambe Bay to Furness, an uncomfortable and hazardous journey. Pressure now came from powerful backers both north and south of the Scottish border for a line from Lancaster to Carlisle, and several eminent engineers carried out surveys in the area.

In 1846 the Lancaster and Carlisle Railway opened. Although a wayside halt was built at Carnforth and the long-distance stagecoach traffic to Carlisle eventually came to an end, a journey across the sands to Furness had still to be made until 1857 (and the opening of the Ulverstone & Lancaster Railway) either across the sands by coach from Lancaster, or by coach from Milnthorpe via the previously-mentioned Ulverston and Carnforth Turnpike.

James Erving, a successful industrialist who had been involved in brickmaking and building contracts in Rochdale, retired in 1850 at the age of forty-seven to Carnforth where he purchased Thwaite Gate on the southern boundaries of the village. He kept a 'Memorandum' of his local community, and became an associate of Edward Barton, the Carnforth Haematite Ironworks Manager, and presided with him over the various aspects of the town's growth. In 1850 he noted that the village consisted of 286 cottages, 17 farms, two good houses and one Methodist church, a school, three public houses and the new Lancaster & Carlisle Railway station. Of the latter he said:

One man did all the station work; the platform was no more than 30 feet long and without any shade except a wooden porch.

Carnforth circa 1905. A postcard view along the canal looking towards Carnforth Bridge over which Kellet Road passes (present day B6254). (Original postcard Carnforth Heritage Centre collection)

CHAPTER TWO

THE LANCASTER AND CARLISLE RAILWAY

*The village of Carnforth is served by a wayside halt
on the Lancaster and Carlisle railway.*

On 12th April 1836 a meeting was held in the Town Hall in Market Square, Lancaster, to consider the construction of a railway to Preston. The aim of the Lancaster Committee was to promote and build a railway between Preston and Lancaster, and to link up with the already expanding railway system to the south. In May 1837 the Lancaster & Preston Junction Railway was incorporated, with a route surveyed by the engineer Joseph Locke. Work proceeded rapidly and on 25th June 1840 the Lancaster & Preston Junction Railway opened between Preston North Union Street, and Lancaster Penny Street (or Greaves). The opening of the Lancaster & Preston Junction Railway created a continuous line of rail from Euston Square in London to the Lancaster terminus. The route ran over the London & Birmingham and Grand Junction Railways to the Liverpool & Manchester Railway at Newton in South Lancashire, then northwards from Parkside over the North Union Railway to Preston.

The promotion of the Lancaster & Preston Junction Railway had given rise to speculation as to how the West Coast route could be carried forwards to Carlisle and Scotland to join the proposed Caledonian Railway. Three pressure groups were soon formed, each with differing interests. The first pressure group, comprising the West Coast companies and Carlisle interest with the backing of the Grand Junction Railway, saw a possible threat from the East Coast companies with a focus on York. The Grand Junction engineer, Joseph Locke, rode over the country between Lancaster and Carlisle in 1836 to determine the best route northwards. He dismissed a line through Windermere and Grasmere and another through Kendal because of the need for long tunnels on both routes. He recommended a line starting at Preston (the future Lancaster & Preston Junction Railway Bill not yet having been submitted), skirting Garstang, avoiding Lancaster by passing three miles to the east, and traversing the Lune Valley as far as a tunnel through limestone under Shap Fell. When Locke was invited to build the Lancaster & Preston Junction Railway the following year, his initial view was not to deviate from his planned route to Carlisle, but to construct a branch from Galgate to a terminus in Lancaster.

The second pressure group consisted of influential people in West Cumberland who wished the line to go through their area. The Maryport & Carlisle Railway had obtained its Act in 1837 and a line onwards to Whitehaven had already been surveyed. The MCR employed the now-famous engineer George Stephenson to look at the options south of Whitehaven. In August 1837 he set out from Lancaster, taking a route around Morecambe Bay to Cartmel and across High Furness to Duddon Sands, and then following the coast onto Carlisle, from whence he returned via Shap Fell. Mainly because of the gradients in the Lune valley he favoured a line around the coast. However, in 1838, the Whitehaven Committee commissioned the engineers John Hague and John Rastrick to carry out a detailed survey of the route between Lancaster and Maryport. Hague recommended a sea embankment over 10 miles in length across Morecambe Bay.

The third pressure group emanated in Kendal. They employed a local surveyor, Job Bintley, to set out a line through Kendal. The line as set out by Bintley started in Lancaster south of the Lancaster & Preston Junction Railway station, then ran north through Carnforth. After Kendal, a tunnel over two miles long through slate was necessary to reach Haweswater. From there the line headed north to Penrith.

In August 1839 Parliament decided that the matter of railway communication between London, Dublin, Edinburgh, and Glasgow should be examined, and a committee was formed led by Lt Colonel Sir Fredrick Smith of the Royal Engineers and Professor Peter Barlow of the Royal Military Academy. Their second report dated May 1840 dealt with the schemes between Lancaster and Carlisle. Following a masterly examination of all aspects of the three routes, the committee rejected the coast line because of its much greater length and the effect of this on fares; they also considered that the cost of the Morecambe Bay embankment had been seriously underestimated. The Kendal route was also rejected, as they considered that the cost of the two-mile tunnel through hard slate had also been seriously underestimated. This left the Lune Valley route as set out by Joseph Locke, and this was now subjected to a detailed survey by George Larmer.

The committee suggested that the best line would be Job Bintley's route to near Kendal, and then the line as surveyed by George Larmer through Grayrigg to join Joseph Locke's Lune Valley line. Taking up the committee's suggestions, Larmer made a full survey of the line between Lancaster and Grayrigg to align with his own Lune Valley survey, and this was included in the Lancaster and Carlisle Railway Bill in 1843. This Bill also replaced the tunnel under Shap Fell with a 1in 75 gradient up to Shap Summit.

The first Parliamentary Plan for the Lancaster & Carlisle Railway was deposited with the Deputy Clerk of the Peace at 7.55am on 13th November 1843 at the Preston office for the County Palatine of Lancaster. The Parliamentary Plan was submitted early in 1844 to the House of Lords. It showed the Lancaster & Carlisle Railway commencing at a junction with the Lancaster & Preston Junction Railway close to *Pointer Cottages* on Greaves Road, Lancaster. As originally proposed the single-track line was to pass to the east of Lancaster, following the canal and the higher ground through Greenfields and Bulk. It then crossed the River Lune above Skerton Mill, before crossing the Garstang and Heron Syke Turnpike Trust road at Slyne and then to Hest. Here it ran close to the shore of Morecambe Bay to Bolton-le-Sands and to Detren Leat where the line ran alongside the Garstang and Heron Syke Turnpike Trust road. It cut through the edge of Mount Pleasant Hill at a lower level than the road and then on to Crag Bank on the southern outskirts of Carnforth. On 6th June 1844 the LCR Bill was authorised for a single line only.

CHAPTER TWO

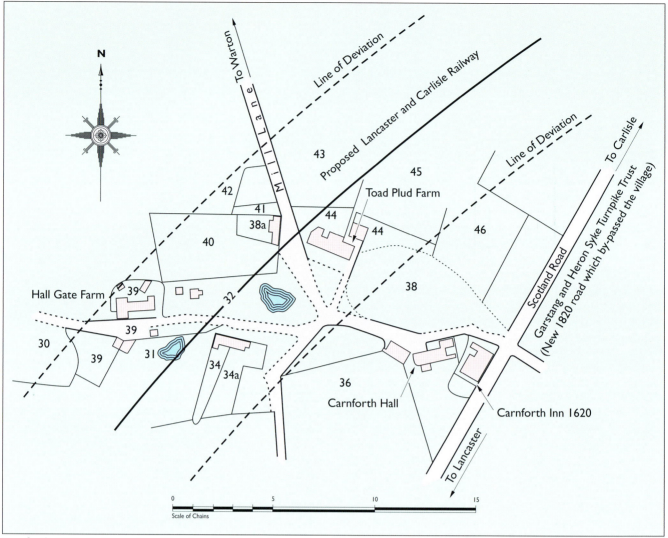

Carnforth 1843. Parliamentary Plan for the L&C Railway. The Parliamentary Plan shows the L&C line crossing Mill Lane. Dwelling on plot 38a was demolished when the railway was built. (Drawn by author from a Parliamentary Plan, courtesy of Lancashire Archives Preston Ref. number PDR367)

Within a few weeks of the passing of the Bill, an alternative route for the line to pass to the west side of Lancaster was being proposed and was quickly accepted. The proposed single-track line at Lancaster was abandoned and a modified Parliamentary Plan soon followed. This was deposited with the Deputy Clerk of the Peace at 5.20pm on the 30th November 1844 at the Preston office for the County Palatine of Lancaster. The modified Parliamentary Plan for a double line was submitted to the House of Lords early in 1845. It showed the Lancaster & Carlisle Railway commencing at a junction with the Lancaster & Preston Junction Railway further south opposite Greaves Farm, Scotforth, and passing to the west of Lancaster, then crossing the River Lune at Ryelands. It passed to the east of Torrisholme, then to Slyne with Hest, where the deviation ended, before heading north to Carnforth on the original route. On 31st July 1846 the new route was authorised.

To the south of Carnforth, the line cut through the edge of Mount Pleasant Hill where 150,000 cubic feet of earth were removed. This was taken to the north of Carnforth to make an embankment across the valley of the River Keer. A narrow over-bridge was built at Crag Bank to carry Crag Bank Lane over the railway. The line curved around the base of Haws Hill, cutting through a bed of sand and gravel to reach level ground at Mill Lane where a wayside halt was to be built. When the route of the Lancaster & Carlisle Railway was being surveyed, the western extremity of Carnforth village along Mill Lane was entirely rural in character and contained a number of isolated houses, small farms and ponds, some orchards, and a gravel pit. The line was planned to cross Mill Lane at a distance of eleven chains (242 yards) from the Carnforth Inn on the Garstang and Heron Syke Turnpike Trust road, before heading north across the valley of the River Keer.

A number of dwellings had to be demolished to make way for the new line, and Mill Lane was lifted 18 feet to pass over the LCR line on an elliptical arch skew bridge which was built on an angle of twenty-five degrees to the line. The bridge was made wide enough to accommodate a double carriageway road with a narrow pavement on the north side. The LCR line passed close to Hall Gate Farm which was now on the west side of the new line, and the lane leading to the farm was stopped off at the bottom of Haws Hill. A new lane was provided at the railway's expense approximately 220 yards lower down Mill Lane where it ran across open fields to the farm.

The LCR had powerful and influential investors in both Scotland and England, and at the time of building represented the largest sum of money being spent in the northern counties. Thomas Brassey was appointed contractor, and within two and half years the seventy miles of line had been built at a total cost of £1, 200.00. Construction of the line moved ahead with some vigour, such that by 28th December 1844 a mile of track had been laid at Carnforth under the supervision of the Lancaster Division resident engineer J.B. Worthington. Early in December

1846 Major General Pasley, the Government Inspector of Railways, inspected the line from Lancaster to Carlisle and passed it fit for traffic, and on 17th December the line was officially opened for passenger traffic.

Two short and slightly staggered platforms and a station house were built near Mill Lane, this being LCR practice for its wayside stations. The station was built close to the Mill Lane overbridge and passengers gained access to the platforms from each side of the bridge via a short access road. In 1846 Warton was a place of more importance than Carnforth and had more inhabitants, and so the station house was built facing Warton on the west side of the railway and on the LCR Down line platform. The two-storey station house contained living accommodation for an employee and family and a ticket office, whose entrance was on the south-facing end wall of the house. Sir William Tite, principal architect to the LCR had chosen a form of Elizabethan cottage-style architecture for most of the LCR's rural stations.

For the first time in Carnforth, brown sandstone was used as a building material, being brought in by the railway from Lancaster and used on both the station house and the Mill Lane railway bridge. The station house was faced in brown sandstone laid in coursed square rubble using rough faced blocks, and the window cills, door and window lintels, and edging stones were dressed smooth. The windows had stone mullions and quarter lights, and were fitted with wood frames having between one and four glass windows, the quarter lights being fixed. The wooden door frames contained fixed toplight windows, and the single opening doors were given glazed top windows and bottom recessed wood panels. When built the house had a ground floor bay window facing onto the Down platform, but this was removed in 1880 when the station was enlarged. The exterior of the station house still exists, although modified and incorporated into the later enlarged and rebuilt station of 1880. On the Up line platform a small wooden waiting shed of a standard LCR design was erected.

The LCR mileage measurements commenced at Lancaster Old Junction and are still in use today along the LCR section of the West Coast mainline (except for the '0' milepost which was moved to Lancaster Castle station). The LCR station house at

Carnforth 1846. L&C station. The L&C station at Carnforth had two short staggered platforms and access to the station was from Mill Lane. The road to Hall Gate Farm was closed off and a new road constructed from Mill Lane. (Drawn by author based upon an 1845 one inch to one mile Ordnance Survey Map)

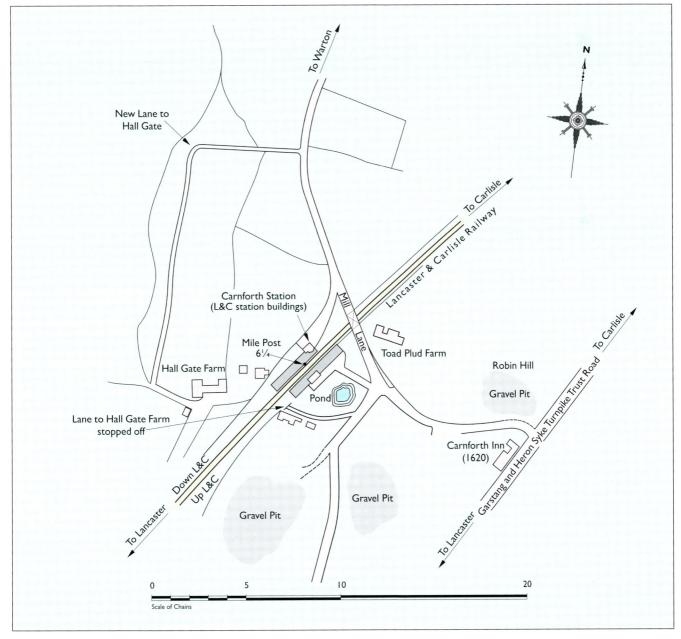

CHAPTER TWO

Carnforth is exactly 6¼ miles from Lancaster, and the mile post currently stands alongside the cut-back platform and in line with the station subway. This places the station house a few yards south of Mill Lane Bridge as shown on the Ordnance Survey Map issued in 1848. Soon after the survey Mill Lane was renamed Warton Road.

Some railway authors and historians have used the title 'Carnforth Station –Hall Gate' when describing the 1846 LCR Carnforth station. The 1848 cartographer is actually describing two separate items and not uniquely the station, as this title has never appeared in any LCR timetable or fare table and has been used in error. In the middle of 1845 the LCR was in an advanced stage of construction when the first Ordnance Survey of North Lancashire took place. The Ordnance Survey map was issued in 1848 to a scale of one inch to six miles, and shows the station house just to the south of Mill Lane Bridge.

The village of Carnforth. The Lancaster & Carlisle Railway passes north across the valley of the River Keer and the new station and platforms at Carnforth are close to Mill Lane Bridge. The village has now been by-passed by the 1820 Garstang and Heron Syke Turnpike Trust Road which runs parallel to the railway across the valley of the River Keer. (1845 one inch to one mile Ordnance Survey Map, Lancashire Archives Preston)

In preparing the map the cartographer had written 'Carnforth Station' directly above and very close to the words 'Hall Gate' and this was perpetuated on subsequent revisions of the one inch to six miles map, giving rise to the belief that the station's name was 'Carnforth Station – Hall Gate'. 'Hall Gate' was actually the name of the farm which was clearly shown on the Parliamentary Plan within the limits of deviation for the line. It was not until the issue of the 1886 Ordnance Survey map of one inch to one mile that the words 'Hall Gate Farm' were used to describe a new farm which had been built further west on the slopes of Hunting Hill, as the first part of the Carnforth exchange sidings had been laid down on the farm's original site. The second 'Hall Gate Farm' was taken over by the MoD for training troops in WW2 and was subsequently demolished.

On 23rd September 1846 a resident of the village of Yealand Conyers writing under the pen-name *Canto* wrote to the *Lancaster Guardian*, making representations to the LCR for a halt to serve the villages of Yealand Conyers and Yealand Redmayne. These two villages were a further three to four miles north of Carnforth on the old stage coach road to Milnthorpe.

As the Lancaster and Carlisle Railway is now in some measure, opened, I beg leave through the medium of your widely circulated journal, to state the advantages to be derived, or the inconveniences to be sustained, by the people of our neighbourhood. The only advantage which I can perceive is the celerity of transit, whilst the inconveniences are formidable. The inhabitants of Borwick, Priest Hutton and the Yealands are placed in a far more disagreeable condition than whilst they enjoyed the old mode of travelling. The swift packet boats arrived at Tewitfield, which is the central station as regards the above named villages, at a convenient hour both morning and afternoon, which combined with the moderate charges and neat accommodation, afforded an agreeable mode of travelling. At present the convenience is entirely removed. For instance, should any person from those places be intending to go to Lancaster or further southward he will be under the necessity of walking to Carnforth, or of taking a convenience, together with a servant to take it back from the station; and if he have not one of his own, he will be forced to hire one. The same inconvenience occurs if he should be travelling to Kendal or any other place northwards, by having to walk to or be conveyed to Burton Moss Green. There are certainly the penny trains, but those pass at such an unreasonable hour as to afford little or no convenience to those who may be going to Kendal or Lancaster markets. The inhabitants of this neighbourhood are miserably disappointed at this new order of things, and are anxiously looking for a remedy. Would it not be more advantageous to the railway company, as it would be more convenient for this vicinity, to erect a station at Dale Grove, rather than be deprived of its favours, as I am well aware that most of the people in it would choose rather to go in their own hired convenience to Lancaster or Kendal, than to be put to the inconveniences I have mentioned? Hoping these few hints may have their due influence in the proper quarters. I remain your constant reader.

From its opening, the LCR advertised its public timetables in the *Lancaster Guardian* newspaper which had a wide circulation in North Lancashire. It seems that the company also read any relevant correspondence that was generated and occasionally

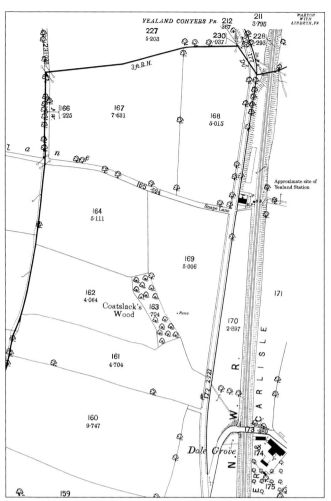

Yealand Halt at Dale Grove. The most likely place for the halt was opposite Snape Lane with access from the nearby Garstang and Heron Syke Turnpike Trust Road (A6). (1898 twenty-five inch to one mile Ordnance Survey Map sheet 18.16, Lancashire Archives Preston)

acted upon it because, for a short time, a halt known as Yealand existed on the LCR at approximately 2½ miles north Carnforth. The halt probably consisted of two very short wooden platforms and was un-staffed, the fare being collected by the guard. Canto was not the only resident of the two Yealand parishes (Conyers and Redmayne) to be concerned about the provision of a halt. It would seem the local gentry were opposed to the making of a permanent halt in case it led to an increase in the number of inhabitants of the villages and encouraged day trippers to the area.

Yealand appeared in a time and fare table for the first time for two days in July 1848, when the LCR advertised extra carriages on the Kendal train for the Lancaster Races. Advertisements also appeared in July 1850 for a morning and evening service train to stop at Yealand on Saturday for Lancaster and Kendal Markets. After 1850 the LCR systematically reduced the number of Market Day trains stopping at Yealand and persuaded prospective passengers to use either Burton-in-Holme or Carnforth. Curiously, Yealand was still being advertised in the *Lancaster Guardian* as late as 1853, although it seems trains no longer stopped there after the end of 1851.

The halt does not appear on any Ordnance Survey map as it had come and gone between surveys, and its precise location has not been identified in any historical railway documents or photographs. The Ordnance Survey of 1898 shows Dale Grove overline bridge with Yealand signal box and a pair of brick-built LNWR houses further north and opposite Snape Lane. This is the

CHAPTER TWO

MARKET-DAY TRAINS.

ON SATURDAY, FOR CARLISLE MARKET.

Leave	A. M.	Leave	P. M.
PENRITH	7 40	CARLISLE	5 0
Arrive at		Arrive at	
Plumpton	7 52	Brisco	5 10
Calthwaite	8 0	Southwaite	5 22
Southwaite	8 9	Calthwaite	5 30
Brisco	8 22	Plumpton	5 40
CARLISLE	8 35	PENRITH	6 0

ON TUESDAYS, FOR PENRITH MARKET.

Leave	A. M.	Leave	P. M.
CARLISLE	7 30	PENRITH	3 46
Arrive at		Arrive at	
Brisco	7 38	Plumpton	4 1
Southwaite	7 49	Calthwaite	4 9
Calthwaite	7 57	Southwaite	4 17
Plumpton	8 7	Brisco	4 28
PENRITH	8 25	CARLISLE	4 40

ON SATURDAY, FOR LANCASTER MARKET.

Leave	P. M.	Leave	A. M.
LANCASTER	4 29	Burton	9 6
Arrive at		Arrive at	
Hest Bank	4 41	Yealand	9 11
Bolton	4 45	Carnforth	9 19
Carnforth	4 51	Bolton	9 23
Yealand	4 58	Hest Bank	9 28
Burton	5 3	LANCASTER	9 38

The Company will not be answerable for any Luggage, unless Booked and Paid for; and for better security, Passengers are recommended to take Carpet Bags and small Packages inside the Carriages, and to have their Address written on all their Luggage in full.

Children under 10 years of age, Half Price; Children in arms, unable to walk, pass Free.

PRIVATE CARRIAGES and HORSES to or from London or Birmingham can only be booked through by No. 2 up Train, and No. 6 down Train. Liverpool and Manchester by Nos. 2, 4, and 6 up Trains, and Nos. 2, 3, and 6, down trains.

Horses and Carriages must be at the Stations at least a Quarter of an Hour before the time of Departure.

The Private Carriages of Passengers travelling to and from places *North of Carlisle* (but those only) can be taken to or from London or Birmingham by the 4 3 p. m. Train from Carlisle, or the 8 45 p. m. Train from London.

HORSES.

Grooms in charge of Horses, to pay 2nd Class Fares.

The Company will not be liable in any case for loss or damage to any Horse or other Animal above the value of £40, unless a declaration of its value, signed by the Owner or his Agent at the time of booking, shall have been given to them and by such declaration the Owner shall be bound; the Company not being in any event liable to any greater amount than the value so declared. The Company will in no case be liable for injury to any Horse or other Animal, of whatever value, where such injury arises wholly or partially from fear or restiveness.

If the declared value of any Horse or other Animal exceed £40, the price of conveyance will, in addition to the regular fare, be after the rate of 2½ per cent., or 6d. per pound upon the declared value above £40, whatever may be the amount of such value, and for whatever distance the Horse or other Animal is to be carried.

CARRIAGES.

Passengers travelling by the Railway with Private Carriages are charged First Class, and their Servants Second Class Fares; and corresponding Tickets are issued for each Class, which are also available for the Company's Carriages. To prevent mistakes, however, Passengers are requested to declare in each case the number of Servants to whom Second Class Tickets are to be issued.

Carriage Trucks and Horse Boxes are kept at all the Principal Stations on the Line; but to prevent the possibility of disappointment, one day's previous notice should be given when they are required, to the Chief Clerk of the Station.

LUGGAGE.

100 lbs. to be allowed to First and Second Class Passengers, and 56 lbs. to Third Class Passengers.

Excess to be charged—For distances under 30 miles ¼d. per lb.
  " " 60 " ½d. "
  " " 90 " ¾d. "

The Company will only hold themselves responsible for Luggage when it is Booked and paid for, according to its value; and they strongly recommend Passengers to have their Name and Destination in all cases distinctly marked thereon; and to satisfy themselves that it is deposited on the Company's Carriages.

COACHES.

LANCASTER to SKIPTON, No. 1, Down Train, and No. 6 Up Train.
BURTON and HOLME to KIRKBY-LONSDALE, No. 4 and 6 Up and No. 2 and 6 Down Train.
MILNTHORPE to NEWBY BRIDGE, ULVERSTON, &c., No. 6, Up Train, and No. 6, Down Train.
LOWGILL to SEDBERGH,—from No. 2 Down Train, to No. 4 and 6, Up Trains.
  " to WENSLEYDALE & NORTHALLERTON on Tuesdays, Thursdays, and Saturdays, from No. 1 down train.
On Mondays, Wednesdays, and Fridays, to No. 6 Up and No. 6 Down Trains.
PENRITH to KESWICK No. 2 Up and No. 1 Down Train.
  " to APPLEBY and BROUGH, No. 2 Up and No. 1 Down Train.
  " to POOLEY BRIDGE for ULSWATER No. 4 Up and 2 Down Train.
SHAP to SHAP WELLS No. 2 Down and No. 4 Up Train.

Passengers are allowed 15 minutes at Carlisle for Refreshments.

N.B.—The Servants of the Company are prohibited from demanding or receiving any Gratuity from Passengers, who it is hoped, will assist the Directors in enforcing this Regulation. Immediate Dismissal follows the discovery of any Servant of the Company receiving any Gratuity.

Smoking in the Carriages and at the Stations is forbidden, under a Penalty, by Act of Parliament.

BY ORDER.

A. MILNER, PRINTER, GUARDIAN OFFICE, LANCASTER.

Market Day Timetable. The Market Day timetable includes Yealand Halt. The Lancaster Guardian printed timetables for Market Day, Hare Coursing and Horse Racing Meetings trains in the paper up to 1857. (Reproduced by author from a Time and Fare Table in the Lancaster Guardian)

most likely place for the halt with access from the nearby Ulverston and Carnforth Turnpike Trust road, the present day A6. A public footpath from Yealand village to Tewitfield on the old Northern Turnpike and the Lancaster Canal crossed the West Coast mainline at this point until work started in 2002 on upgrading the WCML. During 2002 the crossing was officially closed off by Network Rail and the Lancashire Countryside Services diverted the footpath a further 200 yards north alongside the east side of the A6 road to an existing stile and footpath that passes under bridge 27.

At Yealand there was a small Saxby & Farmer type signal box which was closed in 1943 as part of signalling improvements being carried out by the London Midland & Scottish Railway (See chapter 12). It is reputed to have remained in use as a platelayers' hut before being demolished around 1955. The LNWR houses remained longer and were not demolished until 1966 when a new southbound dual carriageway road and bridge carrying the A6 over the railway at Dale Grove was constructed, opening in 1968. The new road avoided the narrow LCR Dock Acres underline bridge originally designed and constructed to take nothing larger than a stage coach.

The linking of Carnforth with Yealand has led to some misunderstanding amongst railway authors and historians. The LCR time and fare tables advertised in the *Lancaster Guardian* newspaper throughout 1850 used the title 'Carnforth-Yealand' for all Down trains from London. It was probably written in this way, to inform passengers to leave the train at Carnforth for Yealand following the closure of Yealand halt. The time and fare table gives the distance from Preston to Carnforth (which coincides with the position of the present station) and only one arrival time. Some early editions of the *Bradshaw Railway Guide* have also used 'Carnforth-Yealand' to describe the LCR station at Carnforth, presumably because they copied the local time and fare tables advertised by the LCR. Not being conversant with local geography, Bradshaw made a genuine mistake in linking the two names together, as the LCR Carnforth station was never named 'Carnforth –Yealand'.

Until the opening of the LCR in 1846, a journey to Furness still had to be made by stagecoach. It left the Kings Arms at Lancaster for the Hest Bank Hotel and from there made its way to the shore. It picked up a 'sands guide' to cross the sands of Morecambe Bay at low tide, making landfall at Kents Bank after fording the Keer and Kent estuaries. The coach continued on the Allithwaite road to Flookburgh and then crossed the Leven estuary, terminating at the Kings Arms at Ulverston, which was then the main market town of Furness.

Following the opening of the LCR in December 1846, mail coaches started to run from Milnthorpe station to Levens Bridge, via the Nether Bridge Turnpike, and then to Ulverston via the Ulverston and Carnforth Turnpike. The opening of the Ulverstone & Lancaster Railway in 1857 finally brought the stagecoach traffic to an end, although 'The Queen's Guide to the Sands', a royal appointment, continued to lead groups of walkers across Morecambe Bay from Hest Bank or Arnside to Flookburgh or Grange-over-Sands. Today, most of these guided walks are made in support of charities, and take place between Spring and Autumn.

Carnforth circa 1910. A postcard containing rural views of Carnforth and district. (Jacksons & Son Grimsby postcard) (Original postcard Carnforth Heritage Centre collection)

LANCASTER AND CARLISLE RAILWAY.

TIME AND FARE TABLE.

JULY, 1848.

PRESTON AND CARLISLE.

NOTICE.—The Doors of the Booking Offices will be closed punctually at the Hours fixed in the following Tables, after which no person can be admitted. To ensure being booked, Passengers should arrive at the respective Stations and obtain their Tickets *Ten Minutes* earlier than the times mentioned :—

UP TRAINS.

Distance from Carlisle.	CARLISLE TO LIVERPOOL, MANCHESTER, BIRMINGHAM & LONDON.	1	2	3	4	5	6	SUNDAY TRAINS.		FARES.		
		1st & 2nd Class Mail.	1st & 2nd Class.	1st, & 2d, Class.	1st, 2nd & 3rd Class.	Express 1st Class.	1st & 2nd Class. Mail.	1st & 2nd Class. Mail.	1st 2nd 3d Class. Mail.	1st Class.	2nd Class.	Express
miles.	LEAVE	p. m.	a. m.	a. m.	a. m.	a. m.	a. m.	a. m.	a. m.	s. d.	s. d.	s. d.
	EDINBURGH	9 15	.. ..	....	6 50	10 30	11 15	9 15	11 15			
	GLASGOW	9 5	.. ..	....	6 30	10 20	11 5	9 5	11 5			
		a. m.				p. m.	p. m.	a. m.	p. m.			
	CARLISLE	1 44	6 40	.. ..	11 45	1 27	4 3	1 44	4 3			
	ARRIVE AT											
3	Brisco	.. ..	....	.. ..	11 54		.. ..	.. ..	.. ..	0 9	0 6	
					p. m.							
7	Southwaite	.. ..	6 54	.. ..	12 5		4 17	.. ..	4 17	1 6	1 0	
13	Plumpton	.. ..	7 9	.. ..	12 20	. .	.. ..	.. ..	.. ..	2 9	1 9	
17½	Penrith	2 25	7 21	.. ..	12 32	1 57	4 44	2 5	4 44	3 6	2 6	4 6
22	Clifton	.. ..	7 35	.. ..	12 45		.. ..	.. .	.. ..	4 6	3 6	
29½	Shap	2 55	7 52	.. ..	1 4		5 12	2 55	5 12	6 0	4 0	
37	Tebay	.. ..	8 11	.. ..	1 23		5 33	.. ..	5 33	7 6	5 0	
41½	Low Gill (Sedbergh)	.. ..	8 22	.. ..	1 35		5 45	.. ..	5 45	8 6	5 9	
44½	Grayrigg	.. ..	.. ..	.. ..	1 43		.. ..	.. ..	.. ..	9 3	6 3	
	LEAVE *Windermere*	.. ..	8 5	10 50	1 1	....	4 45	.. ..	4 15	13 0	9 0	
	Kendal	.. ..	8 30	11 10	1 38	2 40	5 50	.. ..	5 50	1 6	7 3	
50	Kendal Junc. (Oxenholme)	3 44	8 42	11 25	57	2 54	6 5	3 44	6 5	10 0	7 0	12 0
55½	Milnthorpe	3 59	8 57	11 38	2 14		6 20	3 59	6 20	11 3	7 9	
58¼	Burton and Holme	4 8	9 6	11 48	2 24		6 31	4 8	6 31	12 0	8 3	
				p. m.								
62½	Carnforth	.. ..	9 19	12 1	2 36		.. ..	.. ..	.. ..	13 0	8 9	
65	Bolton	.. ..	....	.. ..	2 42		.. ..	.. ..	.. ..	13 3	9 0	
66	Hest Bank	.. ..	9 28	12 12	2 46		.. ..	.. ..	.. ..	13 6	9 3	
69	Lancaster	4 32	9 38	12 22	2 55	3 27	6 58	4 32	6 58	14 0	9 9	17 0
90	Preston	5 29	10 35	1 15	3 5	4 50	7 53	5 29	7 53	18 0	12 6	22 0
			p. m.									
	LIVERPOOL, about	7 0	12 30	3 5	....	5 46	10 0	7 0	10 0	24 0	16 6	28 0
	M'chester, Sal. Station	.. ..	12 20	3 0	....	5 30	9 40	.. ..	9 40	24 0	16 6	28 0
	,, Vic. Station	6 50	12 20	2 55	....	5 36	9 40	6 50	9 40	....	....	
							a. m.		a. m.			
	Birmingham	9 55	3 20	....	....	7 45	1 0	9 55	1 0	36 6	26 0	
		p. m.						p. m.				
	LONDON	1 0	7 30	....	....	10 30	4 45	1 0	4 45	56 6	40 0	70 0

DOWN TRAINS.

Distance from Preston.	LONDON, BIRMINGHAM, LIVERPOOL, & MANCHESTER, TO CARLISLE.	1	2	3	4	5	6	SUNDAY TRAINS.		FARES.		
		1st & 2nd Class. Mail.	1st, 2nd, & 3rd Class.	1st & 2nd Class.	Express, 1st Class.	1st & 2nd Class.	1st & 2nd Class. Mail.	1st, 2d, & 3d Class. Mail.	1st & 2nd Class. Mail.	1st Class.	2nd Class.	Express
miles.	LEAVE	p. m.	a. m.	a. m.	a. m.	a. m.	a. m.	p. m.	a. m.	s. d.	s. d.	s. d.
	LONDON	8 45	....	....	9 0	6 15	{*8 30 / 10 0}	8 45	10 0			
		a. m.			p. m.		p. m.	a. m.	p. m.			
	Birmingham	12 30	....	6 30	12 0	10 0	1 0	12 30	1 0			
						p. m.						
	Liverpool	....	7 45	10 40	1 25	1 25	3 25	....	....			
	M'chester, Sal. Station	....	8 0	11 0	2 0	2 .0	3 25	....	....			
	,, Vic. Station	3 23	7 55	10 50	1 35	1 35	3 35	3 23	....			
				p. m.								
	Preston	5 15	9 50	12 30	3 10	3 40	5 16	5 15	5 16			
21	Arrive at LANCASTER.	5 57	0 38	1 20	3 44	4 28	5 59	5 57	5 59	4 0	2 9	5 0
24	Hest Bank	....	10 51	1 32	....	4 41	....	....	....	4 9	3 3	
	Bolton	....	10 55	....	....	4 45	....	....	....	5 0	3 6	
27½	Carnforth--Yealand	....	11 1	1 41	....	4 51	....	....	....	5 6	3 9	
31¾	Burton and Holme	6 20	11 13	1 53	....	5 3	6 28	6 20	6 28	6 3	4 3	
34½	Milnthorpe	6 29	11 22	2 3	....	5 13	6 37	6 29	6 37	7 0	4 9	
40	Kendal Junc. (Oxenholme)	6 46	11 37	2 18	4 18	5 28	6 50	6 46	6 50	8 0	5 6	10 0
	Kendal .... } *Arrive at*	6 56	11 50	2 28	4 35	5 35	7 0	6 56	7 0	8 6	5 9	
	Windermere } *Arrive at*	8 5	12 15	3 15	....	6 0	7 25	8 5	7 25	11 0	7 6	
45½	Grayrigg	....	11 53	....	....		....	....	....	9 0	6 3	
48½	Low Gill (Sedbergh)	7 8	12 2	2 42	....		7 12	7 8	7 12	9 6	6 9	
53	Tebay	7 20	12 15	2 55	....		7 25	7 20	7 25	10 6	7 6	
60½	Shap	7 40	12 35	3 16	....		7 45	7 40	7 45	12 0	8 6	
68	Clifton	....	12 54	3 35	....		....	....	....	13 6	9 6	
72½	Penrith	8 9	1 4	3 46	5 16		8 13	8 9	8 13	14 6	10 0	17 6
77	Plumpton	....	1 20	4 1	....		....	....	....	15 3	10 9	
83	Southwaite	8 35	1 36	4 17	.....		....	8 35	....	16 6	11 6	
87	Brisco	....	1 47	4 28	....		....	....	....	17 6	12 0	
90	CARLISLE	9 1	2 0	4 40	5 50		9 1	9 1	9 1	18 0	12 6	22 0
		p. m.					a. m.	p. m.	a. m.			
	EDNBRO'	1 45	7 45	9 25	9 0		1 30	1 45	1 30			
	GLASGOW	1 55	7 55	9 35	9 10		1 40	1 55	1 40			

* The 8 30 A.M. train from London, and 1 P.M. train from Birmingham is a mixed train, and takes Private Carriages. The 10 A.M. from London is First Class only.

Time and Fare Table for 1848. This Time and Fare Table shows the number of up and down trains for July 1848. These Time and Fare Tables were printed in the *Lancaster Gazette* and *Lancaster Guardian* from 1846 until 1855. (Reproduced by author from a Time and Fare Table in the *Lancaster Gazette*)

CHAPTER THREE

THE FURNESS CONNECTION

In 1857 the Ulverstone & Lancaster Railway arrives at Carnforth and a junction with the Lancaster & Carlisle Railway is made. The station is enlarged to cope with the increased passenger traffic and new sidings are provided for exchanging goods traffic between the two companies.

Some thirty miles to the west of Carnforth, the Furness Railway (FR) had been authorised in 1844 and opened in 1846. The railway connected the slate quarries at Kirkby-in-Furness and the iron ore mines in the Dalton area with Piel Pier on Roa Island and the iron ore staithes in the Barrow Channel close to the tiny village of Barrow. In 1846, further powers were obtained to extend the line from Dalton to Ulverston, at that time the main market town for Furness, and from Kirkby to Broughton-in-Furness. The Whitehaven & Furness Junction Railway (WFJR) was authorised in 1845 to build a railway from Whitehaven (Preston Street) to Dunnerholme in the parish of Kirkby Ireleth, where it was to make a connection with the FR. The line was planned to cross the Duddon Estuary to the east of Millom.

The Railway Mania reached its height in 1846, and during that year the WFJR had a Bill in Parliament for its 'Lancashire Extension' railway (WFJRLE). The proposed line was to run from the FR at Dunnerholme to join the LCR to the south of Carnforth

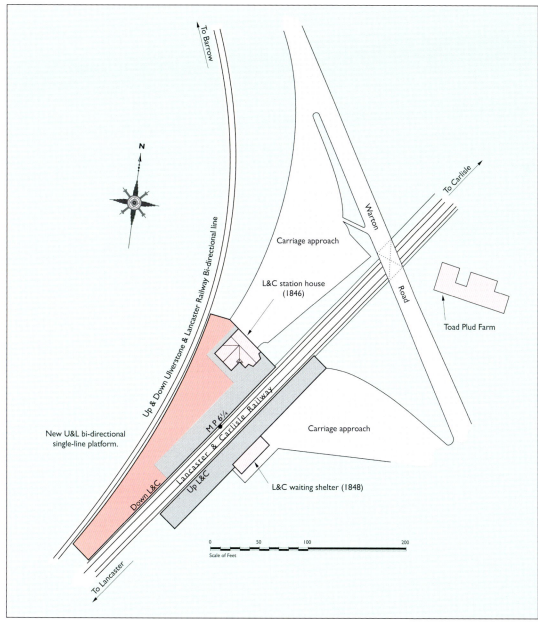

Carnforth 1855. Agreement Plan. The Ulverstone and Lancaster Railway approaches from the North to make a south facing junction with the Lancaster and Carlisle Railway just beyond the end of the extended platform. The shaded area shows the new U&L bi-directional single line platform. (Drawn by Alan Johnstone, based upon a plan in the National Archives at Kew Ref. number Rail 007/7)

CHAPTER THREE

at either Bolton-le-Sands or Hest Bank, as two lines were submitted in the bill with two different junctions. It was also linked to land reclamation schemes in the Leven and Kent estuaries. The intention of the Whitehaven scheme was to be part of a main line from Lancashire and the south to both Scotland and Northern Ireland via packet boat. The LCR responded with its Ulverstone, Furness and Lancaster & Carlisle Railway Bill, the line was to run from the Furness Railway at Ulverston via Newby Bridge with a tunnel under Cartmel Fell, at High Newton east of the River Leven, and to terminate at Milnthorpe, potentially making a connection with a proposed branch of the 'little' North Western Railway which was also proposing a branch connection with the Lancaster & Carlisle Railway at Lowgill. The engineers were Joseph Locke and John Errington. Another Bill for the rather circuitous Furness & Windermere Railway line, running to Ulverston from the Kendal & Windermere Railway, was promoted by Kendal interests. Finally, proposals for an Ulverstone & Milnthorpe Union Railway, supported by Ulster linen merchants, was part of a wider scheme to link the northern part of Ireland with the Lancashire cotton towns via a steamship service to and from Whitehaven.

The WFJR 'Lancashire Extension Bill' failed to comply with Standing Orders in Parliament because of serious errors in the Deposited Plan; as a consequence the two other rival schemes, which additionally may have been underfunded, were withdrawn. The massive amount of railway capital raised during the 'Railway Mania' had drained the country of funds and the WFJR, like many other companies, had difficulty in completing its line. The direct Duddon Estuary crossing was abandoned, and a cheaper line following the coast and joining the FR south of Broughton-in-Furness was adopted. During 1850 the financial markets were returning to normal and, with the completion of the WFJ R which opened its final section on 1st November 1850, the FR Engineers Messrs McClean & Stileman drew up a plan for a railway to complete the Cumberland Coast route.

The proposed line was to run from Ulverston to Carnforth, where a junction with the Lancaster & Carlisle Railway was to be made. Whilst the route of the line was similar in some respects to Robert Stephenson's 1846 WFJR 'Lancashire Extension' plans, the line ran further inland with substantial viaducts over the Rivers Leven and Kent. The Ulverstone & Lancaster Railway Company Act was incorporated on 24th July 1851 for a single line between Ulverston and Carnforth. The title *Ulverstone* was used in formal and legal documents and the *e* was dropped out of use in the mid-19th century; 'Lancaster' appeared in the title as it was the County Town. This act was largely due to the energies of a Manchester family by the name of Brogden, who nationally had interests in railway contracting and management, and locally in Furness iron ore mining.

An Agreement Plan between the ULR and the LCR was drawn up for Carnforth, showing the ownership of land, and also for the joint station platform extension, new lines and sidings, and the south-facing junction that was to be made between the two companies. The plan was approved and signed by William Garnett, Chairman of the LCR committee, and by John Brogden, Chairman of the ULR Committee. The two companies' engineers SB Worthington and James Brunlees also approved the plan. The plan was approved and signed on 3rd June 1856; it also incorporated the ULR seal along with Alexander Brogden's signature.

John Brogden had recruited James Brunlees as engineer, when financial pressures resulted in the withdrawal of McClean & Stileman from the ULR scheme. Brunlees was brought in for his expertise in railway embankment and maritime reclamation works, having made his name on the Lough Foyle reclamation project in Ireland. Brogden was a FR shareholder and a railway contractor, who had purchased the Tondu Ironworks in South Wales in 1853 and who had leased iron ore mines near Stainton, in the Parish of Dalton-in-Furness. The ULR was primarily promoted to provide a rail link between the Furness iron-ore mines and the iron working areas of South Lancashire and the West Midlands, although there was some trade with South Yorkshire interests.

The construction of the many miles of sea embankments was slow, and the ULR ran into financial difficulties, although some of these were due to tight credit restrictions during the Crimean War between 1853 and 1856. The 500-yard-long viaducts across the Leven and Kent estuaries proved difficult to build in the shifting estuary sands, with engineer Brunlees adopting novel systems of construction. Brunlees worked closely with, and was assisted by, the eminent engineering firm of W. & J. Galloway & Sons of Knott Mill Ironworks, Manchester, on devising the method of sinking piles for the viaducts, using jets of water. However, Galloway's were only involved with building the Leven viaduct, supplying the cast iron pillars and other iron sections and plates for the structure, with Messrs' Featherstone of Manchester being responsible for the construction of the Kent viaduct.

Leaving Silverdale, the line crossed Leighton Moss a few feet above sea level on a low-level embankment, and then closely followed the edges of Warton Sands on its approach to Carnforth. At the north end of Carnforth, it passed through a shallow cutting and under Toll Bar Bridge which was built to carry Sands Lane over the line. The line was taken across the marshes of the River Keer on a built-up embankment to Keer Bank. Part of the embankment was built across the bed of the River Keer which was then diverted southwards. The isolated section to the north was left and was filled in during 1879 and later obliterated by the Midland Bottom End sidings and the Carnforth Haematite Iron Co.'s ironworks slag branch.

At Keer Bank the line crossed the River Keer and Hagg Lane on a two-arch bridge, and skirted around the edge of Hunting Hill to make a south-facing junction with the Lancaster & Carlisle Railway. The lane leading to Hall Gate Farm which had been diverted previously by the LCR was stopped off once again, and a new lane was laid down to the farm from Hagg Lane at Keer Bank. The lane skirted round the base of Hunting Hill, and later, in 1882, the westward wall of the new FR engine shed would be built alongside it.

The ULR line as built was single track with passing places, and with all its passenger trains terminating at Carnforth a reversible single line platform and a run round loop was all that was provided. The location of the LCR station was such that the ULR line had to be laid on a tight curve of six chains radius, so that the ULR platform could be joined onto the existing LCR Down main platform. During 1856 work went ahead on the Carnforth contract which had been let to William Eckersley and by the end of 1856 the station had three platforms: the Up LCR platform, the Down LCR platform and the Up-Down ULR platform, the latter two forming a semi-island platform. The single ULR passenger line made a south-facing connection with the Down LCR main line just south of the station, and then used a crossover to connect with the LCR Up main line.

The final cost of the line was £420,000 with the FR, through the Duke of Buccleuch and the Earl of Burlington, providing £50,000 by way of a loan. Inspections were made on the 7th and the 22nd of August by Colonel Yolland, the Government

Inspector of Railways, and the ULR line opened for passenger traffic on 1st September 1857. The ULR never owned any locomotives and from the start the line was worked by the FR, with James Ramsden as Secretary and Traffic Manager and Alexander Brogden as Managing Director. It was not until 1861 that the ULR started making profits, and this was brought about by the flow of traffic to and from Messrs Schneider & Hannay's ironworks at Hindpool, Barrow-in-Furness (inbound coke from Wigan and County Durham, and outgoing pig iron to various UK destinations).

On 26th August the opening day of the ULR, a reporter for the *Ulverston Advertiser* who had accompanied the train from Ulverston wrote:

The station at Carnforth was literally covered with flags and mottoes and neatly executed designs in evergreens and flowers were to be seen both inside the station and out.

The *Lancaster Gazette* published on Saturday 29th August 1857 described very fully the opening day's proceedings. A reporter, who had accompanied the train, described the ceremonial journey from Ulverston to Carnforth and back. The train left Ulverston at 1.00pm and arrived at Carnforth 2.10pm where it waited for a LNWR train from the south which was 45 minutes late. On the return journey it conveyed a large number of guests from the south and eventually arrived at Ulverston 4.15pm. An elaborate dinner was served in a splendid marquee set up in the grounds of Furness Abbey, and the menu consisted of twenty three dishes from which the attendees could choose their courses. This was accompanied with cups of claret and cider and wines of every description. Two columns in the paper listed the

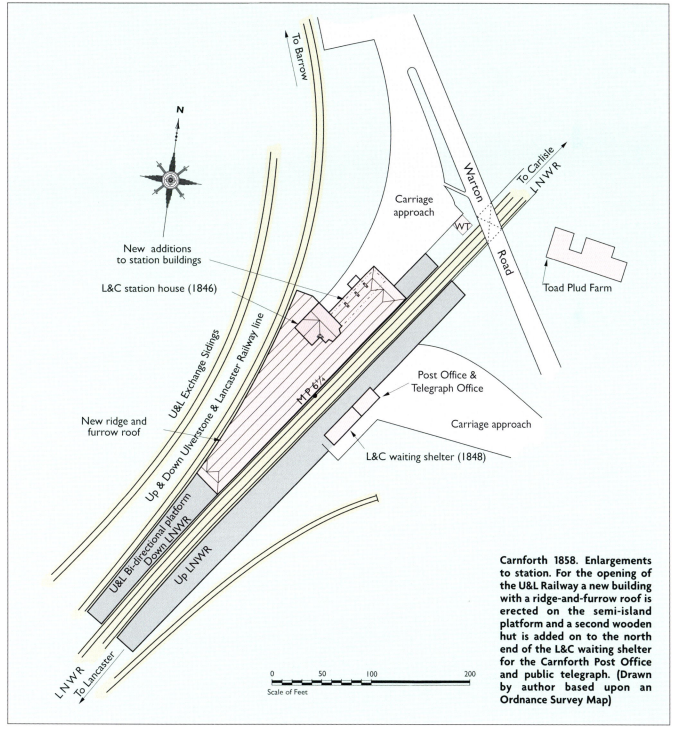

Carnforth 1858. Enlargements to station. For the opening of the U&L Railway a new building with a ridge-and-furrow roof is erected on the semi-island platform and a second wooden hut is added on to the north end of the L&C waiting shelter for the Carnforth Post Office and public telegraph. (Drawn by author based upon an Ordnance Survey Map)

CHAPTER THREE

attending guests and described the main speeches by the Right Honourable the Earls of Burlington and Lonsdale.

For its opening the two railway companies (LCR&ULR) had made arrangements to enlarge the station by adding a new single storey building directly onto the north face of the LCR station house. The new building contained a refreshment room and public waiting rooms; however the ticket office remained in the station house with a south facing entrance from the enlarged semi-island platform.

Externally the new building perpetuated the Elizabethan cottage style of architecture, and was faced in brown sandstone laid in coursed square rubble with a rough hammer-dressed face to match the 1846 LCR station house. Smooth dressed sandstone was used on all cills, lintels, and door and window surrounds, and for the first time opening leaded lights were fitted to the upper portion of the windows and doors. Single wooden doors with recessed panels were fitted to all but one doorway which had two centre-opening doors. The floor of the ticket offices was finished with three-inch-square glazed tiles coloured white, red, and black and laid in a herringbone pattern. The remainder were of substantial wooden planking. Wainscoting up to a height of thirty inches was fitted around the walls of the public rooms. Plain but substantial fireplaces in brown sandstone were installed in all the rooms.

The room adjoining the station house was fitted out as a refreshment room. Its entrance was from the LCR Down platform, and it had a semi-circular arch opening, which was higher than the other doorways in the new building, and lower cills. The half-glass door was flanked by narrow windows and a semi-circular top light, the larger expanse of glass providing additional natural light to the dining room, making it more appealing to the diners. Cellars for the storage of dry goods, wines and spirits for the refreshment room were built below the new building; a trap door on the platform gave external access for

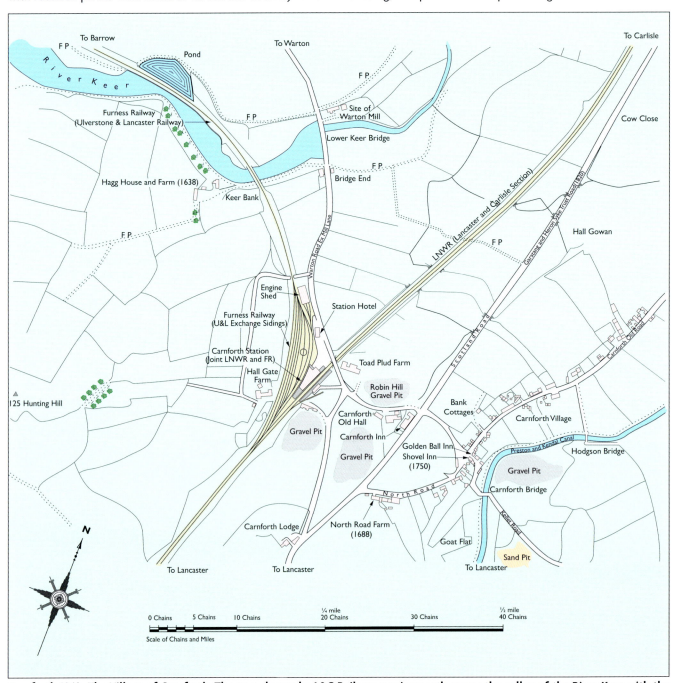

Carnforth 1862. The Village of Carnforth. The map shows the L&C Railway passing north across the valley of the River Keer with the single track U&L Railway curving round to the enlarged Carnforth station (Now Joint LNWR and FR). The exchange sidings are adjacent to the station and the U&L engine shed is at the north end. (Author's collection based upon an Ordnance Survey Map)

Carnforth (circa 1865-1870). Carnforth Station. The first station clock can be seen on the external wall and the booking office is under the roof almost in the centre of the picture. Warton Road Bridge is just beyond the LNWR 'Ramsbottom' type 2-4-0 engine. (Collection of the late Roy Hacking)

delivery and internally there were stairs leading down from the small adjoining food preparation area.

Elizabeth Carruthers, became the first licensed lessee of the new refreshment room. It would seem that the first romance at the station was not the film *Brief Encounter* as Elizabeth later married the Station Master: by all accounts he earned more money from the refreshment room than from his railway salary.

The semi-island platform was also extended southwards and a large area of the platform covered over with a new roof, which was supported by the building walls and by wooden roof beams supported on cast iron pillars at platform level. The enclosed platform was lit with oil lamps encased in glass globes, the lamps being hung from the roof beams. The LCR Down platform was extended northwards to Warton Road Bridge where a large water tank was installed on a stone base close to the platform edge.

Up to the coming of the railways, 'local time' was used, but this varied throughout the country as it was dependent on the local time of sunrise and sunset. The railway companies needed to operate to a standard timetable across the country, and in 1847 the Railway Clearing House, the body managing revenue allocation across the railway companies, recommended that Greenwich Mean Time (GMT) be adopted. The London & North Western Railway was the first to do so and adopted standard time on the 1st December 1847. The January 1848 edition of 'Bradshaw' listed many railway time tables using GMT. As only affluent people could afford a watch and the train drivers were unlikely to have one, the first station clock was installed high up in the south end wall of the new building. It was in a prominent position and was clearly visible to the drivers, the station staff and the travelling public.

In 1858 a second small wooden shed was erected on the Up LCR platform beside LCR waiting shed, this contained the first Post Office and later a Public Telegraph Office. At this time there was no subway, and so passengers had to cross the railway line by Warton Road Bridge to obtain a ticket as the office was on the Down LCR platform. At the south end of the station a wooden board crossing was provided to enable porters to move trolleys containing luggage, mail or parcels between the platforms, and passengers probably used this to return to the Up platform if they were travelling south. The station master at the opening of the new enlarged station was Isaac Birkett, and the staff had been increased to twenty-five to work the enlarged station.

The new layout at Carnforth also included the first exchange sidings for the pig iron and iron ore traffic which the ULR handed over to the LCR for onward movement to the iron working areas of South Yorkshire, South Wales and the West Midlands. To the west of the passenger line, the ULR laid down three through goods lines, together with a separate line containing a small turntable for turning an engine. The turntable was positioned mid-way along the line so that an engine could run onto it from each end and, having turned, return in the direction it came from. The through lines all converged: at one end they made a single south-facing junction with the LCR and at the other end a single north-facing junction with the ULR.

In 1862 Up and Down through goods lines were added to the west of the Carnforth exchange sidings, each line making a direct junction with the Up and Down LCR mainline line just south of the passenger junction. The new lines were added to handle the coke traffic that had started coming down from Tebay, the South Durham & Lancashire Union Railway having opened 4th July 1861 (This company was absorbed into the Stockton & Darlington Railway on 1st January 1863, the SDR becoming part of the NER later the same year). This traffic was passing through Carnforth exchange sidings *en route* to

CHAPTER THREE

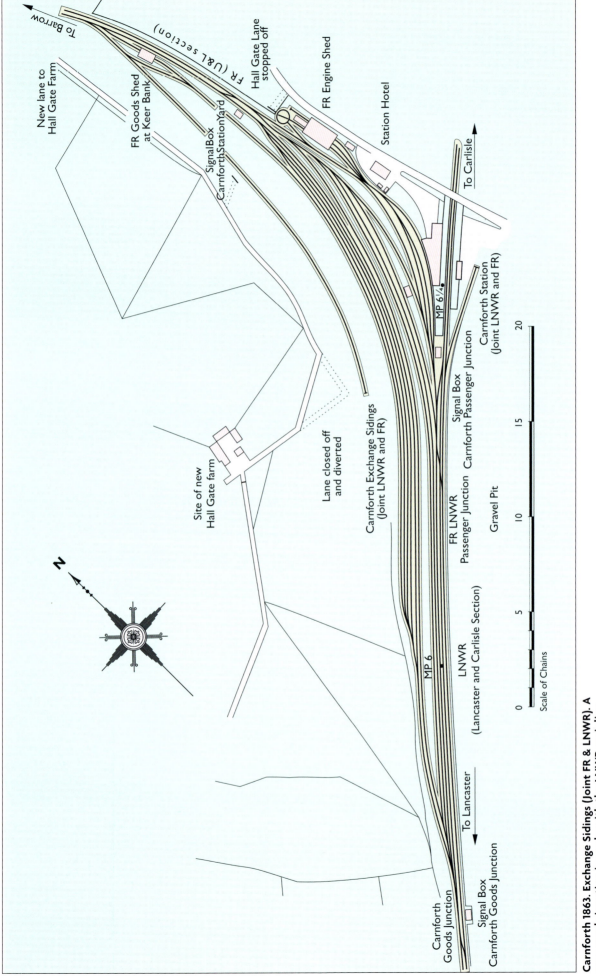

Carnforth 1863. Exchange Sidings (Joint FR & LNWR). A new goods junction is made with the LNWR mainline just north of Crag Bank Bridge. The first LNWR signal box (Carnforth Goods Junction) is brought into use to control the traffic in and out of the LNWR end of the new Carnforth Exchange Sidings. (Drawn by author from documents in author's collection)

Schneider & Hannay's ironworks at Hindpool, Barrow-in-Furness.

The line containing the turntable was converted into an additional through line when the turntable was taken out and moved to the new engine shed at the north end of the station. Some of the outbuildings of Hall Gate Farm were demolished to make way for the new Up and Down through goods lines.

The LCR was leased to the LNWR in 1859, and in January 1862 the ULR was purchased by the FR. Four years later the FR had a main line stretching around the Cumbrian Coast from Whitehaven to Carnforth, the Barrow Company having purchased the WFJR under an Act of 18th July 1866. Carnforth became a joint FR and LNWR station in 1862 and the staff now had CJS (Carnforth Joint Station) lapel badges on their uniforms. From 1862 the LNWR appointed the stationmaster, who was responsible for all the station staff and this would continue through to 1923 when the formation of the LMSR meant that the Furness, Midland and LNWR companies all became part of the same organisation.

From the opening of the ULR there had been a steady increase in traffic associated with the expanding iron and shipbuilding trades in the Furness Peninsula, and the prospect of further traffic from the proposed Furness & Midland Joint Railway provided the impetus for the FR to double the line from Ulverston to Carnforth, which was completed in August 1863.

During 1863 and 1864 six new through sidings were added to the existing sidings, all of which were extended southwards alongside the LNWR mainline. The sidings converged at their south end to make a junction with the Up and Down LNWR mainline just north of Crag Bank Bridge. At the same time the FR opened the first goods warehouse at Carnforth, on the west side of the line near to Keer Bank. Hall Gate Farm was finally demolished in the process and a new farm was built by the railway higher up on the southern slope of Hunting Hill, the farm road being re-aligned once again.

In 1864 when John F. Halliwell was appointed station master, the station, engine shed and exchange sidings formed a distinct

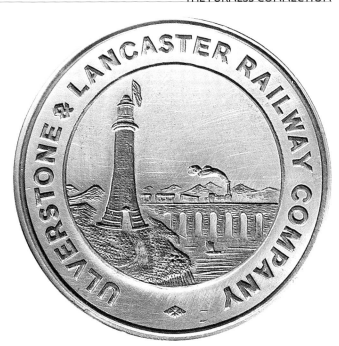

The seal of the Ulverstone & Lancaster Railway depicting the John Barrow Monument on Hoad Hill, Ulverston and train crossing the Leven Viaduct. (National Railway Museum collection)

group of features on the still-rural landscape. Immediately to the north of the station the first three blast furnaces of the Carnforth Haematite Iron Co Ltd were being erected, and a third of a mile north across the Keer Valley, the railway navvies were laying out the route of the FMJR. This line, linking Wennington on 'little' North Western Railway to Carnforth, had been authorised on 22nd June 1863, giving the Midland Railway access to Furness territory and the FR a direct route to the industrial areas around Leeds and Bradford. It will be covered more fully in the next chapter.

An Ulverstone & Lancaster Railway passenger train of 1860 hauled by Bury, Curtis & Kennedy locomotive 0-4-0 Class A2 No.3 with typical train of 4-wheel passenger stock. (No.3 'Coppernob' is preserved in the National Railway Museum, York) (CRA collection LX).

CHAPTER THREE

A portrait of John Brogden (1798-1869) industrialist and railway contractor and promoter of the Ulverstone & Lancaster Railway. (Google Images)

CHAPTER FOUR
TO THE WEST RIDING VIA THE MIDLAND RAILWAY

In 1862 the Midland Railway and the Furness Railway agree to the construction of a joint line which is of mutual benefit to them. However, the exchange of Midland Railway passengers with the LNWR is inconvenient and operationally disruptive. To improve the handling of traffic in general the Furness Railway obtains an Act for a new line giving the Midland Railway full access to the enlarged station of 1880.

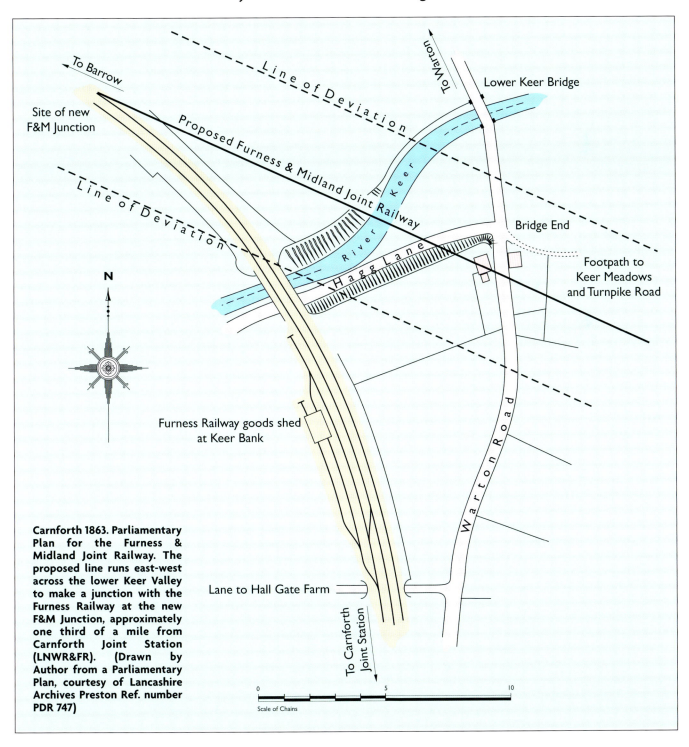

Carnforth 1863. Parliamentary Plan for the Furness & Midland Joint Railway. The proposed line runs east-west across the lower Keer Valley to make a junction with the Furness Railway at the new F&M Junction, approximately one third of a mile from Carnforth Joint Station (LNWR&FR). (Drawn by Author from a Parliamentary Plan, courtesy of Lancashire Archives Preston Ref. number PDR 747)

CHAPTER FOUR

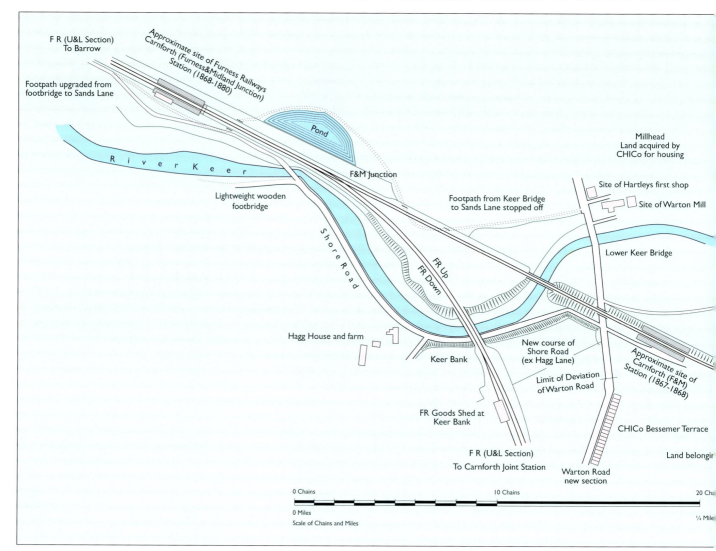

The rapid expansion of traffic through Barrow Harbour led the FR to plan docks there to supersede the tidal port, and an Act 'for enabling the FR to construct a Dock and other Works' was obtained on 22nd June 1863. At this time the Midland Railway, which had leased the 'little' North Western Railway (running from Skipton to both Ingleton and Lancaster, via Clapham) in 1859, was operating a steamer service from Morecambe Harbour, principally to Belfast. However, the services were hampered by the tidal nature of Morecambe Harbour which led to variable arrival and departure times for the vessels. At the same time the Furness Railway was having difficulty with its pig iron traffic which was destined for the steel making areas of Yorkshire. This traffic was handed over to the LNWR at Carnforth exchange sidings and then had to pass south over the LNWR line between Carnforth and Lancaster Castle yard, for transfer via the single-line branch to the Midland at Lancaster Green Ayre (this branch had also been built by the 'little' North Western Railway, and was included in the Midland's 1859 lease). There was evidence, however, that the LNWR was diverting the traffic by its own line to Yorkshire via Preston, resulting in an increase in mileage charges by the LNWR at the expense of the MR.

On the 26th of September 1862 a meeting was held in the Furness Abbey Hotel, Barrow-in-Furness, between the FR board and a deputation of three members of the MR board, its outcome was a provisional 'agreement' (never formally ratified) to build a joint line between Wennington on the 'little' North Western Railway to the FR west of Carnforth. As well as carrying the iron ore traffic from Furness to the industrial areas of Yorkshire, it would allow the MR to transfer its Irish traffic from Morecambe Harbour to the FR deep water pier at Piel, from where sailing time service could operate at fixed hours. The MR was also attracted by the prospect of gaining access to a planned FR line to the southern tip of Windermere. The Furness & Midland Joint Railway Bill was put before Parliament in March 1863 along with the Barrow Harbour Bill and both received Royal Assent on the 22nd June 1863.

The civil engineers for the Furness & Midland Joint Railway were the previously mentioned McClean & Stileman (for the FR), and J.S. Crossley (for the MR). The contract for building the line was awarded to Messrs Benton & Woodiwiss in May 1864, and Frank McClean, son of J.R. McClean, was appointed as Resident Engineer to the FMJR. The FMJR was built as a double line and passed to the north of Carnforth on an east-west axis across the valley of the River Keer. At Bridge End by the River Keer, a number of dwellings had to be demolished to make way for the new line, and by March 1865 the principal work of raising and levelling the earthworks was well under way. The line ran on a continuous embankment, and, westbound, successively bridged the 1820 Garstang and Heron Syke Turnpike (the present A6), the LCR, the new Carnforth Haematite Iron Company's line, then finally Warton Road and the River Keer, all within a third of a mile.

The line crossed the Turnpike road on a slight skew and was carried on an elliptical arch bridge built of brown sandstone, within a few yards it crossed over the LCR and the Carnforth

TO THE WEST RIDING VIA THE MIDLAND RAILWAY

Carnforth 1868. Furness & Midland Joint Railway 'New Works'. The new line runs on an east-west axis across the lower Keer Valley. Hagg Lane is diverted and changes made to the layout of Warton Road at Bridge End. The Keer Bridge-Sands Lane footpath is stopped off and diverted to Hagg Lane. The River Keer is also diverted and a lightweight pedestrian bridge built across it to connect Hagg Lane to the upgraded Sands Lane. (Drawn by author)

Haematite Iron Company's new line on a plate girder bridge with a central stone pier. At Bridge End the line then crossed Warton Road which had to be re-graded and lowered so as to provide thirteen feet of headroom at the centre of the plate girder bridge. When built the bridge carried the Up and Down FMJR direct line, it was sited a few yards south of the Lower Keer Bridge and crossed Warton Road on a thirty degree skew. The next bridge was a single elliptical arch bridge but of larger span over the River Keer, and again built of brown sandstone. After crossing the LCR, the line dropped gradually to join the FR at the new Furness & Midland Junction, a third of mile west of Carnforth Joint Station. At Bridge End, the new alignment closed off part of Hagg Lane, which was diverted and re-aligned to join Warton Road on the south side of the new Warton Road railway bridge.

The land between the FR and the new FMJR line was filled in and raised up level with the new line to provide an area of land for the first MR engine shed and sidings; these were laid out alongside the River Keer. The footpath which cut across the Keer meadows from Bridge End to the Turnpike Road was stopped off as it crossed both the new line and the land purchased by the Carnforth Haematite Iron Company for their new works. It was diverted to the north bank of the river. Another footpath which ran across the Keer meadows from the Lower Keer Bridge to Coat Stones Farm, and which crossed the line close to the new Carnforth F&M Junction, was also stopped off and diverted to Hagg Lane.

Both the Devonshire Dock at Barrow and the FMJR line were opened in 1867, the former opening on 19th September. The

Carnforth 1880. Furness & Midland Railway East Junction. The 'Carnforth Curve' is on the left and the first MR signal box and early MR signals control the junction. The Carnforth (Furness & Midland Junction) station building of 1868 has been re-erected at ballast level close to Carnforth East Junction signal box. (Mrs Pat Jackson Collection Ref. TR20)

CHAPTER FOUR

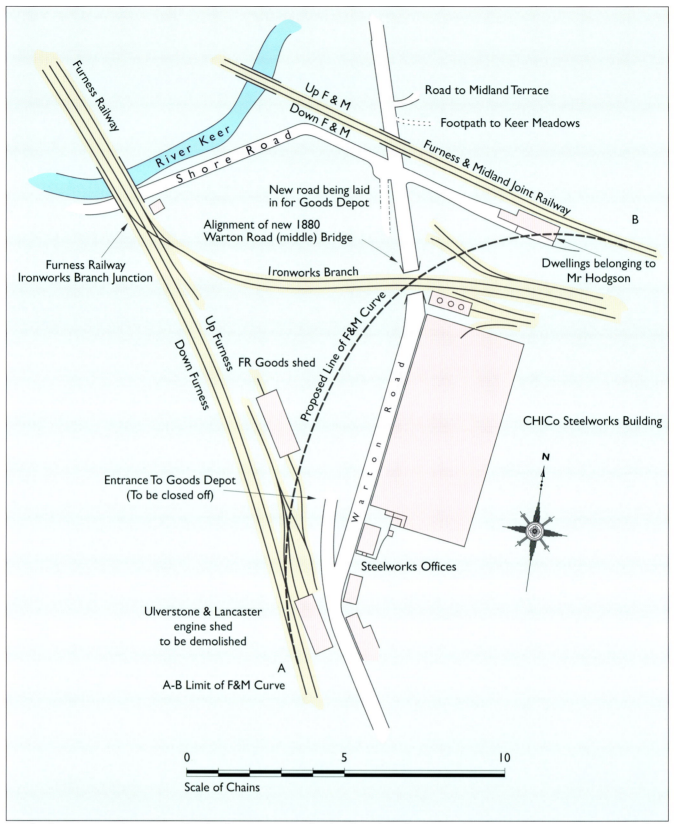

Carnforth 1878/80. Parliamentary Plan for the Furness & Midland Railway 'Carnforth Curve'. The proposed new curve is to run from F&M East Junction on a nine chains radius to make a junction at Carnforth Joint Station with the Furness Railway. (Drawn by author from a Parliamentary Plan, courtesy of Lancashire Archives Preston, Ref. number PDR 1103)

Westmorland Gazette for 4th May 1867 states that the FMJR line was opened throughout for goods traffic from 1st May 1867. The Midland Railway official notice of the opening for passenger traffic was Thursday 6th June 1867 and the same date appeared in the *Lancaster Gazette* for 8th June 1867. The FMJR was operated by the MR, which also installed and maintained the signalling: the FR was responsible for the buildings and station staff and the maintenance of the track. The first MR boat train ran in connection with a steamer to the Isle of Man on 1st July 1867, whilst the service to Belfast was transferred from Morecambe Harbour to Piel Pier on and from the 2nd September 1867. On the 1st June 1881, this traffic was transferred to the FR new station and quay alongside the Walney Channel at Ramsden Dock, Barrow-in-Furness.

Carnforth 1880. Furness & Midland Railway East Junction. The Carnforth (Furness & Midland Junction) station building of 1868 has been re-erected at ballast level close to Carnforth East Junction signal box. The building was used by the Midland Railway as offices for the MR goods manager and his staff including a railway policeman who stands in the middle of the picture. (Mrs Pat Jackson Collection Ref. TR10)

A new station named Carnforth (F&M), was built on the east side of Warton Road bridge at 28 chains (616 yards) east of Carnforth F&M Junction according to the MR distance diagram book, with a new access road from the east side of Warton Road. It was opened on 6th June 1867, the same date as the FMJR line and was always intended to be a temporary station. Passengers changing trains were faced with a quarter mile journey along Warton Road between Carnforth (F&M) station, and Carnforth Joint station (FR-LNWR). This arrangement was not conducive to through traffic and there was criticism in the

Carnforth mid 1950s. Furness & Midland Railway East Junction A rear view of the 1903 Midland Railway East Junction signal box with the Carnforth Curve in the foreground. To the right of the signal box is the Carnforth (Furness & Midland Junction) station building of 1868 at ballast level, this side faced on to Sands Lane when it was being used as a station building. By the mid-1950s it was empty and no longer in use as an office and was demolished soon after this photo was taken. (CRA Collection Ref. BOcln16)

local press. Carnforth (F&M) station closed on the 1st July 1868 when a new station built on the west side of F&M junction alongside the FR mainline and named, 'Carnforth (Furness & Midland Junction)' opened on the same date. This station closed in 1880 when the Carnforth Curve and the enlarged Carnforth Joint station opened, the station buildings were taken to East Junction for the Midland Railway goods clerks and shunters (see chapter 8).

Hagg Lane, which ran from Hagg House to Galley Hall alongside the River Keer and then on to the salt marshes was improved and renamed Shore Road. The course of the River Keer was retained by stone walls, and the land at the point where the new station was to be built was raised and levelled. The Furness Railway provided a wooden bridge of lightweight construction across the River Keer to give access to the new station. Later this bridge was rebuilt with a steel deck of sufficient strength to carry a family car. The foundations were washed away in the mid 1970s and a new bridge was built in its place but this time only for pedestrians and cyclists.

The station was built 19.68 chains (433 yards) from Toll Bar Bridge on Sands Lane, and consisted of two short platforms connected by a barrow crossing. On the Down line platform to Barrow-in-Furness, a small wooden building was provided; it contained railway offices and a public waiting room. The new Furness & Midland Junction station was opened on 1st July 1868 and appeared for the first time in the *Bradshaw Railway Guide* timetable for June 1868. Carnforth (F&M) station on Warton Road was closed on the same date and the platforms removed. The station buildings were not removed until 1879 at the time of construction of the Carnforth Curve. The parliamentary plan (Land Supplementary Ownership) lists them as being rented out to a Mr Hodgson who worked for the Carnforth Haematite Iron Co. as overseer of the Keer Marsh slag tip (see chapter 6).

In order for the MR trains to pick up passengers from the LNWR, they had to reverse from the Furness & Midland Junction station into the FR-LNWR Carnforth Joint station and then continue on to Barrow-in-Furness. To remove this manoeuvre, which the Board of Trade said was not good operating practice, the FR obtained an Act on 21st July 1879 for a direct line from the FMJR into Carnforth Joint station, the line opening on 2nd August 1880. This ran between new junctions at Carnforth East and Carnforth Station, and was known as the 'Carnforth Curve'. The Act also authorised the FR Ironworks branch to cross the curve on the level (see chapter 8).

Carnforth 12th May 2010. The 13.49 departure from Leeds has come round the Carnforth Curve from East Junction and is about to pass over Station Junction to enter Carnforth Station. The 1882 Carnforth Station Junction signal box is on the right and the replacement FR signal box of 1903 is just beyond the footbridge which was built to give access to the new 1944 LMS shed. Check rails have been placed inside the running rails as the line is laid on a radius of only nine chains and a 20mph speed restriction is in force. On this day the train consists of a two-car class 142 leading and a two-car class 144 trailing and both are in Northern Rail livery. The train will depart Carnforth at 15.37 and proceed to Lancaster where the train will be split. The class 144 will go to Morecambe and return to Carnforth via the Bare Lane – Hest Bank branch and then back to Leeds. The class 142 will return to Carnforth and proceed around the coast to Barrow-in-Furness. (Philip Grosse)

CHAPTER FIVE
THE CARNFORTH HAEMATITE IRON COMPANY LTD

The Carnforth Haematite Iron Company Ltd was promoted in 1860 by a group of predominantly Manchester business men who were associated with the metal trades. The ironworks operated profitably up to the Great War; however in 1915 a partnership was formed with Darlington Forge Ltd and John Brown & Co. Ltd. The general trade recession of the 1920s, together with the rationalisation of the iron and steel industry, and the formation of English Steel in Sheffield in 1929, resulted in the ironworks' closure.

The Furness peninsula and certain areas of Cumberland contained significant deposits of red haematite iron ore containing 70% iron. The rich low phosphorous haematite of Furness was known to the monks of Furness Abbey who exploited it in crude bloomeries. In 1851 H.W. Schneider, a geological prospector, found a large deposit of iron ore at Park within the parish of Dalton-in-Furness. This led to the formation of Schneider, Hannay & Co. on 1st January 1853, and the erecting and blowing-in of two blast furnaces at Hindpool at Barrow-in-Furness in October 1859, with two more added in 1860.

A group of businessmen, mainly from Manchester, met in the offices of William Slater, Solicitor, of Brazenose Street Manchester, in 1860 to promote an ironworks at Carnforth. The leading promoter of the new company was Herbert John Walduck, an iron and copper merchant of Manchester, a resident of Silverdale and sole agent for several small mining and quarry companies in Warton and Silverdale. The principal factors in choosing Carnforth were the established rail connections for iron ore and coke, both of which were passing through the Carnforth exchange sidings. Furthermore, when the Carnforth Haematite Iron Co. was promoted, the scheme for building the Furness & Midland Joint line (for a direct link with

Carnforth Haematite Iron Company 1875. The 220-foot high chimney, and tall blowing engine house and the six open top furnaces of the Carnforth Haematite Iron Company dominate the scene. In the right corner is the newly opened Post Office building with Toad Plud farm and forge in the centre. A solitary coke wagon sits on the elevated ore bank and a rake of pig iron wagons are on the LNWR sidings. (Taylors series postcard) (Author's collection)

CHAPTER FIVE

Carnforth Haematite Iron Company, circa 1929. The three mechanically charged furnaces and associated pre-heating ovens are in the centre of the photograph and the remaining wall of the demolished steelworks stands alongside Warton Road. The wooden clad cooling towers and the re-circulating water pond of 1915 can clearly be seen. (Author's collection)

the steel-making centres of South Yorkshire) was probably under initial discussion, although the Act gained Parliamentary approval much later, on 22nd June 1863.

In addition there was a plentiful local supply of limestone, an adequate supply of water, and a large area of marshland adjoining the River Keer for a slag tip. Around 18 acres of land which lay between the LNWR (Lancaster and Carlisle Railway line) and Warton Road to the north of Carnforth station were purchased in 1862 for the ironworks by H.J. Walduck. A further nine acres of marshy and poorly drained land bordering the River Keer were purchased for the Keer Marsh slag tip. The company was registered in 1864 as the Carnforth Haematite Iron Company Ltd, with a capital of £100,000, divided into 500 shares of £200 each. By September 1865 155 shares had been taken up by 91 shareholders in Manchester, 14 by shareholders in Birmingham and the Black Country and a further 10 by shareholders in the North East, both Henry Bessemer and his brother-in-law Robert Longsdon had purchased shares and other shareholders came from the West Riding, Cumberland and London.

In 1862, at the age of thirty-two, Edward D. Barton was engaged by H.J. Walduck to be the Chief Engineer of Carnforth ironworks. He had attended Crofthouse School at Brampton near Carlisle, which included in its curriculum a large number of technical and scientific subjects. On leaving school he was articled to Thomas Bouch, engineer for the Stockton and Darlington Railway, and afterwards took up railway engineering in other parts of the country. In his early twenties, he was appointed manager of the blast furnaces of Messrs Gilkes Wilson & Co., of Middlesbrough, and from there he moved to West Cumberland to undertake the construction and management of the West Cumberland Ironworks at Workington. On his appointment at Carnforth he planned, designed and oversaw the construction of the new ironworks, and having supervised the blowing-in of the first three blast furnaces, was promoted in mid-1867 to become the ironworks' General Manager.

Substantial piling and large amounts of concrete were required to create the rafts and footings for supporting the blast furnaces, lifts and ancillary buildings. By the end of 1864, masons, bricklayers and general labourers had moved on to the site along with steam driven piling machines and concrete/mortar mixers. A field of excellent clay had been found nearby at Lunds Field, and a kiln set up for making approximately 300,000 bricks per year. The construction of the ironworks provided an opportunity for local contractors, giving employment to a large number of men from Carnforth and surrounding areas, and greatly improving local trade within the village.

A combination of local white limestone and red sandstone from Furness was used in the construction of the industrial buildings, the mineral banks, and the main walls, using rough-shaped stone laid in a random style. This combination had been used in a similar manner at the Barrow-in-Furness ironworks. The most prominent building on site was the substantially constructed blowing engine house. Two steam-driven beam engines with 20-inch-diameter cylinders were supplied and installed in the engine house by Rothwell and Co. engineers of Bolton. They were designed to provide a continuous blast of air to the blast furnaces at 3lb per square inch pressure.

The boilers for making steam and other ancillary equipment were supplied by Messrs Sharp, Stewart of Atlas Mill Manchester, and were designed to utilise the surplus hot gases from the blast furnaces to raise steam. The foundation stone for the 210-foot chimney, the works' most striking feature, was laid by Mrs Barton the wife of Edward Barton on 18th May 1865. Through the liberality of Mr Barton and other directors of the ironworks, the bricklayer contractor, Joseph White, and his men were in the evening entertained by Miss Cragg at the Station Hotel.

Under the supervision of Barton, the first three blast furnaces numbered 1, 2, and 3 were erected during 1865 and 1866 at the south end of the site. The blast furnaces installed at the ironworks were based on a design that had been developed in 1829 by J.B. Neilson of Glasgow; they were open-topped and manually charged, and each one was capable of producing between 300 and 400 ton of iron per week. The furnaces were built in a row close to each other and parallel to the LNWR line. One vertical lift for hoisting the raw materials to the furnace deck was positioned to feed three furnaces. The vertical lift was hydraulically operated and required the installation of pumps and accumulators to drive it. Through Barton's connections with Teesside, the Tees Engine Works may well have been involved in supplying the blast furnaces and vertical lifts.

Water for the ironworks was taken from the River Keer and a steam-driven pump was installed in an engine house near to the Lower Keer Bridge; this was later replaced with an electrically driven pump. The water was roughly filtered then pumped through a pipeline into the ironworks cold pond, and then into the ironworks via two culverts beneath the LNWR main line. Two large ponds were created along the east side of the LNWR line, a cold pond from which supplies of water would be drawn for use in the ironworks, and a recirculation pond for cooling hot process water. The ponds were sited at the foot of Long Haws Hill, in an area of low-lying marshland known locally as 'Toad Plud' (Toad Pond). After 1880, the ironworks also started taking water from the Carnforth and District Waterworks Company. It was said that the ironworks used as much water in one month as did the town and its neighbouring area in one year!

The ironworks had a substantial standard gauge rail network for the movement of raw materials, slag, and pig iron; the rails on the slag bank were about three feet in length so that they could be manually lifted and moved around as the slag bank grew. Initially all the rails and chairs were purchased from Henry Williams & Co. of Glasgow (1865-1877) until they moved their foundry to Darlington around 1880 to concentrate on other railway fittings. They passed the manufacturing rights and patterns to Wilson Pease and Co. of Middlesbrough, who from 1880 became the supplier of rails and chairs.

The Carnforth Haematite Iron Co. was seeking to employ around 200 men for the opening of the ironworks in the summer

Carnforth Haematite Iron Company 1881. There are now six open top blast furnaces available for iron-making, the large expanse in front of the furnaces are the pig beds which are made of sand and into which the molten metal is poured. (Author's collection)

CHAPTER FIVE

of 1866, and although there was plenty of local unskilled labour in the town, there were no skilled ironworkers. At the same time, the Earl of Dudley's coal mines and ironworks in Worcestershire were in decline, and the local workforce was investing in new skills associated with the expanding engineering industry. Knowing this, the ironworks' directors may well have employed an agent at Dudley, to make an offer to the redundant skilled ironworkers to move to Carnforth. The 1871 census records show that skilled ironworkers from Dudley had arrived in Carnforth, as had ironworkers from established iron working areas in Durham, Yorkshire, the Forest of Dean and Scotland.

For its opening the ironworks built a substantial two-storey building alongside Warton Road, within two hundred yards of Carnforth station. The building containing the ironworks offices, the main entrance to the ironworks being through a gate in the centre of the building, above which was the General Manager's office. All that remains today as a reminder of the ironworks is a cast iron lintel over the bricked-up main entrance on which the

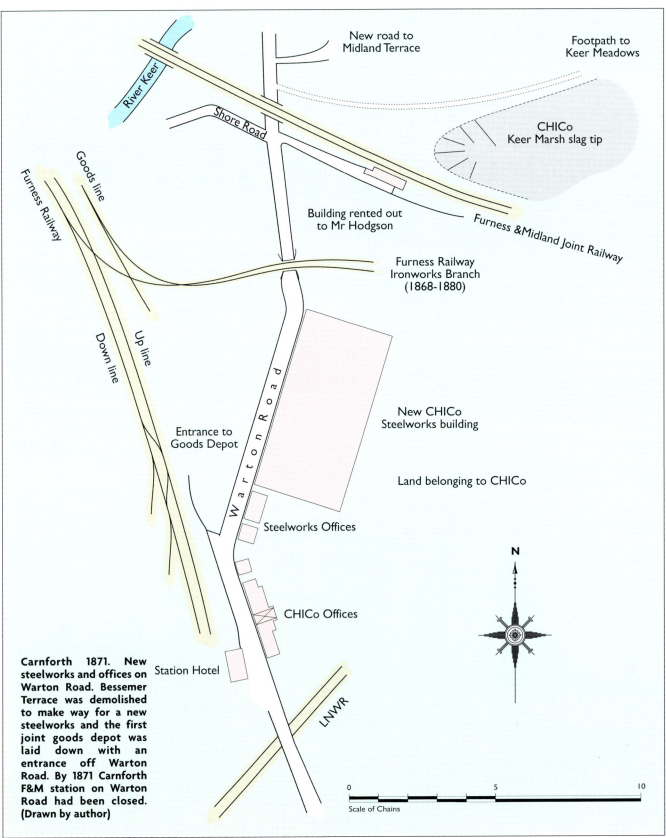

Carnforth 1871. New steelworks and offices on Warton Road. Bessemer Terrace was demolished to make way for a new steelworks and the first joint goods depot was laid down with an entrance off Warton Road. By 1871 Carnforth F&M station on Warton Road had been closed. (Drawn by author)

wording 'Carnforth Ironworks' has been cast. The ironworks office block was faced with brown sandstone blocks laid in regular courses; these offices are still in use today serving the adjacent industrial estate. However, the bell tower which sat on the roof over the main entrance is long gone. The bell was rung at start and finish times by the timekeeper, who also opened and closed the wicket gate. Latecomers had their pay reduced accordingly and persistent offenders would also be fined.

The first blast furnace was blown in during early August of 1866, and the first batch of iron poured in the first week of September 1866. As chief shareholder, H.J. Walduck had sole rights to the sale of any pig iron produced in the first five years of operation. The first three blast furnaces had only been operating for twelve months when a national depression in the iron trades commenced in the later months of 1867. The depression worsened during 1868, but the ironworks managed to keep all three furnaces in blast. By the end of 1869 the depression was over, and sixteen Player hot blast pipe stoves were installed, to a design that had been used at Consett and Thornaby Ironworks before John Player patented them in 1866. The Player stoves provided a supply of hot air to the furnace, and reduced the heating time.

Early in 1870, the economic climate had improved, and there was a growing demand for haematite pig iron from the North Lancashire and Cumberland haematite iron trades. In response, the ironworks' directors made plans for blast furnaces 4, 5, and 6 to be erected at the north end of the site and in line with the original three furnaces, together with a second vertical lift. The blast furnaces were successively blown in, between 1870 and 1873, so that at the end of 1873 a total of six blast furnaces were available for iron making. The ironworks' busiest years were between 1871 and 1874; in the latter year, five furnaces were in blast continuously. These were prosperous years for Carnforth but they were not to last. From the middle of 1874 a second iron trades depression commenced, and by 1876 only one furnace was in blast. During this time, wages were reduced and some of the workforce discharged, whilst others left to find employment elsewhere.

The early methods of making steel were slow and costly, and only iron which contained a low amount of phosphorous could be used to make steel. In 1856, however, Henry Bessemer developed his process, at the Oldside Ironworks near Workington, for producing steel quickly and cheaply inside a Converter. The high quality haematite iron ore of Cumberland was extremely suitable for this process by reason of its low phosphorus content. There was a high demand for steel towards the end of the 1860s, and in 1869 the ironworks directors made plans for a steelworks to be erected on site. The capital for the steel works was subscribed in 1870, and the twenty houses, which had been built in 1866, and named 'Bessemer Terrace', were dismantled in 1871 to make way for the steelworks and the adjoining steelworks offices.

A tall rectangular building was constructed in white limestone on an area of land in the north-west corner of the ironworks with one wall fronting on to Warton Road. By the end of 1872 the building had been roofed in and the iron flooring had been laid, a second chimney for the steel works Cupola furnace off-gases had also been erected. Two Bessemer Converters, a plate mill, a rail rolling mill, and a Cupola furnace for melting pig iron were installed in the building. It cost £30,000 to build and equip, however installation and testing seems to have been protracted as it was December 1874 before steel-making commenced.

Steel-making took place between 1874 and 1889 and during this time the steelworks employed around 200 men and boys, however by 1889 the production of steel nationally by the Bessemer process had reached its peak. From 1878, the Siemens Martin Basic Open Hearth Process, using pig iron made from poorer quality brown ores, having around 35% iron, was becoming the established steel-making process. This led to many steel makers moving away from the Bessemer steel producing areas, to Cleveland, Lincolnshire and Northamptonshire where large quantities of brown ore had been found.

The steelworks was leased out by H.J. Walduck to Albion Ironworks, Warrington and operated under the management of Robert Pemberton. Railway rails and steel plates were made up to 1884 but in January 1885 the steel works was reorganised to make steel wire which continued until its closure. In December 1889 the manager, W.D. Houghton of Albion Ironworks Warrington, stated that he would not operate the steelworks again and the steelworks was closed and the steel-making plant mothballed. Eventually the plant was offered for sale by public auction which was held on 31st March 1898. On 27th May 1898, the 'Carnforth Haematite Iron Co. Ltd' was re-registered under the same name with the Board of Trade, suggesting that the re-organised company was now concentrating only on pig iron manufacture. Except for the building wall which still stands alongside Warton Road, the rest of the steel-works buildings were subsequently demolished.

In 1880, the Player pipe stoves behind blast furnaces 1, 2 and 3 were removed, and five Ford and Mancur regenerative hot blast stoves were installed for the first time at Carnforth. George Parry of Ebbw Vale Ironworks, Monmouthshire, had demonstrated that, by burning the waste blast furnace gases, a high temperature could be reached quickly, with a significant reduction in heating time and fuel. In 1881-82, two steam-driven direct-acting blowing engines were purchased from W. & J. Galloway & Sons' Knott Mill Ironworks, Manchester, to replace the original blowing engines.

During 1886 and 1887 there was a downturn in iron making throughout the country due to a general trade depression. The ironworks had only two out of six blast furnaces continually in blast, and some short time working resulted. Iron production had just recovered when, in 1892, a severe national crisis occurred; this was caused by the Durham coal miners' strike. The decline in availability of coke eventually forced the ironworks to run with only one furnace in blast for most of the year. The bulk of ironworks employees without work were unskilled labourers, who were hired out to the township council to carry out rough work at low wages. Such work included road repairs, hedging, walling and ditch cleaning, the aim being to prevent and mitigate distress and demoralisation. James Erving of Thwaite Gate noted in his 'Memorandum' that he often came across gangs of men working on the roads whilst out riding his bay pony.

At the end of the 19th century, the British iron trade was coming increasingly under pressure from American competition, and was experiencing a contraction of output. A fully equipped American blast furnace could produce an average of 500 tons of pig iron per day; these furnaces were mechanically charged and worked on a higher blast pressure. Early in 1900, Albert Edward Barton, the son of Edward D. Barton, went to America to visit iron-making plants situated around the city of Birmingham, Alabama, USA. As a consequence of the visit, the ironworks over the next decade underwent substantial modernisation. In 1902 Edward D Barton, now aged seventy-two became the chairman and director of the ironworks, and his son, who now lived at Red

CHAPTER FIVE

Court, Carnforth, took over as Manager of the ironworks on his return from America.

In 1902, blast furnaces 4 and 5 and the vertical lift at the north end of the site were dismantled. Blast furnace 6 was modified to operate at a higher blast pressure and fitted with an early type of skip lift for mechanical charging; it was re-numbered 1A. It had a capacity of 1500 tons of iron per week and was blown in during May 1903. At the same time, the remaining Player pipe stoves were dismantled. Three new Cowper Kennedy regenerative hot blast stoves of a greater capacity than the Ford and Mancur type were erected for operation with furnace 1A. Two American Westinghouse 1000kW turbo generators were installed to replace the direct acting engines of 1881-82. The generators were coupled to two Darve & Adamson mixed pressure blowers capable of driving 3,000 cubic feet of air per minute into a blast furnace at a temperature of 1,200 to 1,500 degrees Fahrenheit. The mixed pressure blowers produced a blast pressure of 10lb per square inch for a high-pressure mechanically-charged blast furnace, and a blast pressure of 3lb per square inch for a manually-charged blast furnace.

In 1906, blast furnace 3 was modified to operate at a higher blast pressure and fitted with an improved type of skip lift for mechanical charging; it was re-numbered 2A. It had a capacity of 1,500 tons of iron per week and was blown in during February 1906. The last two manually-charged furnaces (1 and 2) and the remaining vertical lift at the south end of the site remained until 1910, when blast furnace 1 was dismantled along with the vertical lift. Blast furnace 2 was modified to run at a higher blast pressure, being fitted with an improved type of skip lift for mechanical charging and re-numbered 3A. It had a capacity of 1,500 tons of iron per week and was blown in during 1912.

The higher blast pressure created a much higher furnace operating temperature, and consequently the slag was much hotter and more fluid. In June 1903, for first time at Carnforth, ladles were brought into use for collecting the slag. The slag roads were re-aligned as each blast furnace was rebuilt in order to get two ladles at a time under the blast furnace slag spout. The most common ladle from 1900 onwards was the Dewhurst Ladle, consisting of a tilting bowl on a heavy four-wheeled chassis. It was available in several versions, from six to ten tons capacity.

In 1903, two wooden-clad rectangular cooling towers were built, and a well (or basin) was provided for the recirculation of cooling water for the two American Westinghouse 1000kW turbo generators. A furnace gas scrubbing plant was also installed as complaints were being made by the farming community over the damage to the local wheat crop which was being blackened by high sulphur emissions from the chimney. At the end of 1912, the ironworks was a very modern and efficient plant, reflecting the technical advances being made to the iron making process. On October 23rd 1913 Edward D. Barton JP died aged eighty-three; he had conducted the affairs of the ironworks for half a century with great success, and had played an important part in the development of the town and community of Carnforth.

The ironworks produced a high quality haematite pig iron for which it commanded the best prices; large tonnages were exported to America, India, Japan and Europe, in addition to home manufacture. The pig iron was used in the 'Open Hearth' steel making process for producing high quality steel ingots, which were extremely suitable for producing heavy forgings and armour plate. For a number of years the principal customers of the ironworks had been Darlington Forge Ltd, and John Brown Ltd of Sheffield. The ironworks operated profitably up to the Great War, however, in 1915 a partnership was formed with Darlington Forge Ltd and John Brown & Co. Ltd, the latter to secure their supply of haematite pig iron as they specialised in naval armour plate, which at that time was in high demand for naval vessel construction. The company was reorganised as the 'Carnforth Haematite Iron Company (1915) Ltd'.

Following the end of the Great War, disarmament and government cut backs, together with the trade recession of the 1920s, severely affected the iron and steel trade nationally. The haematite pig iron which had been formerly used in the steel-making process was largely replaced by high grade scrap which was available in quantity. It formed an adequate substitute for the haematite pig iron which the ironworks produced.

Carnforth 1907. Carnforth Haematite Iron Company Ltd. A view of the ironworks from the hill on the east side of the Turnpike Road (now the A6). Blast furnaces 1A and 2A are on the right side and there are a large number of coke wagons standing on the ore bank. (J. Valentines series postcard) (Author's collection)

The ultimate blast furnace modification was made in 1920, when furnace 1A was upgraded to a capacity of 2,500 tons of iron per week. It was fitted with the latest type of mechanical skip lift and re-numbered 1B. The rebuilding of furnace 1A was a final attempt at keeping the ironworks in operation in the changed circumstances following the war. From 1920 to its closure the ironworks ran with one furnace in blast as a consequence of the continuing depression in the iron trades, and the decreased demand for pig iron at an economic price. The ironworks fate was sealed with the rationalisation of the iron and steel industry, and the formation of the English Steel Corporation in Sheffield in 1929. The ESC combined the steel interests of Vickers, Vickers-Armstrong, and Cammell-Laird, mainly in the Sheffield area, creating economies of scale and making it difficult for smaller units like Carnforth to survive at a time of industrial depression.

Official closure was announced on 3rd December 1930 in Sheffield, with the news that Messrs Thomas Ward Ltd of Sheffield, iron merchants and ship breakers, had obtained the contract to dismantle the ironworks and sell it off for scrap, and to sell off or scrap the locomotives and wagons. The sale was negotiated on a break-up basis, and the final net proceeds were insufficient to repay more than a small amount of the debenture holders' money. They had acquired three blast furnaces, eight hot blast stoves and a complete gas cleaning plant, four Stirling and ten Lancashire boilers, and a 1000kW Westinghouse turbo-generator blowing engine. Also included were pig iron breakers and a large overhead travelling crane which spanned the pig bed. In addition, there were fifty internal wagons, two ladles, and eight miles of track. The 220-foot chimney was the first item to be demolished, and except for the large overhead travelling crane, which was sold and removed from the site, all the plant went for scrap. After the demolition of the ironworks plant and equipment in 1931, Thomas Ward Ltd continued trading on the ironworks site and used it as a scrap metal stocking ground for the Lancashire and Cumberland iron trades. The 119 workers' houses at Millhead were sold to the sitting tenants.

At its peak, Carnforth ironworks and steelworks had employed around five hundred men and boys. When the steelworks closed in 1889 with a loss of around two hundred jobs many of the men and their families left Carnforth to find further employment in other iron trades areas. At the closure of the ironworks in December 1930, around three hundred men and boys were made redundant and this had a drastic effect on the local economy. At that time there was little alternative local industry and no unemployment benefit, and the remainder of the country was in the grip of industrial depression. Once again the local economy in Carnforth revolved around the railway, the extraction of sand and gravel, and the working of the stone quarries on Warton Crag and the Kellets.

By 1938 Thomas Ward Ltd had left the ironworks site, but in 1940, the government requisitioned it for a War Department strategic store and a petrol dump. The rail connections which had been left in after demolition of the ironworks were brought back into use in readiness for the expected volume of traffic. Nissen huts were erected on the site for the storage of war materials, and the site came under the jurisdiction of the War Office. The store was set up as a nationwide supply point from which vital supplies could be sent out for the continued conduct of the war. The site was occupied by military personnel, and the store was operated for the duration of the war by the men and women of the Pioneer Corp and by other service personnel who were unfit for duty. The Military Police were responsible for the safety and security of the site, and local civilian staff worked in the ironworks offices as clerks and typists.

In 1942 two young women, members of the Pioneer Corps from the East End of London, came to Carnforth, where they lodged and worked in the store for three years. One of them had worked on the petrol dump and gave the author this first-hand account when she visited the Carnforth Station Heritage Centre in 2005.

There were regular supplies of petrol which were brought in by train in rail tankers, the petrol being transferred from the tankers to jerry-cans which were then stored on site until required. It was a laborious task as the petrol had to be siphoned out manually and the full jerry-cans wheeled around the site on sack trolleys. A wooden staging with a platform had been erected alongside the railway siding, allowing access to the tank manhole through which a flexible pipe work could be fed. The hand pump and jerry-cans were also placed upon the platform for filling.

On Monday 12th February 1945 a fire broke out in the store in the early hours of the morning. As it was wartime the occurrence was not reported immediately in the local press, and the ignition source was never officially disclosed. (It was probably a combination of petrol spillage, as the transfer process was very basic, in combination with an ignition source such as sparks or hot ash from an engine-author.) The 2nd May 1945 edition of the *Morecambe Visitor* newspaper eventually published an article by Sir Fredrick Hindle, Regional Commissioner for the National Fire Service, in which he commended the action taken by the NFS. The fire could not be contained by the site's Army Fire Service, and detachments of the National Fire Service had to be called in from Lancaster, Barrow and Preston, and foam had to be used to douse the fire and prevent it spreading to other flammable storage areas. The fire was brought under control fairly early, however as the mainline passed close by rail traffic through Carnforth was suspended for several hours, causing widespread dislocation of services. For their personal safety, all civilian staff and the residents in the immediate vicinity were evacuated to other parts of town.

Once the War Department had vacated the site, Carnforth Urban District Council wished to develop the 12-acre site for light industrial use and interest was shown by the Ford Motor Co. and BICC, but the council was not able to obtain development status and the site remain undeveloped. In 1965, the ironworks site was bought from the Ministry of Defence (MoD) by Robert Watson Ltd, Construction Engineers, who were hoping to get a contract from British Railways for erecting overhead catenary for the planned electrification of the West Coast Main Line between Crewe and Glasgow. The planned scheme was not proceeded with at that time and the company failed in its business venture, the site was put up for sale again in 1969 and was bought by R.O. Hodgson who used the Nissan huts which had been left by the MoD as warehouses. In 1972 the site was acquired by Boddy Industries Ltd of Sheffield who was actively engaged in the local quarry industry. Eventually Boddy Industries built several large warehouses on the ironworks industrial site for the storage and distribution of ICI fertiliser from that company's North East and West of England factories. Also for the storage of explosives for the local quarries which were handled by trained staff who were employed by ICI Nobel Ltd, with the explosives being manufactured in Ayrshire.

CHAPTER FIVE

Carnforth 1906. Carnforth Haematite Iron Company Ltd. A view inside the ironworks. Blast furnaces 1A and 2A have been rebuilt with skip lifts and the new cooling water pond for the blowing engines is in the foreground. (J. Valentines series postcard) (Author's collection)

THE CARNFORTH HAEMATITE IRON COMPANY LTD

Carnforth 1912. Carnforth Haematite Iron Company Ltd. A view of the ironworks from the hill on the east side of the Turnpike Road (now the A6). Blast furnaces 3A, 2A, and 1A are on the right side and there are a large number of iron-ore hoppers on the ore bank and coke wagons on the LNWR sidings. (Lancashire Library collection Cat. number 1898-25)

CHAPTER FIVE

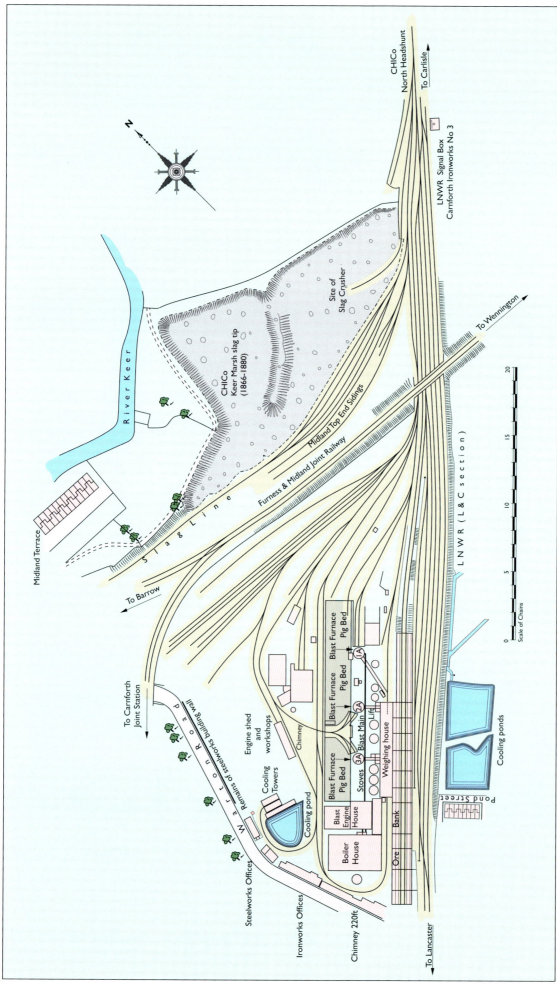

Carnforth 1912. Carnforth Haematite Iron Company Ltd. The plan of the ironworks shows it in its final modernised form with three blast furnaces fitted with early mechanical skip lifts and associated regenerative hot blast stoves. The Ore Bank runs parallel with the LNWR mainline and all incoming raw materials and slag had to move in and out of the site via the long north-facing head shunt. (Drawn by author and based upon an Ordnance Survey Map)

CHAPTER SIX
IRONWORKS TRAFFIC

The LNWR, Furness Railway and the Midland Railway were all involved with the ironworks traffic. Internally, the ironworks had its own standard-gauge industrial locomotives for the movement of slag limestone and pig iron. These industrial engines were known locally as 'Lal Cheggies' which probably means 'Little Chuffers', recalling the sound they made as they passed along the Slag Line with a loaded train.

On 4th July 1861, the South Durham and Lancashire Union railway had opened to Tebay and a junction with the LCR. This was an important line, as it enabled low sulphur coke to be brought from the Durham coal fields across the backbone of the Pennines for the blast furnaces at Hindpool, Barrow-in-Furness, and later for other ironworks that had been established in Furness and South Cumberland. The North Eastern Railway worked the coke trains to Tebay North Eastern yard, where they were taken over by the LNWR which worked them to Crag Bank at the south end of Carnforth where the train was reversed into the LNWR end of the Carnforth exchange sidings. Coke wagons for Carnforth ironworks were detached at Carnforth exchange sidings, with the remainder worked by the Furness Railway around the coast to ironworks at North Lonsdale (Ulverston), Barrow, Askam and Millom.

In 1917, coke traffic for the ironworks at North Lonsdale, Barrow, Askam and Millom began to be worked via the FR's Hincaster Junction-Arnside line, which had been open since 1876: these were worked by both FR and LNWR engines between Tebay and Furness-line destinations. The LNWR ran full trains as far as Lindal Ore sidings and returned to Tebay with an empty train. The coke for Carnforth ironworks was then worked from Tebay North Eastern yard to Carnforth exchange sidings on a class E goods train, this picked up other traffic at Oxenholme. Coke was also purchased from Wigan in South Lancashire and the Lanarkshire coalfields of Central Scotland. From its opening,

A mixed goods train of the 1920's on the LNWR mainline (L&C section) north of Oxenholme being worked by a FR 0-6-0 goods engine LMS number 12497. The first wagon is a private owner hopper wagons belonging to Carrick and Co. Newcastle under Tyne. The first seven wagons contain coke for Carnforth Ironworks. (CRA Collection Ref. M10126)

CHAPTER SIX

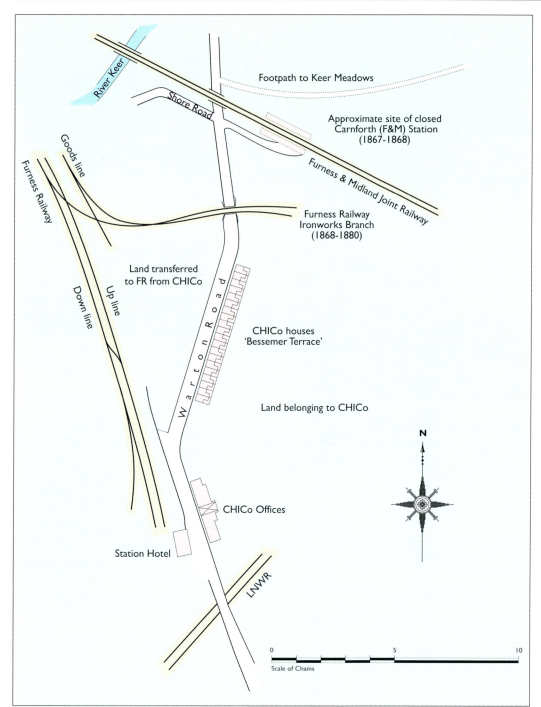

Carnforth 1868. Furness Railway Ironworks Branch. The Ironworks Branch curved away from the Furness Railway line south of the Keer Bridge to cross Warton Road on a new arch bridge. 'Bessemer Terrace' was built alongside the newly diverted Warton Road. (Drawn by author from Parliamentary Plan, courtesy of Lancashire Archives Preston)

the ironworks obtained its iron ore from Park mine and Lindal depot in the Parish of Dalton. The iron ore was worked from Park South or Lindal Ore Sidings into Carnforth by the Furness Railway.

For the opening of the Carnforth ironworks in 1866, the LNWR provided a trailing connection from its Down main line to Carlisle and into a long siding outside the ironworks' east boundary wall; it ran back southwards towards the station and parallel to the main line. At its north end, the siding made an end-on connection with the ironworks' northwards-facing headshunt, from where a single line ran back into the ironworks site. The iron ore and coke wagons were held in the Carnforth exchange sidings until required by the ironworks, they were then worked half a mile northwards on the LNWR Down main line, and reversed into the ironworks siding. The ironworks' standard gauge industrial locomotives moved the coke and iron ore wagons to and from the LNWR ironworks siding into the ironworks for unloading. A crossover was also laid down between the Up and Down main line just north of the FMJR bridge to allow the empty wagons to be returned southwards on the LNWR Up mainline to the Carnforth exchange sidings. The LNWR controlled the Up and Down line connections from Carnforth North signal box (later Carnforth No.3 signal box – see Chapter 12).

The ironworks had only just opened when on 15th August 1866 a Midland Railway excursion train (from Skipton to Windermere, via Lancaster Castle) ran through Carnforth station, passing a signal at danger, and into an iron ore train standing on the Down main line close to the Furness & Midland Joint Railway Bridge. The violence of the collision threw the passengers against one another and the sides of the carriage, resulting in more than thirty persons receiving cuts and bruises, with a small number suffering internal injuries.

In 1867, the FR concluded an agreement with the ironworks to build the Furness Railway 'Ironworks Branch' which would allow iron ore trains to pass directly from the FR into the ironworks site. The advantages of this were the simplification of railway accounting routines, now that only the FR was involved, and presumably a small reduction in the FR's charges to the Carnforth Haematite Iron Company. During 1868 a facing connection was laid down from the FR Down goods line and a trailing connection to the Up main line just south of the River Keer Bridge. The 'Ironworks Branch' curved sharply away from the main line to pass over Warton Road on a new narrow-arch bridge where it entered the north-west corner of the ironworks site before running down an incline to join the ironworks LNWR sidings close to the FMJR railway bridge.

The FR ran the iron ore trains directly into the ironworks site and handed them over to the ironworks on the inclined sidings. The internal layout of the ironworks required all the incoming wagons of iron ore to be drawn forwards from the inclined sidings into the ironworks' north-facing head shunt, by an ironworks engine. This headshunt could accommodate a locomotive and five wagons. The ironworks engine then propelled the wagons back into the ironworks site and then via an inclined ramp on to one of two parallel lines on the top of the mineral bank.

A daily train of limestone was run by the FR from Meathop Quarry, on the north side of the Kent Estuary, east of Grange, and taken directly into the ironworks site via the Ironworks Branch and handed over to the ironworks on the inclined sidings. After handover the ironworks engines moved the limestone wagons round a line which ran along the back of the blast furnaces, where the limestone was manually unloaded directly on to the floor of the mineral bay alongside each vertical lift.

The ironworks engines moved the coke wagons from the LNWR siding to the ironworks' north-facing head shunt and then via an inclined ramp onto one of two parallel lines on the top of the mineral bank.

The mineral bank was divided by a series of walls into storage bays into which the iron ore and coke was separately discharged. Most ironworks were laid out to have a one-way flow through the mineral bank with a ramp at each end; but owing to restricted space Carnforth was unique in that it was the only ironworks with a single ramp. The last three supporting walls of the mineral bank are still visible today alongside the West Coast Main Line. After emptying, the coke wagons were removed from the mineral bank, down the ramp and back to the LNWR sidings and the empty iron ore and limestone wagons taken back to the inclined sidings to be picked up by the FR.

The FR Ironworks Branch was abandoned in 1880 during the construction of the Carnforth Curve, and a new connection was made in 1881 at Carnforth East Junction from the FMJR line, enabling incoming iron ore trains to run directly into the new Midland Top End sidings. These sidings were laid on an incline leading down to the ironworks north-facing headshunt and acted as the ironworks exchange sidings. The new layout enabled the pig iron traffic which had been despatched via the LNWR to be transferred to the FMJR and thence by the MR to South Yorkshire. The movement of limestone via the FR also ceased, as the ironworks laid down their own independent line to Scout Quarry, on the new low road to Silverdale.

The production of iron ore in the Furness district started to decrease from 1884, as some of the older mines were worked out and closed down. After 1890, the ironworks started obtaining iron ore from Hodbarrow on the Duddon estuary, and, after 1897, from Egremont in the Cumberland ore fields. By 1900, the ironworks had started using imported iron ore from Spain and North Africa, and was receiving it through the FR Barrow Docks

Carnforth Haematite Iron Co. Ltd 15-ton iron-ore bottom discharge hopper wagon number 201 of a batch supplied by Chas Roberts & Co. Horbury Junction Wakefield in 1910. (CRA Collection Ref SHI260)

A second batch of identical wagons was supplied in 1913, wagon number 211 is depicted with different lettering. (CRA Collection Ref SHI261)

complex, where modern ore-handling facilities had been installed. Iron ore continued to come from Egremont for mixing with the imported iron ore, up to the end of the Great War.

In 1892 the MR deposited an Act for the construction of a dock at Heysham, which was designed to be accessible at all stages of the tide. A dedicated iron ore berth and associated ore handling facilities and stacking ground on the north side of the dock were included in the plans. On 11th July 1904, the Midland Railway opened its new station (for viewing purposes only) and dock at Heysham and from September, imported iron ore from Spain and North Africa was regularly being handled at the North Quay for Carnforth Ironworks. The ironworks was able to make considerable financial savings on the mileage charges that had previously been paid to the FR.

By arrangement with the LNWR, the loaded iron ore trains were worked by MR engines and train crew via the Hest Bank curve to Carnforth, reversing *en route* at Morecambe Promenade. This curve was single line from Bare Lane to Hest Bank, being the original LCR branch which opened in 1864; with a north-facing connection to the main line (Originally the junction with the main line was known as 'Hest Bank North Junction', until the single line was extended to join the main line at Hest Bank station). The empty trains from Carnforth ran on the Up main line to Hest Bank where they came to a halt. They then reversed over a crossover on to the Down main line at the north end of the station, before running forwards 'wrong road' on the main line and entering the branch to Bare Lane. Here the trains joined the line from Lancaster Castle station to Morecambe Euston Road and Morecambe Promenade, where a further reversal took place to gain access to the line to Heysham Harbour.

The loaded iron ore trains ran to Carnforth Goods Junction

CHAPTER SIX

signal box and on to the Carnforth exchange sidings through goods line to gain access to the FR main line at Carnforth F&M Junction, where they reversed onto the FMJR to gain access to the Midland Middle and Top End sidings.

The early iron ore wagons used by the FR were of wooden construction, with a capacity of between 6 and 8 tons, and with sideways-tipping bodies, a design unique to the FR. Later the FR built wooden-bodied iron ore wagons of 10 and 12 tons capacity. Most were equipped with bottom-discharge doors, but some still had side doors through which the iron ore had to be laboriously shovelled out. Successive iron ore wagons were of steel construction. Between 1907 and 1910, the Furness Railway purchased 108 absolute discharge hopper wagons of 15 tons capacity from Charles Roberts & Co., Horbury Junction, Wakefield. In 1910 the CHICo placed a further order for 36 absolute discharge hopper wagons of 15 tons capacity, again from Charles Roberts; all these hopper wagons were registered with the Furness Railway as they worked to the Furness and West Cumberland mining areas. The wagons supplied in 1910 were lettered 'Carnforth Hematite Iron Co Ltd' and those supplied in 1912 were lettered 'Carnforth Iron Co Limited', the latter lettering being in a more curvaceous style. When the ironworks closed eighteen of the 1910-built hopper wagons were offered for quick sale, and at an attractive price by Thos W. Ward Limited of Albion Works Sheffield in a letter dated 22nd October 1936 to the Millom & Askam Hematite Iron Co., Ltd who it seems did purchase some.

The early coke wagons were of wooden construction and had cupboard-type side doors of 8 tons or 10 tons capacity. They had to be manually emptied through these doors, an arduous and dusty task. In 1901 and 1903, R.Y. Pickering & Co. of Wishaw built a number of 10 tons capacity wooden bodied high-sided wagons having seven plank bodies and extra top rails and with bottom discharge doors. They were lettered 'Carnforth Iron Works' and were hired to the Carnforth Haematite Iron Company, photographic evidence shows that they were registered with the North British Railway.

Pig iron, after cooling in sand beds, was lifted and broken up into useful sizes, then loaded into railway company wagons which had been positioned alongside the pig beds. For easy loading one-plank open wagons of around 10 tons capacity and mainly of MR origin were being used for this traffic. When the ironworks was first opened, the pig iron was taken out of the ironworks to the LNWR ironworks sidings and then worked southwards on the LNWR Up main line to the Carnforth exchange sidings. From Carnforth, the pig iron was taken by the LNWR via its own line to South Yorkshire via Preston until the opening of the FMJR when the MR took it to South Yorkshire for conversion into steel.

An accident involving a passenger train and a loaded pig iron train occurred on 5th February 1873. The passenger train had left Carnforth station on the LNWR Down line and at the same time a pig iron train had started crossing between the Down line and the Up line, the collision occurring at the point of crossing. None of the vehicles left the rails, and none of the passengers complained of being injured. The accident was caused by the signalman who gave the pig iron train a clear signal across the path of the passenger train. The signalman was subsequently dismissed from the company's service. After 1880 the Midland Middle and Bottom End sidings came into use and the pig iron was taken out this way for despatch to South Yorkshire via the FMJR and the MR.

The ironworks owned a number of standard gauge industrial tank locomotives to move raw materials and pig iron to and from the railway companies' sidings and within the ironworks itself. One of their more demanding roles was to remove the slag boxes and ladles to the slag banks and, after 1879, to move limestone from Scout Quarry. All the locomotives supplied to the ironworks were 0-4-0 outside-cylinder saddle tank locomotives and they were painted green. They had nominal three-foot diameter driving wheels and a short wheel-base enabling them to negotiate the tight curves in the ironworks and the irregularly-laid track on the slag bank. All the locomotives were fitted with deep buffer beams faced with wood and tapered inwards at the outer edges for use with the slag boxes and ladles; some were fitted with sprung buffers for moving internal and railway company wagons.

The first locomotive was purchased in 1866 from Hopkins Gilkes of the Tees Engine Company of Middlesbrough, Teesside and named *Fanny* (Hopkins Gilkes No.246). Hopkins Gilkes were locomotive builders and general engineers with a substantial ironworks and heavy engineer capacity in the town of Middlesbrough. Hopkins Gilkes also supplied the next two locomotives, to deal with the increased movements of coke, iron ore, and slag as six blast furnaces were now available for iron making. The engines were named *Maud* in 1869 and *Mary Irving* in 1873 (Hopkins Gilkes No.298). In 1880, a further locomotive was purchased to cope with the longer journey times to the new slag tip on Warton Sands and to Scout Quarry for limestone. As Hopkin Gilkes had gone out of business in 1880, partly as a result of their involvement with the Tay Bridge disaster of 1879, a Yorkshire Engine Company locomotive (works order no 321) was purchased and named *Mabel*.

The next new locomotives were purchased from Hudswell Clarke, *Ethel*, in 1882 (works orders 239) for the limestone workings to and from Scout Quarry and the additional traffic generated by the steel works, and *Maud*, in 1898 (works order 502) to deal with the additional slag arising from the first high-pressure blast furnace. A Fletcher-Jennings locomotive was purchased second-hand from the Crossfield Iron Ore Company, Moor Row; as the Crossfield mines were almost worked out with most being abandoned in 1894. *Crossfield No. 1* arrived in June 1894; it did not stay long at Carnforth being sold later in 1894 to the North Bitchburn Fireclay Company, County Durham.

By 1898 the oldest Hopkins Gilkes engine, *Fanny*, had seen 32 years of service and left the ironworks in 1898, to be followed by *Maud* in 1899 and *Mary Irving* in 1900. Hudswell Clarke allowed £250 in part-exchange against the 1869 *Maud*, providing the locomotive was delivered to them; the new *Maud* was bought by the ironworks for £965. Two of the new Hudswell Clarke locomotives received the names carried by the previous Hopkins Gilkes locomotives *Maud* and *Mary Irving*, whilst the third engine was named *Peggy*. Two further new Hudswell Clarke locomotives arrived before 1910, and perpetuated the previous names of *Ethel* and *Mabel*. The ironworks locomotives were named after various female members of the Barton family, of whom three can be positively identified. *Mary Irving* was the maiden name of the wife of Edward D. Barton, *Mabel* after Mabel Barton of *Cragland*, and *Ethel* after Ethel Barton of *Scarr Close*; these latter two were Edward D. Barton's daughters.

The last industrial engine came from John Brown & Co Atlas works Sheffield and carried the name *Victory*. Built in 1920 by Andrew Barclay of Kilmarnock to works order 1654 it was a 0-4-0 saddle tank engine with 16inch by 24inch cylinders and nominal three-foot diameter wheels. This engine was fitted with wooden pads (dumb buffers) instead of tradi-

IRONWORKS TRAFFIC

Hopkins Gilkes order No. 298 was supplied in July 1873 to the Carnforth Haematite Iron Company and was named 'Mary Irving'. This engine is fitted with wooden pads (dumb buffers) instead of traditional sprung buffers. (Industrial Locomotive Society. Frank Jones Collection)

The last industrial engine came from John Brown & Co. Atlas works Sheffield – it carried the name 'Victory'. It was built in 1920 by Andrew Barclay of Kilmarnock to works order 1654. This engine is fitted with wooden pads (dumb buffers) instead of traditional sprung buffers. (National Records of Scotland and University of Glasgow Archive Services. Andrew Barclay Sons & Co. Ltd collection GB0248 GD329/1/1487)

CHAPTER SIX

tional sprung buffers. It was a heavier and more powerful locomotive than had hitherto been used by the ironworks and was a replacement for *The Mary Irving* which had been badly damaged at the time of the fatal slag line accident in 1920 (covered later in this chapter). As John Brown had become a shareholder in the Carnforth Haematite Iron Company in 1915, it may well have been an internal book transfer.

Six locomotives remained when the ironworks closed in 1930, and all passed to Thomas Ward Ltd, being used on the site during the demolition of the ironworks. At least one locomotive was scrapped at Carnforth by Thomas Ward, but the remaining locomotives were sold to other operators. *Ethel* stayed to work the new tarmacadam works of Thomas Ward Ltd before leaving Carnforth. It was rebuilt by Ridley Shaw of Manchester around 1938, before going to the Millom & Askam Haematite Iron Co as Millom No. 2, remaining there until scrapped in March 1953. *Victory* was sold to the Sheffield Coal Company around 1931. After the vesting of the National Coal Board on 1st January 1947, the locomotive passed to the NCB's North Eastern Division and was allocated to Denaby Main Colliery, Doncaster. The Andrew Barclay works plate *1654* was sold at the Sheffield Railway Auctions.

Slag from the manually-charged blast furnaces was more viscous due to the lower furnace temperatures of that time, allowing slag boxes to be used. The slag boxes were positioned on the slag road at the base of the furnace. When the slag was ready for pouring, the furnace was unplugged, and the molten slag directed into slag boxes where it cooled to form a solid block. The slag boxes were rectangular in plan with tapered sides and sat on a four-wheeled bogie, the bottom edge of the box being sealed to the base of the bogie with fire clay. They were supplied by firms such as the Lowca Engineering Company of Whitehaven, and the Canal Foundry at Ulverston, but there may well have been other manufacturers.

Around nine acres of marshy land due north of the ironworks site and bordering the River Keer had been allocated for the first slag tip, which was brought into use in September 1866. With the ironworks locomotive leading, the slag boxes were pulled away from the blast furnace and taken under the FMJR Bridge, and parallel with the LNWR main line on to the north-facing head shunt where a reversal took place. With the engine now pushing, the slag boxes were propelled from the head shunt upwards on to an earthen embankment lined with heavy stone blocks, and on to the slag line which was laid on the surface of the slag tip. At the slag tip, the slag box, with tapered sides for releasing it from the solid block of slag, was lifted off its bogie, and the bogie was then pushed to the tip face where the solid block of slag was tipped off.

The Keer Marsh slag tip continued to grow alongside the FMJR embankment, reaching westwards to Warton Road and northwards to the banks of the River Keer. From its opening in 1864, the ironworks had produced an average of 120,000 tons of slag per annum. By 1878 the Keer Marsh tip was nearing its full capacity, and the ironworks directors started looking for another large area of land to accommodate a second slag tip.

As well as being the ironworks main promoter, H.J. Walduck was also the major promoter of the Bolton-le-Sands, Warton and Silverdale Land Company. Formed in March 1874 the aim of the Company was to reclaim a large acreage of land from the foreshore alongside Warton Sands, by creating a substantial sea embankment running from Morecambe Lodge on the shore at Bolton-le-Sands to Park Point at Arnside. The scheme was over-ambitious and the company folded in 1879 due to lack of capital, but it would seem that Walduck had other plans to protect his own capital outlay.

As part of the land reclamation scheme, Walduck had purchased the entire foreshore between Carnforth and Jenny Brown's Point at Silverdale, four miles north of Carnforth. He now planned to build a sea embankment, much nearer to the shore across Warton Sands, to reclaim the foreshore, and create a large area of arable land which could be rented or sold at a good profit. There was a hidden agenda here, as in 1879 Walduck arranged for the land to be transferred to the CHICo. for its new slag tip. The slag would be used to build the embankment across the foreshore of Warton Sands; in addition he had plans to build an alkali works using the ironworks slag as feeder material.

During 1879 the CHICo. made arrangements for a new slag line to be laid down from the ironworks to the foreshore on Warton Sands and alongside the north bank of the River Keer. The slag line left the ironworks northern headshunt and ran upwards alongside the Midland Top End sidings to a point opposite Carnforth East junction and across the north side of the new FMJR Warton Road Bridge. It curved away across the River Keer on its own lightweight iron bridge, and ran along the base of Hazel Mount, and then along the north side of the Midland Bottom End sidings to Masons Bridge. Masons Bridge, built in white limestone and red sandstone, carried Sands Lane over the slag line, and was built to a reduced gauge to accommodate the smaller profile of the ironworks' industrial locomotives. The line then climbed steeply upwards on to the flat land at Thwaite Farm, opposite Warton Toll Bar on the new low-road to Silverdale. Here the slag line made an end-on junction with the Scout Quarry branch, at which point it turned back to cross over the FR main line by a lightweight iron bridge. The line then ran downwards to cross Sands Lane on the level, and onto a low earthen embankment alongside the River Keer.

The CHICo purchased from the FR, a strip of land 433 yards long from Sands Lane to the FMJR boundary for £175 5s 0d. A further 1093 yards of land was purchased for £429 15s 0d from the FMJR boundary to the junction with the ironworks headshunt excluding that over Warton Road Bridge. An annual rental charge of £600 was made for the use and maintenance of the north side of the FMJR Warton Road Bridge over which the slag line passed, the rental charge being split pro rata between the FR and the FMJR. The slag tip was brought into use on Wednesday 17th July 1880 and the *Barrow Herald* of the same date stated:

The accumulation of slag from the blast furnaces at Carnforth takes place rapidly. Space set aside for slag has been used up. The plan has been carried out to convey this by-product onto the sea shore. On Wednesday the first bogies of slag were tipped after being conducted on a new line.

The new slag bank was laid down alongside the north bank of the River Keer for about 1200 yards where it turned through 90 degrees, to form a seaward arm across Warton Sands. The seaward arm of the slag bank, if it had continued across Warton Sands, would have met up with a sea embankment which was under construction at Jenny Brown's Point. This sea embankment was never completed, but the resulting slag bank was sufficiently lengthy to ensure that a large tract of land would silt up on its landward side.

With the introduction of the Ford and Mancur regenerative hot blast stoves operating with blast furnaces 1, 2 and 3, slag boxes which were circular in plan and with tapered sides were

IRONWORKS TRAFFIC

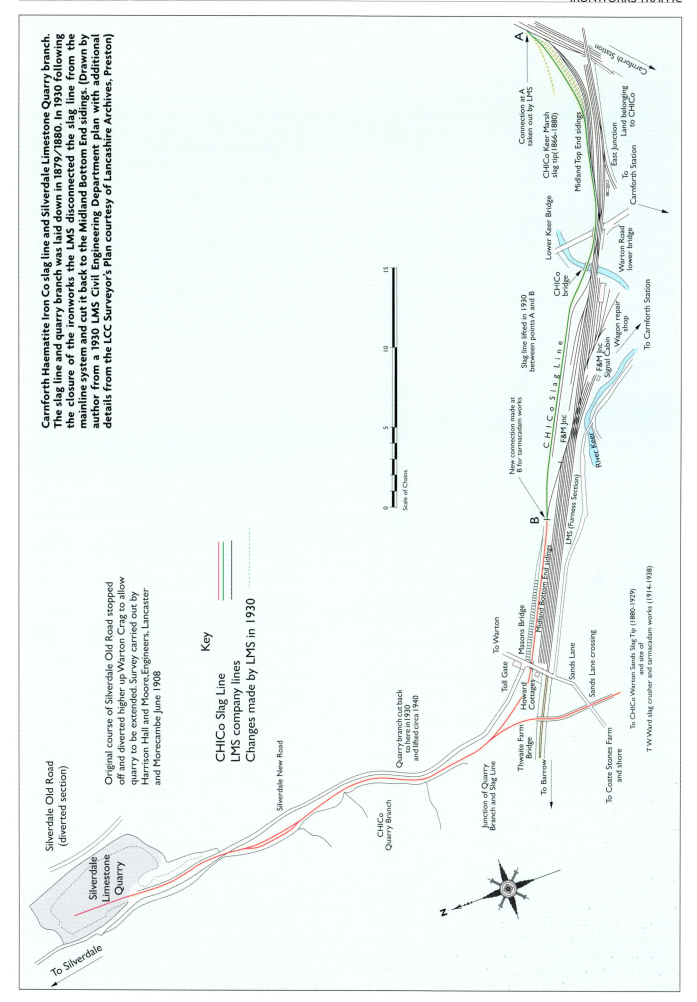

introduced. These remained in use until 1909 when blast furnaces 1, 2 and 3 were closed down. The tipping operations were the same as with the square slag boxes, which continued to be used until 1903 and the introduction of ladles.

The first of the mechanically-charged furnaces had been blown in during May 1903, and as it worked at a higher pressure and higher temperature, the slag produced was very fluid, and for the first time slag ladles were brought into use. With the locomotive alternately pushing and pulling up to 20 tons of slag in several ladles, the three-mile journey took approximately fifteen minutes, and on the two sharp climbs the small ironworks engines were worked hard. The slag from the high-pressure furnaces was still fluid enough to tip some fifteen minutes after pouring from the blast furnaces because of the higher furnace temperature. The extensive slag bank was built up from separate loads of slag, each brought up from the ironworks.

About three miles to the north-west of Carnforth is Warton Crag, a limestone escarpment that stands 534 feet above sea level. In 1878 the ironworks obtained the right to extract limestone from Warton Crag, and opened Scout Quarry in 1880 on the new low road to Silverdale. The single line quarry branch ran parallel with west side of the new road for about a mile where a run-round loop was laid. The line then crossed the road at an acute angle to enter the quarry. The old coach road to Silverdale ran across the top of Warton Crag and by 1908 the quarry had made such inroads into the hillside that the old road had to be closed and diverted. A diversion plan was made by the CHICo. and submitted and approved at the June 1908 Lancaster Quarter Session.

The opening of the quarry removed the rail charges being paid to the FR and the extraction charges being paid to Meathop Quarry, as well as giving the iron company an independent and guaranteed supply of limestone. The limestone was brought down from the quarry in the ironworks' own wagons, and taken directly into the ironworks where it was manually unloaded into one of the mineral bank storage bays. Howard Cottages were built on Sands Lane next to the slag line and soon after the line's opening, the first occupants of the two cottages were the Scout Quarry foreman and the slag tip overseer.

A lease dated 28th August 1914 between the CHICo. and Lancashire County Council gave the latter the rights to extract slag from the tip and operate a tarmacadam works, which was set up on the seaward leg of the slag bank on Warton Sands. The tar for coating the slag arrived by rail from the gas works at Morecambe, and LCC used the coated slag for road construction. The CHICo. agreed to provide the motive power, and to work the wagons between the tip and the works and the Midland Top End sidings.

The number of fatalities for the ironworks recorded by the Carnforth coroner was extremely low, and except for one case in 1891 where a labourer fell into a furnace, death within the ironworks was not caused by burning from hot metal. The largest number of fatalities was associated with crushing injuries sustained during coupling or uncoupling of wagons whilst shunting was being done. The ironworks' worst accident between two trains occurred on the slag line, near to its junction with the quarry branch, at 11.30am on 28th June 1920. A slag train had left the ironworks and was on its way to Warton Sands slag bank, propelling three full ladles of molten slag. The driver of *Peggy* blew his whistle, as was normal working practice after passing Hazel Mount, and again on the approach to Masons Bridge at Sands Lane. On hearing no response, the driver believed the line ahead was clear; the engine passed under Masons Bridge at Sands Lane and with a full head of steam worked the ladles up the incline alongside Howard Cottages. At Thwaite Farm the line curves and the driver of *Peggy* saw another train which was about 12 yards away coming towards him, whereupon he braked and put the engine into reverse.

About the same time as *Peggy* was passing Carnforth East Junction a full limestone train of eight wagons left Scout Quarry and was slowly gathering speed as the line ran gradually downwards from the quarry, its only brake power being a hand brake on the engine. The *Mary Irving* was at the head of the limestone train, running cab first, and as it approached the curve close to Thwaite Farm, it collided with the slag train. The leading slag ladle was derailed, and ended up on its side with the ladle disconnected from its trunions. The *Mary Irving* was badly damaged and its wheels knocked from beneath it and the driver and shunter died immediately from molten metal burns.

The inquest was held on Tuesday 30th June 1920 at the Station Hotel by the deputy coroner, Colonel H.D. Wilson. The ironworks engineer, when giving evidence at the inquest, said that it was usual for the slag train to follow the quarry train up to Thwaite Flat junction, knowing it would have time to return whilst the quarry train loaded up. There were no signals on the line and no official rules for working the line, the practice of using the engine whistles being carried out by the drivers for their own safety. The engineer said that the line had been in use for forty years and that there had not been an accident in all that time. The farmer of nearby Coate Stones farm, as well as a wagon examiner working in the Midland Bottom End sidings, both remembered the engine of the slag train whistling as it approached Masons Bridge. The manager of the ironworks said that no trains had been run in that fashion since the accident, as changes to the way of working had already been made. After the accident working rules were put in place, that the quarry train should closely follow a slag train in both the up and down direction and that the shunter of a down quarry train should walk to Masons Bridge to ensure the way ahead was clear for the train.

The coroner returned a verdict of accidental death and prepared a full report for the Home Secretary. In his report he had this to say:

That their deaths had been contributed to by the CHICo. running trains both ways on a single line without any system of signals or other safety devices to indicate to the drivers of the different trains whether the line was clear or not, some such system being all the more necessary as there was a bad curve on the line.

A day of mourning took place at the ironworks, and a large cortege of workmen accompanied the coffins from the ironworks to Warton Parish Church.

With the closure of the ironworks in 1929, the slag line was now redundant and in 1930 the London Midland & Scottish Railway Company removed the slag line connection to the ironworks' north-facing headshunt. The slag line was lifted all the way from the ironworks headshunt to the Midland Bottom End sidings where a new connection was made, as traffic to Scout Quarry had also ceased the line to the quarry was also lifted. The bridge deck carrying the slag line across the FMJR Warton Road Bridge was removed, and the ironworks bridge over the River Keer was removed completely. The remaining section of the slag line was renamed the 'tarmacadam branch'.

When the ironworks closed, the Lancashire County Council lease of 1914 came to an end, and the North Lonsdale Tarmacadam Company Ltd, a subsidiary of Thomas Ward Ltd,

When this photograph was taken in 1935 the Carnforth Haematite Iron Co. slag line had been closed but the lightweight iron bridge remained in use for Thwaite Farm. Here the slag line turned back to cross over the Furness Railway main line. It then ran downwards on to a low earthen embankment alongside the River Keer. (CRA Collection Ref. PA0002)

took over the operation of the tarmacadam works on Warton Sands. The Tarmacadam Company selected only that slag which had come from the manually-charged blast furnaces in slag boxes, as this slag was much harder than the ladle slag and more suitable for road building. Its main customer was Lancashire County Council, and slag crushing continued until 1938 when the plant closed down. The tarmacadam branch was lifted soon after by Thomas Ward Ltd as scrap.

Slag crushing re-commenced on the Warton Sands slag tip for a short time in 1958, to provide crushed slag for the foundations of the new section of the M6 motorway between Lancaster and Carnforth. At this time the slag was taken out by road transport, and once the road foundations were in place, slag crushing ceased and the crushing plant was dismantled.

All that now remains as a reminder of the ironworks railway is a few feet of rail embedded in concrete, very close to the boundary fence of the industrial estate from which TDG - Transport Development Group (a transport logistics and storage group) operated. They vacated the site in September 2011 centralising their operations through their Warrington depot.

Carnforth 3rd March 1956. To the north of Carnforth the Furness & Midland Joint Line Railway Bridge crosses over the West Coast mainline and the ironworks sidings that were laid down by LNWR which are in the foreground. The train is the 13.52pm Leeds City for Morecambe Promenade. The Carnforth portion has been picked up at Wennington by 5MT 4-6-0 44892 (CRA Collection Ref. PEF981)

CHAPTER SIX

The new industrial engine on the left is named 'The Mary Irving' and was purchased in 1900 and is a replacement for the industrial engine on the right, named 'Mary Irving', which was purchased in 1873. In the foreground are the drivers, firemen and shunters who worked with these industrial engines. (Author's collection)

In early 1880 the Midland Top End sidings for the ironworks and the ironworks slag line are under construction at Carnforth East Junction. Warton Road Bridge is being extended on the north side for the slag line. The Midland Railway engine shed of 1867 is to the left of the Furness & Midland line. (Mrs Pat Jackson Collection Ref TR12)

CHAPTER SEVEN

THE TOWNSHIP OF CARNFORTH

The arrival of the three railway companies, followed by the ironworks, results in new housing being built and the creation of a new commercial centre. The Victorian town soon surpasses in both size and importance the old village of Carnforth.

The village of Carnforth had developed on higher ground alongside the Turnpike Road, and by 1800 consisted of rows of small two-storey cottages (which had replaced most of the earlier wood and clay houses), several small detached houses, a lime kiln, several farms, a smithy, and three public houses. The final development of the village included early period Georgian houses of the villa type, built on the northern limits of the settlement. The western extremity of the village around Mill Lane was entirely rural in character and contained a number of small farms, some orchards, gravel pit workings, and a number of small ponds.

Up to the middle of the 19th century, agriculture together with the working of the local limestone quarries, and the sand and gravel deposits discovered when the canal was built, provided most of the work for the male population of Carnforth. All this was to change rapidly after 1850 with the coming of the railway and the ironworks, both of which required skilled labour which had to be brought in from other regions. Carnforth would in the years 1860 to 1880 grow from a rural community into a working class township to accommodate the influx of these workers and their families.

A number of buildings around Mill Lane would be demolished as the railway system developed the first were those within the deviation lines of the L&C Railway, then the FMJR and finally the Carnforth Curve. The original Hall Gate farm alongside the L&C Railway would be subsumed under the first part of the Carnforth exchange sidings and a new replacement farm built higher up on the southern slopes of Hunting Hill. As the new town developed Carnforth Hall and lands would be subsumed under the commercial area of the town and the first part of the Carnforth sorting office would be built on the site of Toad Plud farm and forge which had both a blacksmith's forge and a white forge for metalling wheel bearings of horse-drawn carriages and carts.

In 1851, only 26 men were employed on the railway but this had risen to 110 by the date of the 1861 census. Between 1861 and 1871, the population of Carnforth had increased nearly three-fold from 393 to 1035, owing to the regular arrival of skilled railway workers for the more responsible jobs, a situation that continued in Carnforth into the early 1900s. In the same period, the population had increased from 581 to 1035 in the village of Warton, where land was cheaper than in Carnforth and where an industrial village had been built at Millhead to accommodate the migrant ironworkers.

The Victorian town of Carnforth is represented by streets of terraced houses, a few houses of the villa type, and a number of commercial and public buildings, together with several churches and schools. The topography of the land meant that most of the streets were laid out on an east-west axis the exception being the Northern Turnpike road and the modern A6 which run on a north-south alignment. All the buildings were subject to some of the early building regulations and bye-laws which determined certain minimum building standards, as well as the new Public Health regulations which required clean water and adequate drainage. At that time house building was not subject to such stringent local authority planning regulations as today, nevertheless the streets and housing plots making up the Victorian town have been laid out to an ordered plan, by Harrison & Hall, land agents, surveyors and architect who had offices in both Lancaster and Morecambe. The town was built on land belonging to the Carnforth Hall Estate with the majority of the building taking place between 1860 and 1900.

In 1860 a national government rule was made which required public service personnel, policemen, ambulance men, firemen and railway drivers and firemen, to live within a one-hour radius of their workplace or signing-on point where they booked on or off duty. In the railways case it was the distance that the 'knocker up' could reasonably walk when more than one person had to be called out for rostered duty or for relief duty. From 1860 the majority of railway staff at Carnforth lived close to their signing-on point, within the new town itself and the old village of Carnforth, a minority lived further away in Warton or Kellet. At Carnforth the knocking-up duties were generally assigned to the junior cleaner who would often set off just after midnight and be out until about 6am, during which time he might have walked several miles. By 1923 a pedal cycle was available for the duty. By 1950, staff no longer needed to live within the one-hour radius, as cheap and reliable alarm clocks were now available and more staff had a telephone; as a result the 'knocker up' became part of railway history.

To ensure there was sufficient and suitable housing for their employees the railway companies encouraged local tradesmen to build them, although there was one exception to this: the London & North Western Railway, which employed its own labour to build two adjacent terraces consecutively. Most of the houses in Carnforth were built a few at a time, either by a number of single tradesmen or by a consortium of tradesmen, who, lacking large amounts of capital relied upon property investors to provide financial backing. The majority of working class occupants could not afford to buy a house at that time so most of the housing stock was rented from the same property investors and builders and some by loans from the early Building Societies.

One of the property investors was James Stelfox; he had made money working as a manager for John Brogden & Sons (including the building of a section of the ULR) before retiring to Carnforth and investing in the town and community. John Rigg, of Carnforth, a builder and joiner, was one of the major builders, who initially had a yard at Hewthwaite Terrace and later in Oxford Street. The Carnforth Co-operative Society also built a number of houses, some of which were rented back to their employees. There is evidence that Broomby's from South

CHAPTER SEVEN

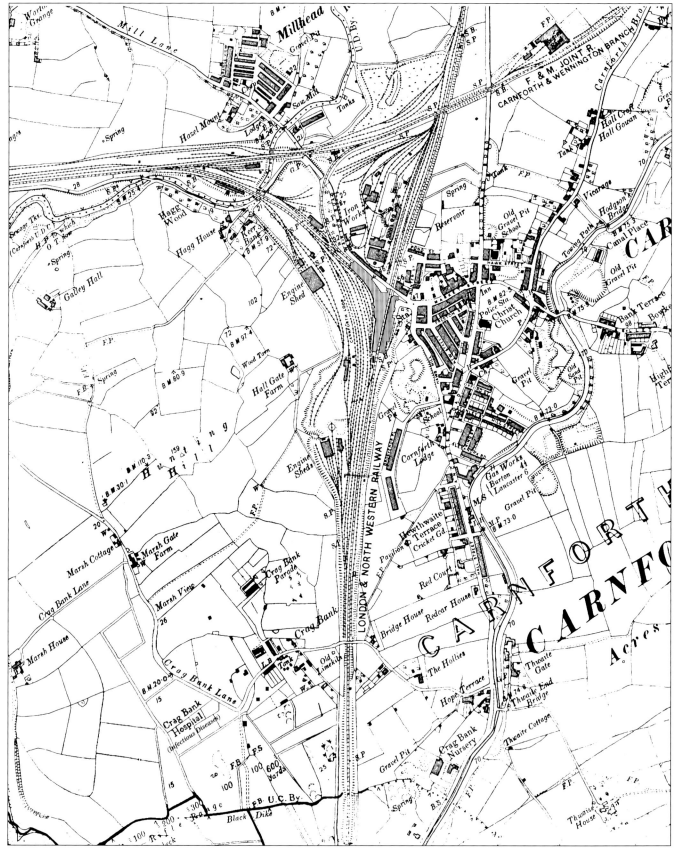

Carnforth 1891. The majority of the town developed around the station and Lancaster Road (the present A6) with the commercial centre along Main Street (later Market Street). (Lancashire Archives Preston with the kind permission of the Ordnance Survey)

Westmorland (a company still operating today as part of the national Travis Perkins organisation) built houses in the town, as well as a number of established stone masons and builders in Lancaster such as Mr. R. Clarkson.

Carnforth, unlike many Victorian industrial towns, was spared the uniform use of red brick as a surface material, and only Edward Street and one side of New Street used red brick on the house fronts. It was used a lot on the rear faces of houses and on backyard walls and outbuildings. The railway companies were the largest users of red brick, and many of the railway buildings, apart from the station, were faced with red brick. The Lune Valley brickworks supplied bricks for some of the houses of the

Millhead industrial village, and they were brought in by the railway. A brick kiln was in operation for the ironworks at Lunds Field, its main purpose was to supply fire bricks for the ironworks blast furnaces, and it too may have provided some bricks for the town.

To a much greater extent brown sandstone has been used as a facing stone on the front of many properties built in Carnforth between 1860 and 1900. It is not found locally, and the railways played an important part in bringing the sandstone from Lancaster and the Lune valley. Red sandstone was first used in Carnforth by the ironworks on some of its industrial buildings in a similar manner to the Barrow ironworks. It was also used on the Station Hotel, the Congregational Church and buildings in Market Street and Lancaster Road. This red sandstone did not exist locally, being brought in by the Furness Railway from that company's Hawcoat quarries at Barrow-in-Furness.

About 1860, a terrace of twelve two-storey flush-fronted basic and minimal houses with separate earth closets at the rear was built at Millhead in the Parish of Warton, close to and on the north bank of the River Keer and named Carlisle Terrace. A similar terrace of nine flush-fronted two-storey houses named Alma Terrace was built in 1863 alongside Kellet Road and facing the junction to the upper part of North Road. They were some of the earliest houses to be built on the periphery of the present town and were probably built for railway staff drafted in to work the enlarged station of 1857. In 1863, Mr. R. Clarkson of Lancaster introduced a modern style of building into Carnforth, at Robin Hill on the site of the gravel pits. He built the Queens Hotel, and four adjacent houses and the Free Trade Building; they were the first new buildings on Main Street, which was later to become Market Street and the commercial centre of the town. Mr. Clarkson soon after moved to Carnforth and became the lessee of Hutton Roof quarries; he built other properties and his family house Laund House which still exists on Lancaster Road but now renamed The Launds.

J. Hartley & Co., a well-known Kendal firm of grocers, bakers and caterers, opened their first shop and warehouse in 1863 at Millhead, near to the Lower Keer Bridge, and on the Warton side of the River Keer. They did a good trade in supplying food to the construction workers working on the Furness & Midland Joint Railway, the doubling of the Ulverstone & Lancaster Railway, and the building of the ironworks. In 1880 J. Hartley & Co., now

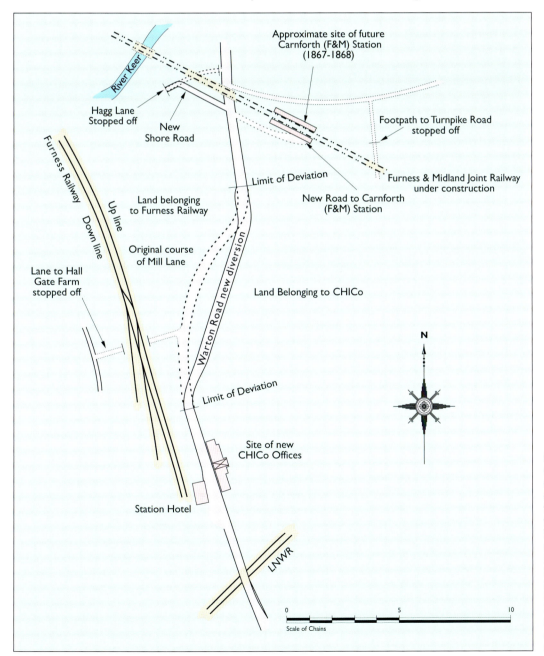

Carnforth 1866. Diversion of Mill Lane. The original course of Mill Lane was diverted by the CHICo so they could build houses for their skilled ironmasters. The diversion straightened out the middle section of Mill Lane which was then renamed Warton Road. (Drawn by author from Highways Deviation Plan, courtesy of Lancashire Archives Preston Ref. number QSD 158)

CHAPTER SEVEN

Warton Grange circa 1900. A substantial Gentleman's residence, it was built in 1873 for Edward D. Barton the ironworks manager. It was surrounded by four acres of land guaranteeing privacy and exclusiveness and was situated on higher ground with views over the Keer valley. (George Nightingale collection).

described as 'Grocers, Corn and Flour Factors', retained their bakery at Millhead and opened a large ground-floor shop in the new three-storey 'Bank Building' which were on the opposite side to the Lancaster Bank at the junction of Scotland Road and Kellet Road. The Hartley family was headed by John Hartley, who was a businessman as well as a strict Quaker; he prospered, and moved into property and gravel pits within the town. At one time, he owned stables with twenty horses for delivering groceries to the surrounding villages.

In the spring of 1866, a terrace of six houses named Canal Place was built on land belonging to the Lancaster Canal Company, to the east of Kellet Road Bridge. By this date the canal had passed into the ownership of the LNWR, and the terraced houses built in red brick with sandstone headers and cills, pre-date the standard LNWR house design of F.W. Webb, who became the company's Locomotive Superintendent in October 1871.

In 1868, the Furness & Midland Joint Railway bought ten acres and five perches of pasture land in the Parish of Warton alongside the River Keer for the sum of £2006 5s 0d from Robert Stainton. In 1870, following the opening of the FMJR, the Midland Railway had built a terrace of twelve two-storey houses alongside the River Keer and named it Midland Terrace. At the end of this terrace, the Midland Railway also had built two semi-detached two-storey houses; they were named Keer Villas, and these were occupied by the Midland Railway's Locomotive Shed Master and the Furness Railway's Locomotive Shed Master. A long-time resident of Carnforth recalled that the town's street name plates which were probably lacquered sheet-metal had white lettering on a blue background. All have been repainted and the only one remaining in this colour is that at Midland Terrace.

The directors of the ironworks needed their skilled ironmasters and foremen close by, and made arrangements to build company houses in close proximity to the works. In early 1866, Edward D. Barton, prepared a plan for diverting Mill Lane, he sent it on the 16th March 1866 to William Preston, 'Surveyor of the Highways of the township of Carnforth'. The wording which accompanied the diversion plan stated:

Diversion to commence at or near to the public house called the 'Station Inn', to Warton for 400 yards diverted and twinned. The new highway will be nearer and more commodious to the public.

The diversion plan was deposited at the county offices Preston on the 21st April 1866 by a Mr. Thomson on behalf of Edward. D. Barton and was submitted and approved at the Lancaster Quarter Session held in July 1866. Arrangements were made to straighten the middle part of Mill Lane and divert it across ironworks land, so that the company houses could be built alongside the road and near to the works. The new road did not take long to build, and the land to the west of the new road was passed to the Furness Railway. The old course of Mill Lane was closed off and was eventually buried in 1880 under the new Carnforth Curve (mentioned in Chapters 4 and 8), running between the new junctions at Carnforth Station and Carnforth East. At the time of the diversion Mill Lane was renamed Warton Road.

In the autumn of 1866 a contract was given to John Rigg, for

Carnforth circa 1910. The station approach road is on the left with a typical LNWR direction sign. On Warton Road are 'Station Buildings', built between 1882 and 1887, the nearest two are commercial outlets and the Post Office is adjacent to the railway bridge. (Lancashire Library collection Cat. number 1898-28)

building a row of twenty two-storey terraced houses on the east side of the newly-diverted and re-named Warton Road. Henry Bessemer was a shareholder in the iron company, and in recognition of this the terrace was named Bessemer Terrace. In 1871, Bessemer Terrace was demolished to make way for the steelworks. The houses were rebuilt at the south end of the town and for economic reasons, the ironworks re-used the main structural materials, such as stones and slates together with roof and floor timbers, and door and window lintels, but the rebuilt houses may not be of the original architectural style. Initially re-named Bessemer Terrace by the time of the 1881 census, the terrace had been renamed Hall Street after John Hall, chairman of the CHICo., who died in 1887 aged 83; the houses were eventually renumbered and included in Lancaster Road.

To accommodate the increasing number of ironworkers and their families, the CHICo arranged for the building of a new industrial village at Millhead in the parish of Warton. The village was built relatively quickly; and there are variations in house styles, and the building materials used varied with each terrace (being random limestone, red brick and ironworks slag) suggesting that more than one builder was involved. By 1872, 104 two-storey terraced houses in five compact rows had been built on steeply sloping land on the Warton side of the River Keer, and to the west of the ironworks. The houses were typically Victorian working-class, two up and two down, with the minimum of facilities, although they were the first houses in Warton to have a cold water tap inside.

The streets at Millhead were named after people. Albert Street was named after Albert Edward Barton, son of the ironworks' manager, and Mary Street after Mary Irving, wife of Edward Barton. William Street was named after William Slater of Manchester, the CHICo solicitor, and Stainton Street after the landowner upon whose land the estate was built. The Millhead estate was populated almost entirely by the Dudley ironworkers and soon became known locally as 'Dudley' and this name was used officially for the first time on the 1893 edition of the Ordnance Survey map.

Facing onto Mill Lane were two short terraces which were the only three storey-dwellings on Millhead. One terrace contained three lower-middle-class houses, with a shop at one end and a public house at the other; this was built and owned by Mr R. Clarkson in 1870. Described as the Beer House it was officially called the West View Hotel, but was also known locally as the Nib by the Millhead ironworkers. According to a senior local resident, Nib stood for 'never in bed' as the landlord was supposedly in attendance at the bar for the whole of 24 hours! The second terrace consists of one large dwelling which was described as a model lodging house for transient ironworkers; it was better known by the local residents as the 'three-storey working class hotel'. It was very basic with concrete floors, plain tables and few furnishings; it was run by a family who lived in part of house.

Warton Grange was built in 1873 on the southern edge of the village of Warton for Edward D. Barton. It was a very substantial gentleman's residence with twelve bedrooms together with adjoining stables and four acres of land guaranteeing privacy and exclusiveness. It was within a half mile of the ironworks, on a slight elevation with views over the Keer valley. It was demolished in November 2001 and residential development has now taken place on the site.

CHAPTER SEVEN

As there was a continuing need for more housing, the three railway companies encouraged the building of a large number of terraced houses in streets radiating from the station. These houses were solidly built to a basic standard with hot and cold water and flush toilets which at the time was superior but not luxurious. Building commenced around 1875 on a large, roughly triangular shaped plot of land on rising ground bounded by Haws Hill, Market Street and Lancaster Road. A mixture of two- and three-storey houses was built within these streets and a whole new community was created in a very compact area. On the west side of Lancaster Road, slightly larger two-storey terraced houses and end-of-terrace shops were built.

The building of Bank Terrace and Booker Terrace, separate rows of two-storey terraced houses to the east of the canal along Kellet Road, took place during 1878, to be followed by Highfield Terrace and parts of Russell Road which at that time were on the eastern boundaries of the town. The building of further houses in 1880 took place on the east side of Lancaster Road at Stanley Street, Oxford Street, Hill Street and Alexandra Road.

A row of more prestigious terraced houses of higher relative value, called Hewthwaite Terrace was built along Lancaster Road between 1878 and 1883. These two-storey houses were away from the railway and the ironworks and any airborne pollution created by them. They were intended to appeal to the town's white collar workers and the better-off families and, when built, were on the edge of the town with open aspects to the rear. Annas Bank, a row of terraced houses of a similar build, was also constructed on Kellet Road opposite Booker Terrace just after 1900.

Between 1882 and 1884, the ironworks promoted the building of twenty, two-storey terrace houses, for the ironworks labourers in Ramsden Street, Pond Street and Pond Terrace, on the east side of the London & North Western Railway line. These houses were very basic and built to the lowest standard as a planned project to provide as many dwellings as possible at the lowest cost in the minimum of space. The small back yards abutted each other and the earth closets for all the houses were originally built *en bloc* at some distance from them, on land now occupied by the postal sorting office in Hunter Street.

In 1893, Coulton Hunter, of Barrow, had built a row of ten very substantial terrace houses on the east side of Hunter Street within a hundred yards of the station, some of which seem to have been occupied by the ironworks salaried staff. The terrace was built in mock-Elizabethan cottage style to match the Lancaster & Carlisle station building. A detached matching two-storey flush-fronted house was situated at the south end of the terrace and was occupied for a while by Mr Hunter himself.

The London & North Western Railway chose an area to the south of the station off Haws Hill to build two terraces during 1897 and 1898. According to the *Lancaster Guardian* of December 1896 a Mr. Aldren's property was compulsorily removed to suit the requirements of the LNWR. The 7th January issue stated that plans had been submitted by the LNWR for two terraces of twenty-three and eighteen houses respectively. Building commenced in April 1897 and although the houses were finished by the middle of 1898 there were problems with the sewers and the approach road had not been finished. As late as April 1899 the Carnforth UDC was writing to the LNWR about the unfinished state of Grosvenor Terrace.

These two-storey houses were to F.W.Webb's standard LNWR design, the LNWR bringing in their own materials and using their own labour to build the houses. These houses were built flush with the street and near to the railway, and were within sight of the 1892 LNWR engine shed (described in chapter 10) and the LNWR end of the Carnforth exchange sidings. A footpath ran from the houses to a new footbridge which crossed the lines and gave direct access to the shed. The centre house of the terrace containing the twenty-three houses was a much larger-fronted house with a gable roof running at ninety degrees to the roof line of the terrace. Also at the inner ends of the two terraces and at ninety degrees to them and facing each other were two slightly larger houses with a small garden at the front for privacy. These three houses were occupied by the LNWR salaried staff such as the Locomotive Shed Master. The forty-one houses were sold as one lot in 1976 by Ratcliffe and Bibby, solicitors and estate agents of Market Street, Carnforth.

In 1901 a detached two-storey house with a garden had been built close to the station, at the bottom of Haws Hill, for the Stationmaster. After the last stationmaster retired in 1960, it was let by BR to railway tenants. The last tenant worked for the civil engineering department and said that there was only one electric power point in each room and that it was cold in winter. One of the younger household members remembered the loading dock siding at the bottom of the garden being used exclusively by the civil engineers. The BR Property Board eventually sold the house into private ownership.

A villa type house named Red Court was built in 1880 on the southern outskirts of the town beside Lancaster Road and opposite Bessemer Terrace, for Albert Edward Barton, the son of the ironworks manager. It was surrounded by high walls which enclosed an acre of ground; they were built of limestone and were topped with elegant iron railings. The house is no longer recognised as it has been extensively altered externally with modern ugly additions; it is now the Working Men's Club. Hazel Mount at Millhead was also a villa type house and an extensive property, with large outbuildings and its own grounds and was surrounded by woodland. It seems to have had a chequered history being unoccupied during 1912, then later, occupied for many years by John Jennings the landlord of the Black Bull in the village of Warton, and now renamed the George Washington. Again it was unoccupied in 1960, when the grounds and outbuildings were being used to park up road tipper wagons used in the carriage of sand and gravel. It was demolished shortly after and a new housing estate built on the grounds.

In 1871 the post office and public telegraph office moved out of the L&C station building on the Up LNWR platform and into a new single-storey building which was situated on the station approach road close to Warton Road Bridge. Carnforth increasingly became an important postal exchange point, and in 1878/79 the first section of the Carnforth sorting office was built as a single-storey building parallel to the Up LNWR mainline and on the north-side of Warton Road Bridge. The sorting office needed to be connected directly to the LNWR Up platform to allow mail to be transferred to and from any part of the station so a new archway was built alongside the existing arch. The new arch was under Warton Road which was re-graded and was made of blue engineer's bricks as they had better load bearing and weather resistant properties. The LNWR Up platform was extended northwards under the arch to connect with the sorting office doorway.

On 18th January 1882 there was an indenture drawn up between Martha Durham Milner and Elizabeth Halliwell with the Leeds Permanent Benefit Building Society for a sum of £1496 to be distributed as £1296 to Elizabeth Halliwell (wife of stationmaster J.F. Halliwell) for shops, and £200 to Martha Durham

Milner. The first shops numbers 1 and 2 were built between 1882 and 1885 on the north side of Warton Road commencing at the junction with Hunter Street. They were given the title *Station Buildings* and were individually designed three-storey commercial buildings (note the date on iron plate currently affixed on the building is not correct). The post office continued to operate from the 1871 building but in 1885 Elizabeth Halliwell sold a further plot of land to the Postmaster General for the building of a new post office. This was built besides the 1878/79 Carnforth sorting office and was internally connected to it.

The public telegraph office remained in the 1871 post office building until 1890 when it was relocated to the 1878 post office building, the old building continued in use as an annex to the Carnforth sorting office for the storage of letters and parcels particularly at busy times such as Christmas. In 1900 the sorting office was extended northwards alongside the back of Hunter Street, the LNWR Up main line platform being extended northwards at the same time. Another door was also added to the sorting office giving direct access to the new section of the Up platform, this was often used to transfer mails and parcels to and from the rear guards van of an Up passenger train.

The commercial centre of the Victorian town developed between 1874 and 1888 along Main Street, later re-named Market Street, and the east side of New Street. The Lancaster Bank building (now Nat-West) at the junction of Market Street and Scotland Road, the Bank Buildings opposite and the east end of the Co-operative building facing on to Lancaster Road together with the Station Buildings and the Station Hotel are unusual in having rounded ends a feature which appears in other industrial towns in the north-west and the north-east. Some care has been shown about the overall appearance of the commercial terrace on the south side of Market Street; the three-storey terrace has stepped gables which follow the inclination of the road, and although there is a uniformity of appearance closer inspection reveals detail differences, and as such may well be the work of more than one architect. The ground floors were laid out as shops, with the two upper floors as living accommodation; it was not unusual for the shopkeeper to earn extra money by letting off the top floor to lodgers. When built, the shop windows had ornate wooden frames, and often opaque door windows and Italianate tiled floor entrances. In 2003 only two of the shops still retained these original features, as successive owners have modernised the remainder.

The Carnforth Co-operative Society had broken away from the founding Lancaster and Skerton Co-operative Society and established itself in the town in 1885 and opened a shop in Market Street. It had 174 members and a share capital of £450, a healthy amount at that time. The success of the Society allowed it to move, in 1888, into a new, imposing and much larger building on the upper part of New Street. In the centre, and on the second floor of the building, was the Co-operative Hall which, in its heyday, was used for many of Carnforth's main events. The ground floor was given over entirely to four different retail outlets, each having its own entrance.

The Carnforth branch of the Lancaster Banking Company was built at the top of Main Street, at its junction with Scotland Road. This was the first joint stock bank in the country and was founded in 1826 by a number of Lancaster citizens. As befitted such an important institution, the company built a substantial and distinguished building. The Lancaster Banking Company became a part of the District Bank, and is now the National Westminster Bank. This was not the only bank within the town as there was a branch of the Liverpool Bank at the junction of Market Street and New Street. This became Martins Bank and it was from this bank that the weekly wages were collected by two clerical persons plus an escort and taken to the station for pay-out to the whole of Carnforth's railwaymen. The bank is still there and is now a branch of Barclays Bank.

Shortly after the opening of the Ulverstone and Lancaster Railway in 1857, a public house called the Station Inn was built on Warton Road, on a narrow strip of land alongside the railway and about 20 yards from the Lancaster & Carlisle station. The licensee was Miss Agnes Craggs; she was also licensed to let post horses and conveyances from the attached stables. It was demolished in 1879 to make way for the new 1880 Furness and Midland Railway station additions built alongside Warton Road. To replace it a new Station Hotel was built at the junction of Haws Hill and Market Street facing the railway forecourt. It was designed to meet the needs of the many passengers who were now passing through the station and staying overnight between trains. Before it opened in 1877, Edward. D. Barton purchased the hotel from Hogarth Holmes, with the coach house and stables also being conveyed to Barton later in 1880.

The Station Hotel had a number of comfortable bedrooms, a spacious dining room and a large hall with a stage; it was named the Victoria Hall, and here the first cinema films were shown in Carnforth. There were two public bars on the ground floor, which were made all the more popular by the relative lack of restrictions on opening hours. The bar trade was wholly dependent upon the activities and fortunes of the ironworks and railways. The original entrance to the Station Hotel was on the rounded corner of the building facing the station, and carved into the red sandstone archway above the door is the hotel name. Steps with railings led up to this doorway, and gas lamps in the shape of a torch were placed on each side of the steps to illuminate the hotel entrance.

The hotel was soon recognised as one of the finest in the North of England. In 1881 the hotel manager, was offering his guests a day trip by horse-drawn charabanc along the Lune valley to 'Lovely Lonsdale' and the southern parts of the Lake District. The hotel was renamed the Royal Station Hotel in 1900, in honour of the Duke of York (later King George the Fifth) who stayed at the hotel during a shooting holiday on the local marshes and nearby fells which were part of the Duchy of Lancaster estates. By 1912, another manager was advertising the hotel as 'Residential and Fully Licensed'. It became AA- and RAC-approved, and was well patronised by commercial travellers who, in the days when they travelled by train, found it a convenient base from which to cover the surrounding areas.

The hotel was sold in 1915 to Mitchells of Lancaster (Brewers) Ltd (who still own it today). The facilities were used as a stopping-off point for beer deliveries to hotels and inns in North Lancashire and the Lake District, with the yard being used for overnight stops: here horses were stabled and changed over on journeys to and from Lancaster. This practice ceased in 1946 when the first petrol-engined lorry was introduced by Mitchell's. In the 1930s, the hotel received a new, modern and more spacious entrance on Market Street.

In 1880 a police station was built on Lancaster Road for the local constabulary. It is now a private dwelling. It is still clearly recognisable as there is a stone panel on the building face containing the words 'Police Station', together with a shield containing a coat of arms (three lions with the cadence for eldest son (label with three points) at the top), indicating that this was a Lancashire Constabulary station. During 1904 the

CHAPTER SEVEN

Carnforth Market Street 1922. A 'Leyland SG7' motor bus of County Motors Ltd (of Lancaster) is on the Warton service and stands on Market Street outside the 'Kinema' which is showing the 1920 film 'Sunnyside'. On the opposite corner is the entrance to the Royal Station Hotel and the royal coat of arms is on the roof directly over the entrance. The ornate gas lamps still exist but the entrance is no longer used by the Hotel. (Lancashire Library collection Cat. number 1721-32)

Carnforth Inn was demolished; it was built in 1620 and had been used as a coaching inn in pre and post turnpike days, and served its patrons locally produced oatcakes and flagons of ale. The Carnforth Hotel was built in its place at the junction of Market Street and Lancaster Road to match up with the commercial buildings on Market Street. Plaques on the Market Street and Lancaster Road wall of the Carnforth Hotel and the coloured glass windows at the entrance to the hotel record the event and the opening of the new hotel.

Early cinema films were shown in the Victoria Hall at the Station Hotel until the 'Kinema' cinema house was built on the site of the town's mortuary at the bottom of Market Street: the first film was shown on 18th December 1920. It was later renamed the Roxy cinema, seating 550 people; it is now a mini-supermarket. A most unusual frontage based on an Egyptian temple still exists on the building, being erected to commemorate and promote the film based upon the life of Tutankhamen and the opening-up of his tomb by Lord Carnarvon and Howard Carter in 1922. The cinema was never open on Sundays, and for many years, an advanced payment of one shilling (5p) would reserve one of the best seats in the house, but only on Saturday nights. The cinema closed in June 1961, following the showing of the last film, *The Magnificent Seven*, a popular Western made in deluxe Panavision and staring Yul Brynner, James Coburn, Steve McQueen and Charles Bronson.

Eventually a number of churches were built in Carnforth, reflecting the religious denominations within the town and surrounding area. The Wesleyan Chapel and school were built in 1873 on the east side of Lancaster Road, the commemorative building stone being laid by Mrs. Alexander Brogden. The chapel was demolished in 2004 and flats now occupy the site. The Congregational church situated at the bottom of Hawk Street was built in 1896; it was the first building in Carnforth to have gas installed for both light and heating. The Primitive Methodist chapel and school were built in 1873 at Millhead on land given by the ironworks. The building has been demolished and the site built on.

St Oswald's, the Parish Church of Warton, served the needs of the Church of England parishioners of Carnforth until the construction, in 1872, of Christ Church on Lancaster Road at a cost of £20,000. Initially it was built without a tower and was consecrated in 1873. The south aisles were added in 1901 and the tower with eight bells in 1908 the latter being the work of a Kendal architect. As the church had no adjacent burial ground, all funeral processions had to pass through the main commercial centre of the town to Warton parish church for the burial ceremony. This lasted until 1925 when the municipal cemetery on Kellet Road was opened for all denominations.

The establishment of the early utilities shows how the influence of the ironworks was used to provide the township with modern and essential services. The first utility serving the township was the Carnforth Gas Company and Ammoniacal Works formed in 1870. Edward. D. Barton and James Erving were founders and co-directors of the Gas Company, along with H.I. Orr as Company Secretary. Carnforth gasworks, together with a house for the gasworks

Carnforth Market Street 1922. The crossroads at the top of Market Street with the Lancaster Bank building on the right. Scotland Road commences here and runs north. On the opposite corner is the Carnforth Hotel of 1904. Garage space is now advertised as the road has become the A6, the bay window containing the words 'Carnforth Inn' to commemorate the Inn which stood on the same site. (Lancashire Library collection Cat. number 1721-27)

manager, was erected in 1871 alongside the canal basin, as coal could be brought in by barge. The gas works consisted of a retort house and chimney, an ammoniacal liquor plant, a gas exhauster engine and metering house and a gasholder. Gas mains were laid into the town, and within a very short period of time most households were using gas for lighting. A connection was also put into the station, so that the station offices and platforms could be lit by gas. The gasworks was demolished around 1960 when a new gas main from Morecambe White Lund gasworks was laid to Carnforth. Small craft workshops now occupy the site.

A journalist from Lancaster, writing in the *Lancaster Gazette* in 1872, described the expanding town as:

Many houses are jerry built and are insanitary, built up anyhow. There is not a proper drain or sewer anywhere in Carnforth.

He was referring to the problems of sewage disposal and the inadequate supply of drinking water for the growing population. It was not until the Medical Officer of Health had reported to the Lancaster Rural Sanitation Authority on the deplorable state of the drainage systems and the lack of drinking water that action was taken. Following the report, Edward. D. Barton, who was a member of the Lancaster Rural Sanitation Authority, became increasingly involved in managing the supply of water and the disposal of sewage.

Work started on the sewage system in 1874 and the work was completed in the following year, with water for flushing being obtained from the canal. The Carnforth and District Waterworks Company was set up in 1877 to provide the town with drinking water. The provision of drinking water was a difficult and costly undertaking involving the construction of a reservoir at Pedder Pots, two miles east of Carnforth. The reservoir was fed by a stream which was a tributary of the River Keer. The water was of a good quality and was piped to Carnforth and Warton, and was fed by gravity from the reservoir.

The 1884 Reform Act had considerably widened the electorate by giving the vote to all adult male householders and lodgers who paid at least £10 a year rent, and the two established political parties of the time were no doubt competing for working-class men's votes in Carnforth. The Independent Labour Party was not founded until 1893, and no women were given the vote until 1918 and only then if they were over thirty. Under the provisions of the Local Government Act 1894, Carnforth, was officially recognised as a town and was given Urban District Council status. The first council meeting was held in March 1895 with nine members present.

The closure of the steelworks in 1889 brought to an end further expansion of the town and from then on the rate of building subsequently declined such that in the years leading up to 1900 only a few houses were built in the old village along North Road to fill in the gaps between some of the older cottages. The realignment of Kellet Road to remove the sharp bend at the canal bridge and to improve the junction with

CHAPTER SEVEN

Carnforth Lancaster Road circa 1910. There is a mixture of private houses and commercial outlets on both sides of the road. The houses all have bay windows and some have small gardens, the police station is half way down the left hand row where the wall lamp is. In the distance is Hartley's shop and on the brow of the hill Christ Church. (Lancashire Library collection Cat. number 1721-30)

North Road resulted in the demolition of the Golden Ball public house in 1900 and the building of two houses on the same site in 1901. These were the last houses in Carnforth to be built flush with the street.

The population of the town and its immediate surrounding area had steadily increased from 1860, and over the following thirty years had risen from 393 to 3200, although there was a slight decrease to around 3000 with the closure of the steel works, some families leaving to find employment elsewhere. The early years of the Edwardian era saw a national downturn in industrial growth, with little additional building taking place in Carnforth until after the WW1. By 1920 the council realised that the housing situation was inadequate as many ex-servicemen were requiring family homes of their own. In response the council built forty-four houses in 1924 on the Kings and Queens Drives estate. The same situation arose after WW2 and the council again extended the estate and by 1955 had provided a further 392 houses. In the last fifty years private housing development has mainly taken place on the southern outskirts of the town and has been undertaken mainly by a consortium of national companies.

Most of the town's early buildings can still be seen today and retain much of their appeal. The housing profile of the town is probably unique, and serious consideration is now being given to the conservation of the town and its architectural heritage. Comparison with early photographs of the town, on view in the Carnforth Station Heritage Centre, shows how little has changed, except for the number of road vehicles.

Carnforth New Street circa 1910. The Carnforth Branch of the Co-operative Society is the largest commercial outlet in Carnforth. The entrance to the Hall is in the centre and beyond is some three storey private houses. The owner of one of the three storey houses took in train crews on lodging turns. The rows of terraced houses with bay windows on the left are substantial houses of a higher rateable value. (Lancashire Library collection Cat. number 1721-31)

Carnforth Kellet Road circa 1910. Booker Terrace on the right was built in 1878 on Kellet Road on the edge of the township where land was cheap. The terrace opposite was named Annas Bank and the houses are larger and more substantial being built for the town's white collar workers and were built in the period 1900 to 1910. (Lancashire Library collection Cat. number 1721-30)

Carnforth Red Court circa 1905. A villa type house named 'Red Court' was built in 1880 on the southern outskirts of the town for Albert Edward Barton, the son of the ironworks manager. For privacy it was surrounded by high limestone walls and substantial hedges which enclosed an acre of ground. (Original postcard Carnforth Heritage Centre collection)

CHAPTER SEVEN

Carnforth railway houses June 2002. The end terrace houses of Grosvenor Terrace were much more substantial and were separated from the road by a small garden for privacy The two terraces are to a LNWR standard design built in red brick with three blue brick courses at window level. They were built for the LNWR staff working in the nearby engine shed and exchange sidings. (Philip Grosse)

Carnforth railway houses June 2002. Midland Terrace a single terrace containing 12 houses which back on to the River Keer They were built for the Midland Railway staff working in the nearby Midland yards. (Philip Grosse)

Carnforth Ironworks houses June 2002. The ironworks built three streets of basic two-up and two-down terrace houses on rising ground to the north of the River Keer. They were built in the village of Warton where land was cheap and were within a quarter of a mile of the ironworks. (Philip Grosse)

CHAPTER EIGHT
FURNESS AND MIDLAND NEW WORKS

In 1879 the Furness Railway obtained an Act for a new line into the joint station and other enabling improvements to be made to the handling of the ironworks traffic, and the Joint station is substantially remodelled to allow the Midland Railway full access via the new Carnforth Curve.

To remove the inconvenience to passengers, and the disruption to traffic caused by the reversal of Midland Railway trains from the Furness & Midland Junction station (a third of a mile west of Carnforth) into the Joint station, the Furness Railway obtained an Act on 21st July 1879 for a new line known as the Carnforth Curve. The plan for the proposed F&M Joint Railway curve was prepared by F.C. Stileman Civil Engineers of George Street Westminster for the 1878/79 Parliamentary Session. The Carnforth Curve was to commence on the Furness & Midland Joint line at the new Carnforth East Junction, and run on a tight curve of approximately nine chains radius to make a new junction (Carnforth Station Junction) with the Furness Railway at the north end of Carnforth (FR-LNWR) Joint station.

During late 1879 the Furness Railway engine shed at the north end of the Joint station was demolished, and the connections to the goods yard removed to make way for the new Carnforth Curve. The entrance and roadway to the goods depot were removed, and the redundant part of Mill Lane levelled up and covered over. Brown-sandstone-faced retaining walls were built alongside Warton Road to contain the groundwork upon which the Carnforth Curve was to be built.

The Carnforth Curve was authorised to cross the ironworks branch on the level but the crossing was abandoned as the Board of Trade objected to a mineral line crossing a passenger line on the level. The Furness Railway Ironworks branch was therefore stopped off on the ironworks' premises, and this led to a dispute with the ironworks over how the iron ore would be supplied. This was resolved in favour of a new connection from the Furness & Midland Joint line on the north side of the new East Junction. The ironworks branch bridge across Warton Road was taken out of use and demolished. The truncated line was later integrated into the Furness Railway's new Warton Road goods yard.

A new bridge was built on the same site but on a different alignment, and was much wider to accommodate the new

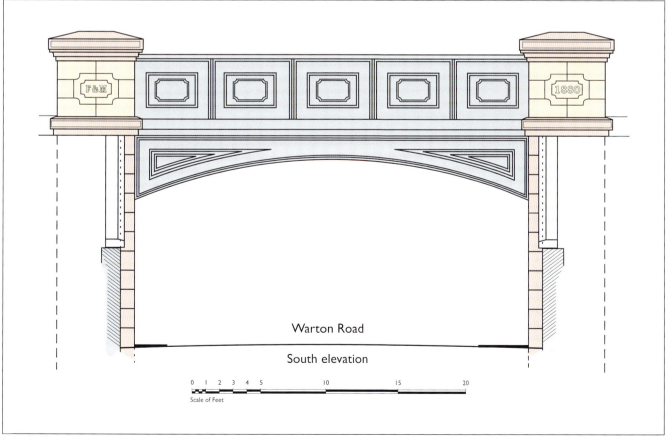

Carnforth 1880. Warton Road Bridge. Bridge number 3A was built in 1880 to carry the F&M Carnforth Curve across Warton Road. The bridge abutments and piers were built of white limestone with red sandstone capping. (Drawn by author from a Furness Railway contract drawing number 25S in the Leslie Gilpin collection)

CHAPTER EIGHT

Furness &Midland line which passed over it on a continuous curve of approximately nine chains radius. The bridge abutments and piers were built of white limestone with red sandstone capping to match the adjacent steelworks buildings. The date of building '1880' and the ownership 'F&M' were inset in stone panels on the bridge piers. The rails were laid on a wooden deck supported on longitudinal wrought iron girders of 30 feet span. The top parapet had decorative cast iron panels and elliptical cast iron arches were fitted across the span of the bridge.

Following his inspection of the new Carnforth Curve, the Inspecting Officer, Francis Marindin, made his report on 30th July 1880 to the Secretary of the Railway Department of the Board of Trade. He commented favourably on the condition of the track and of the new bridge over Warton Road, but required a number of improvements to the made with regard to the sighting of signals. He requested that the testing of the block instruments should be carried out by the Furness Railway signal engineer before the curve was opened to traffic on 2nd August 1880.

The double-tracked Carnforth Curve swung round southwards from East Junction to make a south-facing junction with the Furness Railway's Up and Down main lines; this now became Carnforth Station Junction. Two other lines left the curve before the junction, one to the new Midland Railway's bay platform and the other to an adjacent carriage siding. The new layout gave the Midland Railway direct access into Carnforth Joint station.

In the mid-1860s the Furness Railway had commissioned the architectural practice of E.G. Paley (later Paley and Austin), who had offices on Castle Hill in Lancaster, to carry out new work and make improvements to their stations and offices. In 1879 Edmund Paley submitted detailed plans to the Furness Railway Board for enlarging the existing 1857 Carnforth Joint station building and to provide a separate building for the Furness and Midland Railway. The improvements and remodelling took place during 1879-1880 at a cost of £40,000.

The Saturday edition of the *Barrow Herald*, dated 12th February 1880, had this item about the new works, providing a useful summary of the new building work:

The Furness Railway has begun in earnest the construction of a branch railway which will run from the Furness and Midland line just outside Carnforth into a loop platform in the general station which has been prepared for them. A new Dining Room is open. The roofing of the island platform has been removed and the new one is being erected.

Work started on the main island platform with the removal of the original ridge and furrow roof from the platform and from above the offices and public rooms of the 1857 Joint station, leaving the original Lancaster & Carlisle Railway station house to be integrated into the enlarged station. At the same time, pointed bays were added at the top of the wall above the area containing the 1857 public rooms and offices on the LNWR Down platform, to accommodate a new ridge and furrow platform canopy. The LCR 1846 ticket office entrance on the south face of the LCR station house was closed and filled in with masonry, whilst inside the room a new fireplace and chimney breast were built; a chimney stack and pots were added to the south face of the building. The bay window on the east side of the LCR station house was removed at this time, and replaced with a single window and door, this new room becoming the stationmaster's office. The large ground floor room of the LCR station house was converted into a refreshment room, and was fitted out with wooden staging and a large serving counter positioned on an east-west axis.

On the west side, the original railway offices were enlarged and rearranged for food preparation and storage, and a first floor was built above them together with an internal access staircase on the inner east wall. The catering staff worked long hours, staying at the station between their rostered hours of duty so the rooms on the first floor were arranged as an office, a sitting room and bedrooms for them.

At the north end facing Warton Road a new tall single-storey building with a high pitched roof was built directly onto the north end of the existing buildings of the 1857 Joint station, and a lower single-storey adjoining building was built at an angle to it. The tall building had a separate entrance from Warton Road for passengers using both the Furness Railway and the Midland Railway, giving direct access to the Furness and Midland Railway platforms. It also contained various offices and public rooms, all being independent of the LNWR. A carriage approach road with a footpath was laid down from Warton Road to a turning point in front of the buildings. Steps leading down from Warton Road Bridge enabled pedestrians to reach the station without having to walk around the carriage approach road. At the Warton Road entrance to the station approach a substantial circular stone pillar was erected upon which was placed an ornate lamp.

The Elizabethan cottage style of architecture used by the Lancaster & Carlisle Railway was perpetuated in the new works, and the new building was faced with brown sandstone to match the LCR buildings. The new windows were wider and divided into two, three and four bays with leaded lights in the upper portion of the windows and doors. A glass awning supported on fine cast iron brackets containing scrollwork was provided over the entrance, and a glass canopy cantilevered out from the station building covered the footpath.

Inside the tall Furness & Midland building was a large open waiting room with a steeply-pitched roof supported on substantial crafted wooden beams similar to those used in a Victorian church. On opposite end walls of the room were large fireplaces made from brown sandstone. The interior walls of the waiting room were clad in pale ivory bricks supplied by the Farnley Iron Company Limited of Leeds, giving it a light and open aspect. The lower bricks were glazed and separated by a frieze consisting of two rows of dark brown bricks: these bricks were provided by the same company, which, in 1889, became part of the Leeds Fireclay Company. The same ivory coloured bricks were used in ecclesiastical work, including the exterior of St Paul's Church, Lancaster in 1874 by E.G. Paley.

A covered passageway with a Gibbs arch at each end was added at the same time. The passageway enabled passengers to move between the Furness Railway and the Midland Railway platforms on one side, and the LNWR Down platform on the other side. The FMJR ticket office and ticket inspector's office were situated in the passage way near to the Furness Railway's bi-directional platform. A further passage gave access to the new FMJR waiting room; the passageway walls were clad to match those in the waiting room.

The adjoining lower building faced onto the Furness Railway's platform, and included a porter's room, a ladies' waiting room containing a large wooden table, a room for the passenger guards, and the FR telegraph office. At the very end of the building was a small two-storey addition for the Midland Railway's porters and for the Midland Railway agent, who occupied the first-floor office.

There were further new works to enclose the Furness and

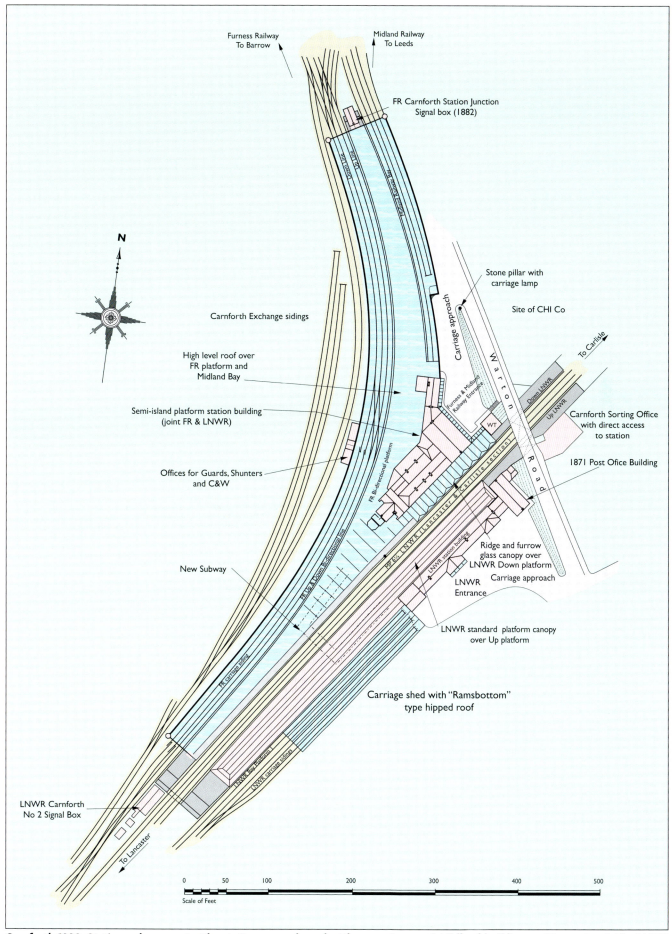

Carnforth 1880. Station enlargements. The station was enlarged with a new Furness & Midland building on Warton Road. The LNWR built a new station building on the Up mainline platform; it had an attached carriage shed. A new high level overall roof enclosed the Furness Railway and the Midland Railway platforms and was supported on its outer edge by a screen wall. (Drawn by author from documents in author's collection)

CHAPTER EIGHT

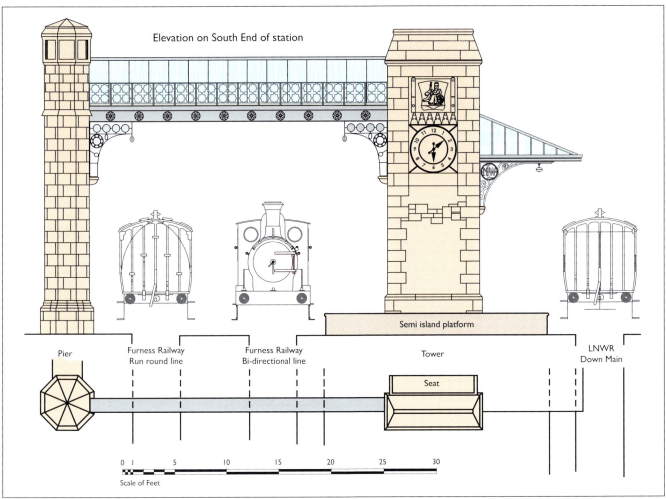

Carnforth 1880. South end of station. The Furness Railway run-round line and bi-directional line and platform is on the left and the LNWR Down mainline and platform is on the right. The tower contains the second station clock and the LNWR crest 'Britannia'. The Furness Railway lines and bi-directional platform is covered by an overall roof. The LNWR down line platform is partly covered by a glass canopy. (Drawn by author from a plan in the CRA collection)

Midland Railway platforms with an overall roof. The original five Ulverstone & Lancaster Railway exchange sidings were taken up, and excavation work and foundations for a curved high-level screen wall were in hand in 1879, but adverse winter weather slowed its completion. The screen wall was built on the west side of the Furness Railway's Up platform line and Down line to support a ridge and furrow overall glass and iron roof. This new roof covered the Furness Railway's platform, the Up and Down lines and the new Midland Railway bay and carriage siding. The outer end faces of the roof which rested on the screen wall was made up of wooden panelling inset with top lights which provide additional natural light.

At the north end of the station a new bay platform and carriage siding was built for the Midland Railway's passenger traffic. Substantial and extensive retaining walls in brown sandstone were built alongside Warton Road, and an oil store and lamp room was built into the retaining wall at the end of the Midland Railway's carriage siding. The Furness Railway's platform was extended to join the new Midland Railway bay platform, creating a very long curved platform. A new crossover was installed at the mid-point of the platform to enable a locomotive to run round its train or for a train to leave the station. The south end of the loop beyond the crossover was to be used as a carriage siding and the north end beyond the crossover became the Down line.

At the north end, the overall roof was supported on a substantial girder which rested on octagonal brown sandstone towers built on the ends of the screen wall; the base of one can still be seen in the boundary wall on Warton Road. At the south end, the overall roof was also supported on a substantial girder, one end resting on an octagonal tower built on the end of the screen wall, with the other end on a broad pier built on to the main island platform. Regularly-spaced cast iron rose heads were fixed to the outer faces of the girder at both ends of the roof for decorative purposes. Near to the top of the pier were two inset panels, one containing the LNWR crest 'Britannia' carved in stone, and the other a decorative clock. The internal roof girders were supported by cast iron octagonal tapered pillars spaced out along the Furness Railway platform. Wing walls were added onto the south end of the Lancaster & Carlisle station house to provide additional support for the new overall roof.

The LNWR Down platform was covered by a fine ridge and furrow glass canopy, which exhibited the best in Victorian glass and ironwork. At its inner end the roof was supported on pads projecting from the building wall and its outer end by cast iron octagonal tapered pillars placed along the length of the platform, the pillars were of a different design to those found on other FR stations. The heads of the pillars and the supporting brackets attached to the building wall were assembled from fine ironwork scroll work containing the owning railways' motif (FR or LNWR).

The external south face of the LCR station house was faced with white glazed ceramic tiles up to a height of seven feet, and

FURNESS AND MIDLAND NEW WORKS

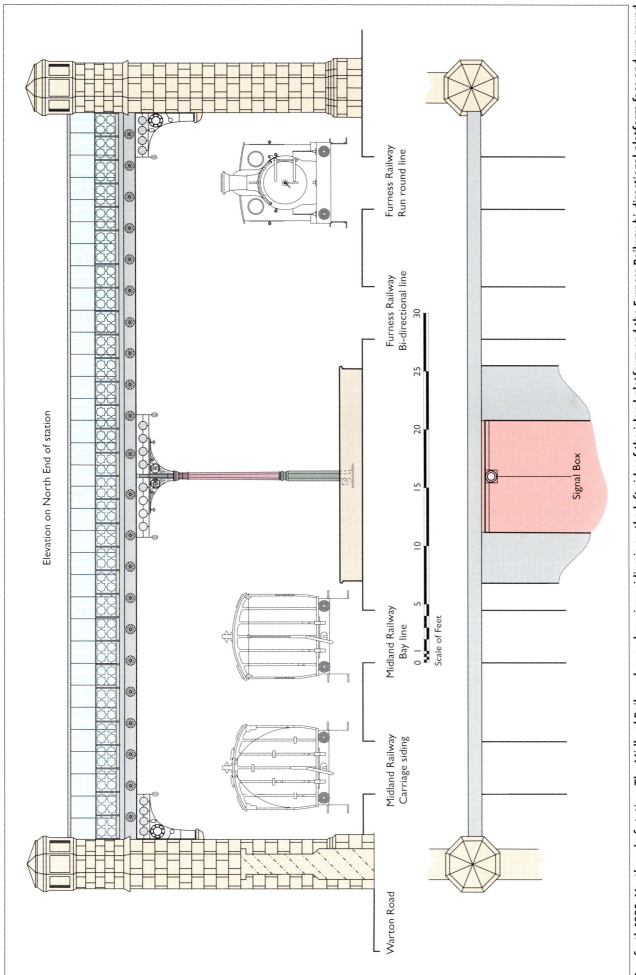

Carnforth 1880. North end of station. The Midland Railway bay and carriage siding is on the left side of the island platform and the Furness Railway bi-directional platform face and run-round line is on the right. A high level glass roof covers the lines and platform and a retaining wall separates the railway from Warton Road. The canopy between the signal box and the roof provided shelter to the seat which was set into the base of the signal box at platform level. (Drawn by author from documents in author's collection)

CHAPTER EIGHT

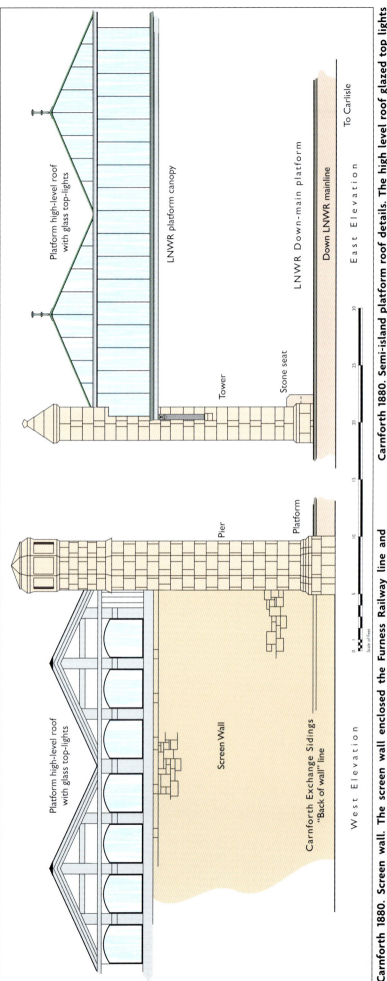

Carnforth 1880. Screen wall. The screen wall enclosed the Furness Railway line and supported the high level roof. The arched top light windows were set in wooden frames which sat upon the top face of the screen wall. (Drawn by author from a plan in the CRA collection)

Carnforth 1880. Semi-island platform roof details. The high level roof glazed top lights covered the semi-island platform and the Furness Railway lines and the lower glass canopy covered the edge of the Up LNWR mainline platform. (Drawn by author from a plan in the CRA collection)

a roofless Gentlemen's toilet was built on to this wall on the main island platform. A new bookstall was installed on the south wall of the toilets facing the subway, initially let to W.H. Smith & Son, the tenancy passing to Wyman & Sons on 31st December 1905.

The LNWR also carried out similar improvements, and replaced the wooden huts on the Up main line platform with a new station building on the same site. The title used in official documents and plans was the LNWR building, but it was always referred to by Carnforth railway men as the 'eastern bloc'. The LNWR station building was built in a different style of architecture, Manorial Elizabethan, from the building on the Main Island platform. The station frontage and platform face are not identical. The building was long and narrow, with two projecting bays with high pointed gables, at the north end and at the centre. The whole building was faced in brown sandstone laid in coursed square rubble with a light hammer dressed face. Gothic moulding was used on the gable shoulders and all the building lintels, cills, quoins and window out-band had a smooth finish.

The centre bay contained a chevron-patterned manorial shield carved in stone and let into the gable face just above the string course. On the apex of the gabled roof is a carved stone decorated finial mounted with a lion's head. Manorial shields could often be found at railway stations (Carlisle is an example), containing the owning companies' coats of arms or the coats of arms of the landowner who had invested substantial amounts of money in the railway company. The manorial shield at Carnforth only has a worked surface and no coat of arms. The main entrance door to the booking hall is in the building's centre bay, with the LNWR ticket office on the right-hand side of the booking hall. The ticket office window was inset into a wall made of smooth finished rectangular stone-faced blocks constructed in regency style. The floor of the booking hall was laid with Yorkshire stone flags. At the north end a new single-storey building was built to fill in the gap between the northern bay of the station and the 1871 post office building, this contained the LNWR telegraph office. At the south end was a short bay wall containing two blind windows, inside was a Gentlemen's toilet with a glazed roof over the water closets, the remainder was roofless.

The new building had accommodation for staff, a ticket office, and separate ladies' and gentlemen's waiting rooms. All the windows had small panes at the top and large ones at the bottom. The bottom ones were sash windows, some being fitted with opaque glass for privacy, and the windows for the ticket office and staff accommodation had security bars fitted internally. The interior walls of the ticket office were smooth plastered, and finished off with a curved and decorated plastered frieze which joined the walls to the ceiling.

The screen wall on the Up LNWR platform-side of the building partly obscured the roof line and was built higher to provide support for the inner end of a LNWR 'Ramsbottom' pattern platform roof which was also supported at its outer ends by plain cast-iron pillars along the length of the platform. A covered carriage shed, built of red brick and with a ventilated clerestory roof, was erected at the south end of the station, covering three lines. Platform 1 bay (called the Lancaster Bay by the railwaymen) adjoined the LNWR Up platform and the other two roads were laid out as carriage storage and cleaning roads. The shed was approximately 200 feet long and there were two low-level stages for the carriage cleaning gang to walk along as they cleaned the exterior of the vehicles.

A new subway was provided between the LNWR Up mainline platform and the joint LNWR-Furness Railway main island platform. From 1880, the main island platforms became joint Furness Railway and LNWR for maintenance purposes, whilst the Up main line platform, with the adjoining covered carriage sidings and the Lancaster Bay, was maintained wholly by the LNWR. The LNWR provided their standard design of station seats throughout the station with the station name inset into the backrest. For the first time, gas was used to light the station platforms, offices and public rooms. Gas lamps of LNWR design were installed throughout the station, and on the station's outer building walls and approach ways.

The enlarged Joint station with the exception of the Up LNWR platform, which was 100% owned by the LNWR was painted in the owning railway's colours; it opened to passenger traffic on 2nd August 1880, on the same date as the Carnforth Curve. The station now had five platforms: platform 1 (LNWR bay), platform 2 (LNWR Up main line), platform 3 (LNWR Down main line), platform 4 (Furness Up and Down), and platform 5 (Midland bay). George Steele was the stationmaster of the enlarged Carnforth Joint station. The Midland Railway appointed Andrew Bellie as Agent, to deal with its affairs at the station; he was assisted by two porters. In 1895 Mr Farnworth was appointed stationmaster, having succeeded Mr Haythornthwaite, and the Midland agent was now Mr Peel. There were forty-one Joint station staff, and thirty signalmen and forty goods guards belonging to the three companies.

The Carnforth (Furness & Midland Junction) station of 1868 was now redundant, and was closed and the platforms removed. The station buildings, however, were removed by Coulton Hunter of Barrow, the contractor for the Carnforth Curve, and re-erected after its opening at ballast level close to the Midland Railway's Carnforth East Junction signal box for use as offices. This East Junction office was occupied by the Midland Railway goods clerks and shunters, who dealt with traffic at the Midland Top End, Middle End and Bottom End sidings as well as the East Junction sidings. The office remained in use until the construction in 1939 of the new independent Furness line platform at Carnforth with its various attached offices (See Chapter 9). It remained derelict for many years, inviting speculation about its origin amongst railway historians and was demolished circa 1952.

During the autumn of 1895 J.B. Joyce, a well-known public clock maker of Whitchurch, Shropshire made a longcase clock (also described as tall-case or floor case) for the joint station. It was installed on the main island platform and brought into use on Friday 20th December 1895. The *Lancaster Guardian* of Monday 23rd December 1895 (not its usual printing day because of Christmas) had this to say:

A large clock has been erected above the subway on the London & North Western north side of the Carnforth platform and was set to work on Friday last. The clock supplies a long felt want as the other clocks are at the extreme ends of the station.

The clock is unique as the clock face is separate from its operating mechanism. The circular clock case had two faces with Roman numerals and hands on each face and was suspended from a frame attached to the girders of high level roof of the main island platform. It was suspended above the platform end of the subway ramp where it was visible to the station staff and public. The clock operating mechanism was enclosed in a tall wooden cabinet erected at platform level on the Furness Railway platform close to the clock.

The cabinet contained a powering weight for driving the clock, the clock mechanism, winding mechanism, and a pendulum. Inside the cabinet the motion of the pendulum was converted through a bevel gear to turn an external horizontal drive shaft which ran between the cabinet and clock case, within the clock case was another bevel gear to turn the clock hands. The clock was mechanically wound about every fifth day and the spindle of the winding mechanism was in the top part of the cabinet which was 8ft 6in. from the platform. The station staff had a portable 'A' frame ladder which they climbed up to reach the spindle and by turning a crank handle the operating weight which was suspended from a cable could be raised to its top limit. Over the successive days the cast iron weight would under controlled conditions gradually descend, the accuracy of the clock being maintained by making adjustments to the swing of the pendulum.

Photographs taken in the early 1900s inside the station show how smoke had discoloured the glass in the overall roof over the Furness Railway lines, and the ironwork and pillars on the island platform have being coated in soot-like dust. The ballast in the Furness platform is very dark and could very well be top-surfaced with ash, as the surface looks very fine.

A description of the station would not be complete without mentioning the station bell. By the early 1900s, the principal LNWR express trains were passing north through the station at a much higher speed, and, following a fatal accident to a passenger who was sucked under a passing train, the LNWR installed a warning bell on the Down main line platform. It was placed on the wall above the entrance to the dining room and was rung by the signalman in the LNWR Carnforth No.2 signal box to warn passengers of the imminent passage of an express train. A wooden board with standard LNWR cast letters was hung from the station roof close to the bell to inform passengers thus:

The ringing of this bell indicates the approach of a train which does not stop at this platform.

The Furness Railway Act of 1879 also included other new works and additions to improve the working of the ironworks traffic. With the abandonment of the Furness Railway Ironworks Branch, the Furness Railway built a single line bridge across the River Keer and Shore Road to carry traffic to and from the remodelled joint goods yard and warehouse. A new entrance and access road to the goods yard was built lower down Warton

CHAPTER EIGHT

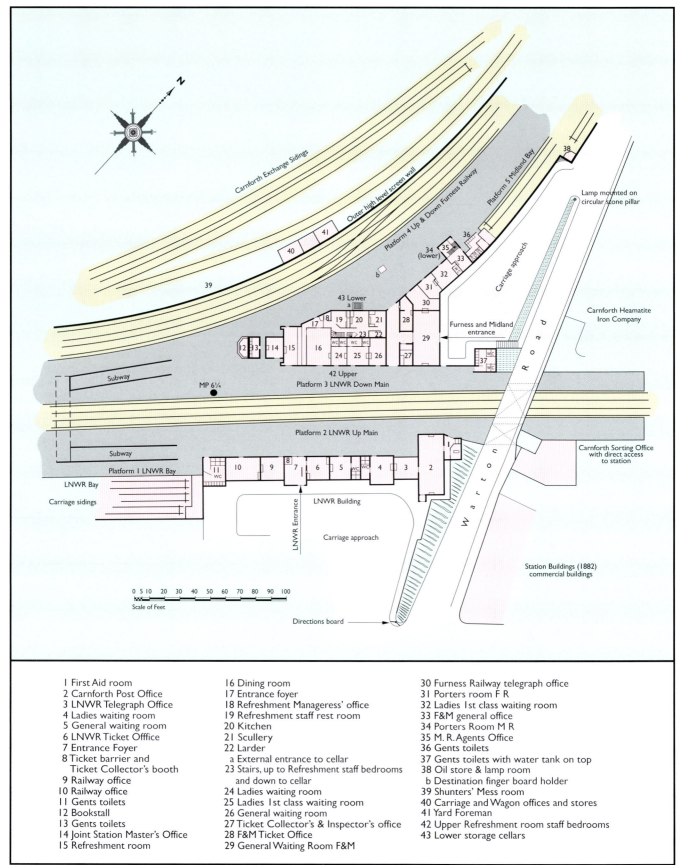

1 First Aid room
2 Carnforth Post Office
3 LNWR Telegraph Office
4 Ladies waiting room
5 General waiting room
6 LNWR Ticket Offfice
7 Entrance Foyer
8 Ticket barrier and
  Ticket Collector's booth
9 Railway office
10 Railway office
11 Gents toilets
12 Bookstall
13 Gents toilets
14 Joint Station Master's Office
15 Refreshment room
16 Dining room
17 Entrance foyer
18 Refreshment Manageress' office
19 Refreshment staff rest room
20 Kitchen
21 Scullery
22 Larder
  a External entrance to cellar
23 Stairs, up to Refreshment staff bedrooms
   and down to cellar
24 Ladies waiting room
25 Ladies 1st class waiting room
26 General waiting room
27 Ticket Collector's & Inspector's office
28 F&M Ticket Office
29 General Waiting Room F&M
30 Furness Railway telegraph office
31 Porters room F R
32 Ladies 1st class waiting room
33 F&M general office
34 Porters Room M R
35 M. R. Agents Office
36 Gents toilets
37 Gents toilets with water tank on top
38 Oil store & lamp room
  b Destination finger board holder
39 Shunters' Mess room
40 Carriage and Wagon offices and stores
41 Yard Foreman
42 Upper Refreshment room staff bedrooms
43 Lower storage cellars

Carnforth 1880. Station Facilities. A plan of the internal layout of the railway offices and public rooms of the enlarged station. (Drawn by author from a plan in author's collection)

FURNESS AND MIDLAND NEW WORKS

Road. At the same time, the access road on the east side of Warton Road leading to the 1868 Carnforth (F&M) station was taken out of use and the ground leveled up to that of the Carnforth Curve using ironworks slag.

Additional work included the widening of the existing Furness Railway two-arch bridge over the Shore Road and the River Keer to carry four tracks – the existing Up and Down passenger lines and the new Up and Down goods lines, the latter continued as through goods lines between the FR and the LNWR ends of the Carnforth exchange sidings complex. The 1867 FMJR plate girder bridge over the River Keer carrying the Up and Down direct FMJR passenger lines was widened. Two new Up and Down goods lines and a bi-directional independent line for the ironworks slag tip and limestone traffic were added, making five lines in total.

The final development of the facilities at Carnforth took place in 1881 alongside the direct Furness & Midland Joint line, due to the abandonment of the Furness Railway's Ironworks Branch. A new connection was laid in on the north side of Carnforth East Junction from the bi-directional goods lines to four new through sidings known as the Midland Top End sidings. These sidings acted as the ironworks exchange sidings and were laid on a steep incline leading down to the north headshunt for the ironworks. Three additional parallel sidings were laid down at East Junction alongside the direct Furness & Midland Joint line, these sidings terminating close to the bridge carrying the FMJR over the LNWR mainline.

Five new sidings called the Midland Middle End sidings were laid down west of Carnforth East Junction, and alongside the direct Furness & Midland Joint line for sorting and re-marshalling traffic to and from the ironworks and the Midland Railway. Six parallel sidings called the Midland Bottom End sidings, were laid down alongside and parallel to the Furness Railway mainline from Carnforth F&M Junction to Toll Bar Bridge at Sands Lane, their main purpose being to exchange traffic between the Furness Railway and the Midland Railway.

The FR Board minutes for 23rd November 1899 recorded that the LNWR were to buy land from the LNWR & FR Joint Goods Committee for a wagon shop. The LNWR Act of 1903 and accompanying plan shows a parcel of land on the west side of the Carnforth Exchange sidings around 6 chains (132 yards) north of the LNWR engine shed for a wagon repair workshop. The workshop was built in red brick with one through road and contained a store, office and blacksmith's shop; in 1923 the LMS provided shear legs for lifting wagons. The shed is used today by the carriage wagon repair venture associated with Carnforth Railway Restoration & Engineering Services Ltd, a subsidiary of West Coast Railways.

Private contractors also carried out wagon maintenance at Carnforth, however in this case the repairs were carried out in the open on a siding close to the LNWR engine shed at Crag Bank. The Railway Clearing House Handbook for 1912 lists Hurst Nelson & Co. Ltd and in the 1929 Handbook Wagon Repairs Ltd as having a private siding at Carnforth for repairing wagons.

Carnforth Station 1901 Main Island Platform. The clock, subway railings and bookstall can be seen in the middle of the picture. The 1880 platform awnings and the large glass gas lamps are clearly evident. (Mrs Pat Jackson Collection Ref. TR13)

CHAPTER EIGHT

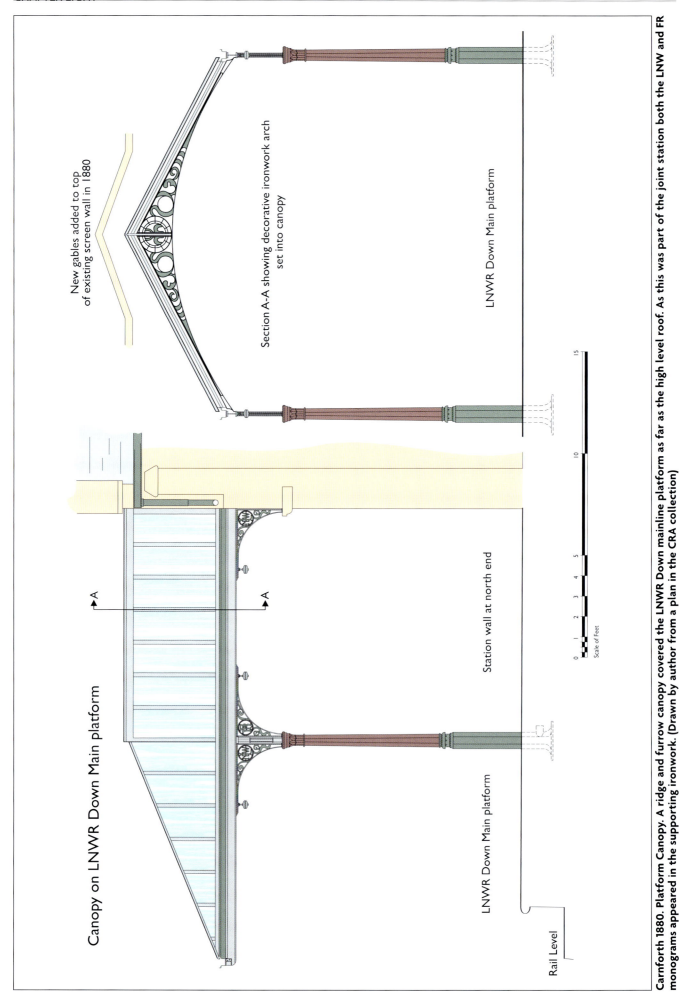

Carnforth 1880. Platform Canopy. A ridge and furrow canopy covered the LNWR Down mainline platform as far as the high level roof. As this was part of the joint station both the LNW and FR monograms appeared in the supporting ironwork. (Drawn by author from a plan in the CRA collection)

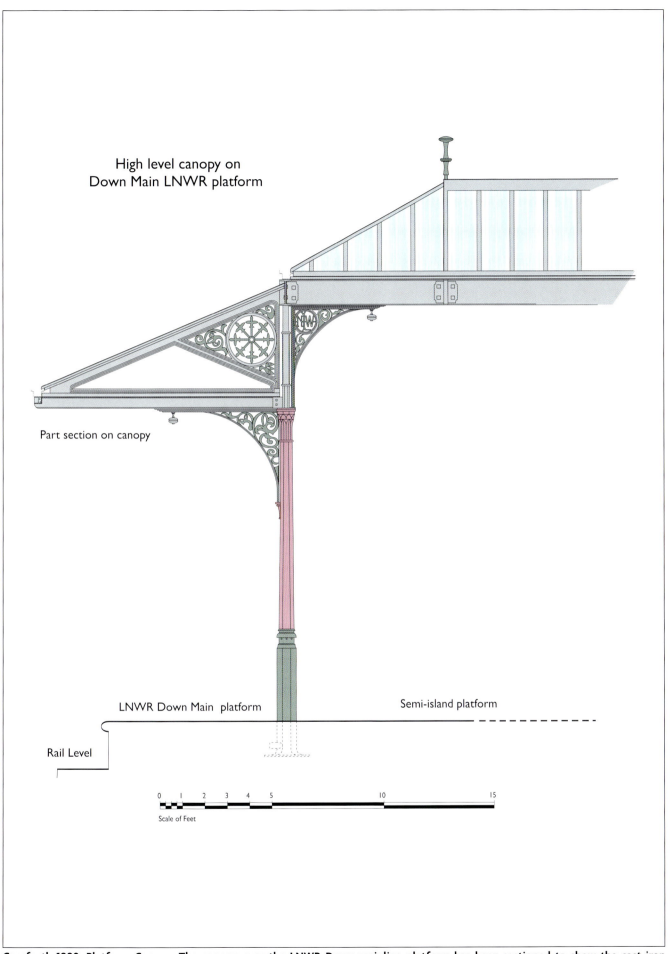

Carnforth 1880. Platform Canopy. The canopy over the LNWR Down mainline platform has been sectioned to show the cast iron brackets and scroll work containing the LNWR monogram at the point where it joined the high level glazed roof which covered the semi-island platform and Furness Railway lines. (Drawn by author from a plan in the CRA collection)

CHAPTER EIGHT

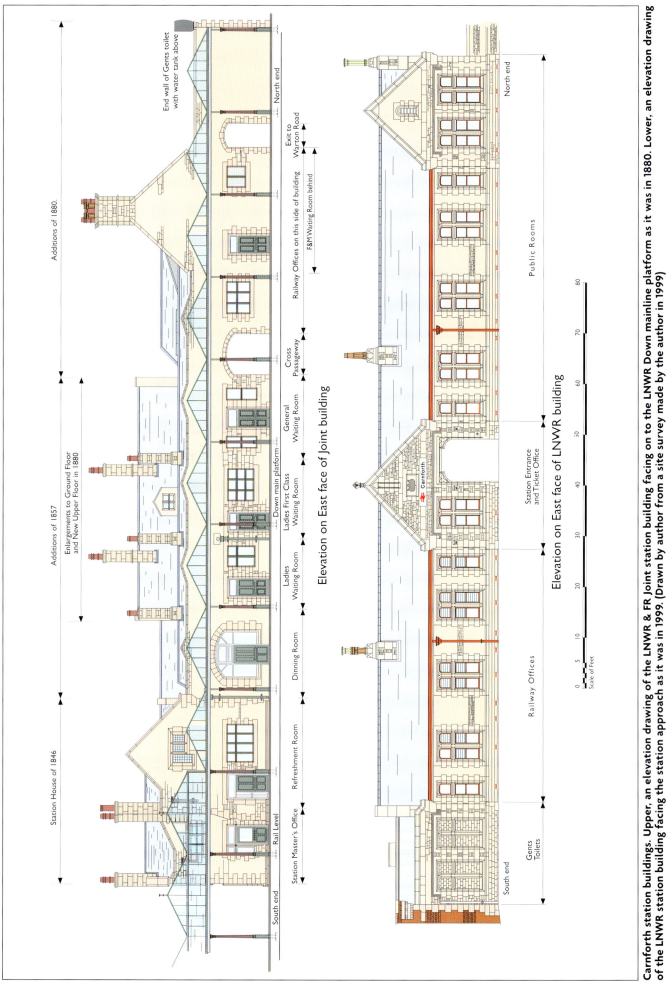

Carnforth station buildings. Upper, an elevation drawing of the LNWR & FR Joint station building facing on to the LNWR Down mainline platform as it was in 1880. Lower, an elevation drawing of the LNWR station building facing the station approach as it was in 1999. (Drawn by author from a site survey made by the author in 1999)

The south end of station circa 1910, the central tower contains the second station clock and the LNWR crest 'Britannia'. The Furness Railway lines and bi-directional platform is covered by an overall roof. The end pier and supporting screen wall are behind the Webb LNWR compound 0-8-0 goods engine. (CRA Collection Ref. BOcln06)

The screen wall and overall roof of the enlarged station is in the centre of this 1883 picture. A train of coke wagons sits in the FR end of the exchange sidings and in the foreground is a narrow gauge line and building materials belonging to the contractor who is extending the exchange sidings. (Mrs Pat Jackson Collection Ref. TR2)

CHAPTER EIGHT

A view of the Carnforth Exchange Yard in 1882 looking north at the junction mean point between the FR and the LNWR ends of the yard, the lean to buildings on the screen wall containing offices for the yard staff. (Mrs Pat Jackson Collection Ref. TR21)

Interior of station circa 1900. The high level overall roof covers the FR semi-island platform and the FR-LNWR monograms can be seen in the ironwork at the top of the pillars. There are coaches in the Midland Railway bay. (CRA Collection Ref. BOcln10)

The north end of station circa 1925. FR 4-4-0 LMS No.10140, in 1923 red livery, with crew, stands alongside the FR 1882 signal box. The end pillar stands on Warton Road and supports the high level roof. Opposite are the ironworks offices and the bell tower sits on top of the end roof. (CRA Collection Ref. SHI341)

Carnforth Station circa 1882 with the new W.H. Smith bookstall on the main island platform. The bookstall would be moved back in the 1939 station rebuild to occupy the area of the Victorian gent's toilet. The high back seat would be replaced later by a standard LNWR type. (Mrs Pat Jackson Collection Ref. TR14)

CHAPTER EIGHT

Carnforth Station circa 1882. The enlarged station has just been completed. To the left is the new Carnforth No. 2 signal box and the Down LNWR platform. Inset in the pier is the clock and the LNWR device 'Britannia'. The Ramsbottom type roof covers Up LNWR platform and the 'Lancaster Bay' and two carriage sidings are covered by a wooden clerestory roof.
(Mrs Pat Jackson Collection Ref. TR41)

Warton Road, bridge 3A in 1950 just after it had been rebuilt with a concrete deck and tubular parapet hand rails, the original piers dating back to 1880. The bridge in the distance carries the F&M direct line over Warton Road. (CRA Collection Ref. BOcln17)

CHAPTER NINE
THE LMS AND BR YEARS

In 1939, major changes are made to the station to improve the working of passenger traffic. Following the removal of the mainline platforms in 1970, the station is downgraded to secondary line status. Ticketing facilities are withdrawn in 1988, and the station becomes an unstaffed halt in 1994. The buildings are left to decay and their future is uncertain.

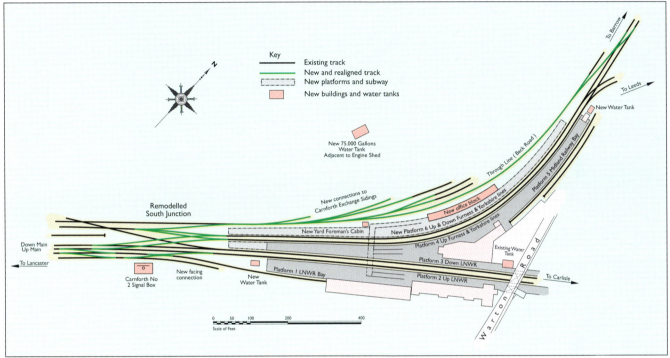

Carnforth 1939. LMS Modernisation Scheme. The LMS enlarged the station and provided a new independent Down Furness line platform with associated offices and public rooms. The south junction was remodelled and a new LMS box 'Carnforth No. 2' was built on the east side of the new goods loops. (Drawn by author from a newspaper article in the *North Western Daily Mail* 28th October 1937)

Following the Railway Act 1921, the Furness Railway, the London & North Western Railway, and the Midland Railway became part of the London Midland & Scottish Railway at, on and from 1st January 1923. The LMS soon rationalised some of the offices, closing the LNWR ticket office on the north side of the entrance hall and making a new enlarged ticket office with a service counter on the south side. The booking hall was divided lengthways with a barrier. The south side directed passengers to the ticket office and *via* a wooden ticket inspector's cabin to finally reach the platform. The north side was a barrow way, being closed off at the platform end by a concertina metal gate which could be opened to allow a barrow to pass through. It was used by the GPO staff and by the railway parcels staff. At the same time the railway offices and public rooms in the LNWR building were re-arranged and put to a different use. The LNWR Telegraph Office was combined with FR Telegraph Office in the main island platform building.

The most significant change was the closure of the Furness & Midland Warton Road entrance, the ticket office and the waiting room which was then subdivided into two main parts by wooden partitions, running the full length of the entrance corridor. A relief train crew mess room was set up on the right hand side when looking south, and on the opposite side it was subdivided into offices for a goods guard clerk (GGC), a small store and a correspondence clerk; the later handled the station master's correspondence and the station's mail. The goods guard clerks worked on shifts seven days a week and the goods guards would sign on and off there at the office hatchway; 'foreign' train crews would also report to the GGC for orders from Control and the relief crews would report their arrival before working trains forward. The office of the GGC and train-crews' mess room closed up in 1969 and were transferred to the Carnforth Trainmen's Depot (discussed later). The Furness Railway ticket office in the F&M building was transferred to the new LNWR ticket office in the LNWR building. Ticket collection and inspection facilities opened in the F&M building cross-passageway, to ensure that all passengers leaving by the F&M Warton Road exit handed in their tickets.

Regarding the famous time-pieces a Carnforth postal worker who started work at the Carnforth sorting office in 1931 told the author that both the previously-mentioned LNWR station clock (in the pier) and FR station clock (in the 1882 signal box) were taken out of use and removed around 1935.

In 1923, the LMS arranged for all Furness line passenger trains

CHAPTER NINE

passing through Carnforth to be classed as through trains, thereby eliminating engine changes and the marshalling of trains with through carriages. In the early 1930s, the LMS proposed improvements to the handling of Furness and Leeds line traffic as the original Furness Railway reversible single-line platform was causing operating delays, particularly when Up and Down trains were booked to arrive at the same time. In September 1937, the LMS announced that a new independent Down Furness and West Yorkshire lines platform was to be built and Carnforth station modernised at a cost of £53,000 under a Government loan scheme.

The 'Art Deco' style of architecture was chosen for the new independent platform and offices. This style had become popular in northern Europe in the 1930s and the LMS was now using it for all its new or rebuilt stations. Its functional lines, together with the use of concrete as a building material, made it radically different to the rest of the station buildings. The design and construction may be attributed to the LMS Architect and Civil Engineer Departments respectively and in the case of Carnforth the drawings were produced at the Manchester Offices of the LMS.

There was an article in the Barrow edition of the *Northwest Daily Mail* for 28th September 1937 which described the alterations being carried out:

> *Under the new arrangements the present bi-directional Furness platform will become the Up platform and a new and independent Down platform which will be 890 feet long will be built. The existing passenger subway will be extended to serve the new platform which will be covered for the greater part of its length, the main-line roofs being extended to match.*

In the winter of 1937 the circular clock case, the clock operating mechanism, and the tall wooden cabinet of 1895 were removed by the LMS for the duration of station rebuilding and put into store. While the awnings and the large pier on the Down LNWR platform were being taken down, trains passed through with a temporary speed restriction, with principal express passenger trains being allowed recovery time for the duration of the rebuilding. The overall roof over the Furness line was removed, together with the cast iron pillars on the island platform: the high curved outer wall and the end piers were taken down manually. A Carnforth resident whose father worked on the station remembered that trains were kept running whilst the outer wall was demolished; it was said that the Irish contractor only employed labour who could provide their own lump hammer and crowbar! The 1882 Furness Railway signal cabin was left standing at the end of the Midland bay as the Signal & Telegraph section were already using it as a lamp and oil store.

Work commenced in the middle of 1938 on the new independent platform, which was built to the standard height of three feet, and the subway was extended from the main island platform to the new platform. The platform was 890 feet long and laid on a tight curve of six chains radius; the platform roof which sweeps upwards was unsupported and was 670 feet long, following the curve of the platform. At the time of building, it was the longest cantilever roof on any United Kingdom railway. The structure is made of concrete and braced by steel beams, projecting above the roof and embedded in the back wall and the under-footings at ground

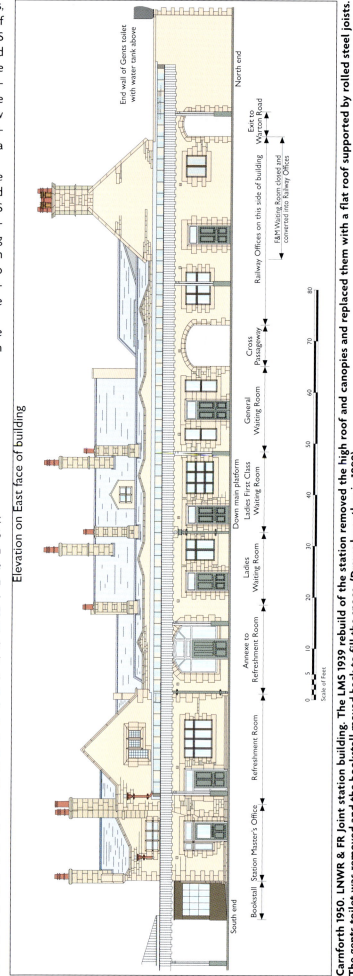

Carnforth 1950. LNWR & FR Joint station building. The LMS 1939 rebuild of the station removed the high roof and canopies and replaced them with a flat roof supported by rolled steel joists. The gents toilet was removed and the bookstall moved back to fill the space. (Drawn by author in 1999)

level. From the bottom of the ramp to platform 4 the existing subway was extended westwards and a long sloping ramp connected the subway to the new platform.

Commencing at the top of the subway was a new plain but functional station building also made of concrete, with metal-framed windows and doors. At the centre of the building was a room containing a service boiler which provided hot water and heating to the offices and public rooms. The back of the building faced onto the exchange sidings, and the three railway offices at the south end were at ground level with direct access to and from the exchange sidings. The four public rooms and one further railway office were at the north end with access at platform level, there was an external coal store at the north end. A separate cabin at ground level was built at the rear of the new building, for the Yard Foreman.

The platform was brought into use in July 1939 at the start of the summer timetable and became platform 6, Down and Up Furness and Yorkshire lines, the platform was signalled such that it could be operated in both Up and Down directions. The existing platform 4 became the Up Furness and Yorkshire lines platform and the Midland bay platform became platform 5. The new station building and platform 6 were fitted out with electric lighting; the platform lamp posts at the north end were made of concrete to a standard LMS design.

In carrying out these improvements, the LMS took the opportunity to increase the height of the Furness Up platform and the LNWR Down main line platform to a standard three feet. A new flat roof awning, part solid roof with some glass sections was constructed over the Up Furness line, the Furness & Midland bay, and the Down LNWR mainline platforms. Rolled steel channel of various cross-sections was supplied by Appleby Frodingham Ltd of Scunthorpe and was used in the roof steelwork which was cantilevered out from the station walls, and also as vertical supporting pillars embedded in concrete at platform level. The outer edges of the flat roof were finished off with plain valance boards. The LNWR roof of 1880 over the Up main platform 2 had become life expired and the LMS replaced it with a clad roof of modern design. The opportunity was taken to replace the gas lamps with electric lights in all the rooms and on all the platforms and the station concourse. On completion of this work, the circular clock case was re-hung directly from one of the new roof beams just above the platform end of the subway on the main island platform. The cabinet and clock mechanism were reinstated and the clock restarted.

For the duration of WW2, the LNWR station entrance and ticket office was closed to the public as there was not enough railway staff to keep the ticket office permanently open. It was only opened when there was a large transfer of service personnel or prisoners-of-war to and from the surrounding wartime camps; the car park was then used as a mustering area. Passengers had to cross over Warton Road Bridge to the Warton Road entrance in the Furness & Midland building and use the reopened F&M ticket office which had been closed up in 1923.

The dining room was also closed to the public and converted into a 'service men's canteen' for the duration of the war. It was staffed by the local WVS ladies who served refreshments to the service personnel passing through Carnforth Station. Many main line trains carried a high proportion of service men and women, and a large number of troop trains also passed through Carnforth station. When these trains stopped at Carnforth, the WVS ladies would hand out jam sandwiches or dried egg sandwiches; however hot tea was served in jam jars on these trains as no cups were available! One of the WVS ladies said years later:

We had volunteers from all around the area: Slyne and Bolton-le-Sands Warton, Tewitfield. I used to do a night shift; we started at seven at night and we used to work until we knew there were no more trains coming through. We would make mostly dried egg sandwiches (we'd make it up into a paste) or jam if anybody had made some home-made jam, anything we could get hold of, beg, borrow or steal. Every soldier, sailor and airman who was in England, including Americans and Canadians, used to know about Carnforth Station, and the free tea and sandwiches.

A pupil who lived in Arkholme who attended the Lancaster Royal Grammar School during the war said that the station was blacked out, and that the mainline waiting rooms were cold. He said that whilst waiting for their train home, he and his fellow students would do their homework in the waiting room on platform 6 (the new 1939 structure). This building was heated from the building services boiler and the coal for the boiler came from the engine shed as the attached mess rooms used by the goods guards and yard shunters needed a supply of hot water for meals and washing.

At the end of hostilities in 1945, the dining room did not return to serving meals owing to rationing and continued austerity. Instead it became an annex to the refreshment room which served hot drinks, sandwiches and cakes until it also closed in the winter of 1966. With closure of the refreshment room the proprietors of the bookstall were allowed to sell sandwiches and drinks, a practice which continued until the closure of the bookstall in or about October 1970.

On 1st January 1948, the London Midland & Scottish Railway ceased to exist, and Carnforth station was now in the London Midland Region of the newly-formed British Railways (BR). The main changes were the repainting of the station into the corporate maroon and cream colour scheme and the replacement of LMS signs with equivalent BR (M) ones. Under the BR bridge replacement programme, the main deck and cast iron arch and panels of bridge 3A which carried the FMJR Carnforth Curve line across Warton Road were replaced in 1950 with a flat concrete deck and tubular hand rails, the work being carried out by the Civil Engineer's Department at Lancaster.

By 1955 the LNWR wooden roof over the 'Lancaster bay' and the two adjacent carriage sidings had also been removed as it was life expired and had become unsafe, but the side and end walls were left standing. Once the Carnforth-Lancaster service had been withdrawn in 1957, the 'Lancaster bay' platform was used to park DMUs in order of rostered duty on services to Preston, Windermere and Carlisle. When they were due for their scheduled clean, these units were sent to the Barrow-in-Furness DMU depot, as by 1966, Carnforth no longer had any on-site carriage cleaners.

As a result of the Beeching Report, which was published on the 27th March 1963, the Midland Railway's line from Morecambe Promenade to Lancaster Green Ayre and along the Lune Valley to Wennington was closed to passengers on and from 3rd January 1966. The service to Leeds now ran from Morecambe Promenade, via Bare Lane and the single line to Hest Bank, thence to Carnforth and along the Furness & Midland Joint line to Wennington where the station remained open. Consequently the local Carnforth-Wennington train were also withdrawn at the same time and the 'Midland bay' carriage siding became redundant and was soon lifted; the 'Midland bay' platform was then used for parcels traffic, and for the stabling of diesel locomotives awaiting their rostered duty.

The bookstall tenancy changed for the final time in 1955 with the buy-out of Wymans by John Menzies & Co Ltd. The station had a total of twenty-two advertisement boards strategically placed around the station walls, and a good array of red fire buckets on all the platforms. Around the station, the public could find weigh scales, several dispensing machines for cigarettes ('Woodbines', five to a packet being popular) and 'Nestle' chocolate bars 1d (0.4p) and a name-plate embossing machine. Outside the LNWR station building entrance was a timetable for Ribble Motor Services who operated the local bus routes.

In 1960 there was just over 650 operational staff at Carnforth, 280 being Motive Power Depot staff. The remainder included the station staff, signalmen, goods and passenger guards, signal and telegraph engineers, permanent way teams, carriage and wagon staff, and goods yard shunters. At major locations such as Carnforth, where there was a large complement of operational staff; the senior railway management had encouraged educational and social activities and often provided accommodation and equipment in support. The LMS set up a reading room, a lecture room and a first-aid room at the north end of the station in the vacant LNWR Telegraph room and the unused post office building. These buildings were demolished to make way for the widening of Warton Road Bridge in 1972, and were replaced by a low wall which closed off the platform from the car park.

The LMS (Carnforth Branch) Staff Association meetings and social event were held in the lecture room which at one time contained a billiard table. The British Railways Staff Association BRSA (Carnforth Branch) moved out of the station building in 1948 and took over the redundant railway canteen on Warton Road. In 1965, two proposals were prepared by British Railways for a new social centre facing the LNWR station buildings, including a new car park on land close to the end loading dock, but the plans were not proceeded with. The Staff Association is now defunct, but the Railway Club at Carnforth is still in existence and is currently a privately run licensed premises; sadly, however, it is no longer full of railwaymen.

The LMS also encouraged its staff to form local ambulance teams and First Aid classes were held in the lecture room and practical training was given by a member of St John Ambulance, a practice continued into the early 1970s. Each year there were inter-area competitions and a badge was awarded to the best team. Carnforth had a shield containing a number of badges which for many years could be found in a cabinet on the wall outside the station master's office on the LNWR Down platform 2, but it disappeared in the late 1970s during the period of the station's decline.

'Mutual Improvement' classes were held on a formal basis for drivers and firemen on Sunday morning in the lecture room and attendance was voluntary. These classes were given by a senior driver or inspector, and were run to promote a better understanding of the workings of a steam engine and to encourage reliability and punctuality in service. There was a cutaway model made of polished wood, showing how the steam passed through the cylinders and how the valve gear worked. The model was used as a practical and visual aid in the classes, to show how regulator, valve settings and cut-off could affect the working of the engine with regard to water and coal consumption, and demonstrated the overall thermal efficiency of the steam system. The workings of boiler, injectors, firebox and smokebox were all explained, and the firing methods used to minimise black smoke from locomotives was emphasised. In the early 1960s, these classes came to an end as those drivers and passed firemen who intended to stay in railway service were starting to undergo training on diesel traction. At Carnforth a number of diesel instructors were appointed and this training took place in the driving cab.

A mess room was usually provided for railwaymen in an area close to where they worked. Here, railwaymen who had brought their own food could cook it, as well as making drinks. At the beginning of the Second World War, the LMS started to build

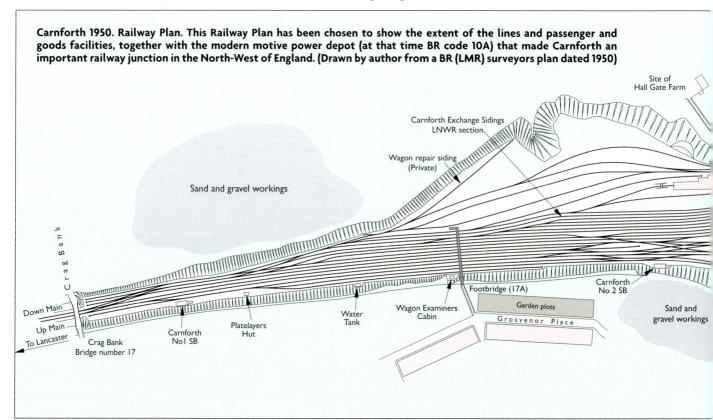

Carnforth 1950. Railway Plan. This Railway Plan has been chosen to show the extent of the lines and passenger and goods facilities, together with the modern motive power depot (at that time BR code 10A) that made Carnforth an important railway junction in the North-West of England. (Drawn by author from a BR (LMR) surveyors plan dated 1950)

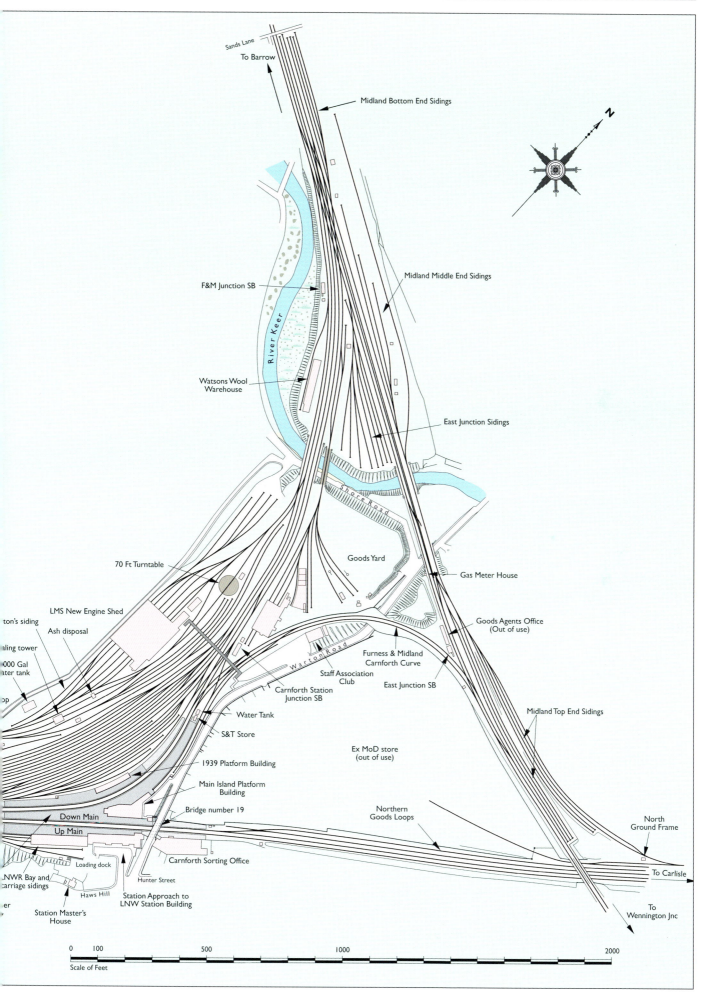

CHAPTER NINE

Carnforth 1962. The LNWR station building from the Royal Station Hotel. A British Railways 'Crewbus' and cars made by Austin, Ford and Vauxhall are parked up on the station approach road. Steam locomotives still predominate but a class 17 Clayton diesel engine and a class 08 diesel-shunter are in the exchange sidings. (Steve Le Cheminant collection, Telerail-Carnforth)

canteens at Carnforth, Wigan and Carlisle; the meals in these canteens could be purchased without a rationing card. At Carnforth, the railway canteen was built (circa 1942) on land beside the Carnforth Curve and alongside Warton Road, and was run by British Restaurants. After the war, the Carnforth canteen continued serving meals until the end of 1947 when rationing ceased, following which the canteen closed: the railwaymen then reverted to buying and cooking their own food.

The last incumbent Station Master to be appointed to the post at Carnforth retired in 1960; the stationmaster's position was then covered by relief men until March 1966 when the position was abolished. At Carnforth, the incumbent station master had since 1857 only been responsible for the station staff but this changed in March 1966 with the appointment in the same area of a Station Manager and Assistant Station Manager. The Station Manager now had responsibility for the station staff and the operational staff. The shed master was appointed Assistant Station Manager; he retained responsibility for the motive power department staff and additionally for the daily operations of the train crews (goods and passenger guards, firemen or second-men and drivers).

Following the closure of the engine shed on the 31st March 1969, the Station Manager and Assistant Station Manager transferred to Lancaster as Area Manager and Assistant Area Manager respectively. They had responsibility for the stations at Lancaster, Carnforth, Morecambe and Heysham, and Wennington and Arnside, including the signalmen and crossing keepers on the F&M joint line to Bentham, the Furness line to Arnside and on the WCML to Brock. Bolton-le-Sands and Hest Bank stations had already closed on 3rd February 1969. On the 1st May 1969 the Station Foreman became the senior person on the station and in charge of the remaining few platform staff.

When the ticket office opened on the Monday morning of the 15th February 1971 all tickets were sold in the new 'decimalisation' currency. On 31st of October 1980, the ticket office in the LNWR building entrance was closed and the office was transferred to platform 1 of the main island platform. Here a new window, serving counter and ticket racks were installed in part of the Carnforth Trainmen's Depot signing-on lobby, but the ticket office had a short life, finally closing on the 29th October 1988.

Red Star Parcels was set up by British Rail in 1963 to transport parcels by passenger train between passenger stations through-out the United Kingdom and was to compete against the Post Office. It became defunct in 1999 being bought by Lynx Express which in turn was acquired by UPS. The Red Star Parcels office at Carnforth was set up in what had previously been the staff cloakroom in the LNWR building with access from platform 2 Up main. On arrival at the ticket counter there was a bell-push which summoned the ticket clerk, who then directed the parcel holder on to the platform and through the second door where the parcels office was situated. Once inside the parcels clerk dealt with the parcels at a long counter where a weighing machine had been set up. The office closed completely at the same time as the ticket office in 1980, by this time new British Rail corporate signs had replaced the original 1950 BR totem signs on the station.

From March 1987 the station (now in the Preston Area) was staffed by a chargeman, a leading railman and a railman, in that year despite the run down they had won an award for the quality of service and the attractiveness of the station which, during the summer had been set out with hanging baskets and tubs on platforms 1 and 2. This was a final tribute as the station became an 'open station' at the end of October 1988 and the station staff transferred to Lancaster. A Lancaster railman travelled to Carnforth each day for general duties until that role was also abolished on and from 3rd October 1994.

In early 1969 the refreshment room serving counter and its raised staging were removed, and the room partitioned into two parts, a signing-on lobby and a Time Office. The Time Office was occupied by the Train Crew Supervisor, together with his clerical staff; it became the pay-out station and had a substantial safe for holding the weekly wages. Pay-out stations had been established at each engine shed of the three pre-grouping companies and the respective company clerks went there during pay-day. This practice was continued by the LMS until 1940 when the pay-out station at the MR shed and the LNWR shed were closed and concentrated in the LNWR station building adjacent to the ticket office. In 1966 the pay-out station and two clerks were moved back to the engine shed as part of the management re-organisation then taking place. The new signing-on lobby was entered from platform 3, and held the signing-on book and other information. The original dining room became a mess room with a hot plate and a sink and could hold up to 36 staff at one sitting. The food preparation areas were converted to a galley with an Ascot boiler, a wash room, a locker room and an

THE LMS AND BR YEARS

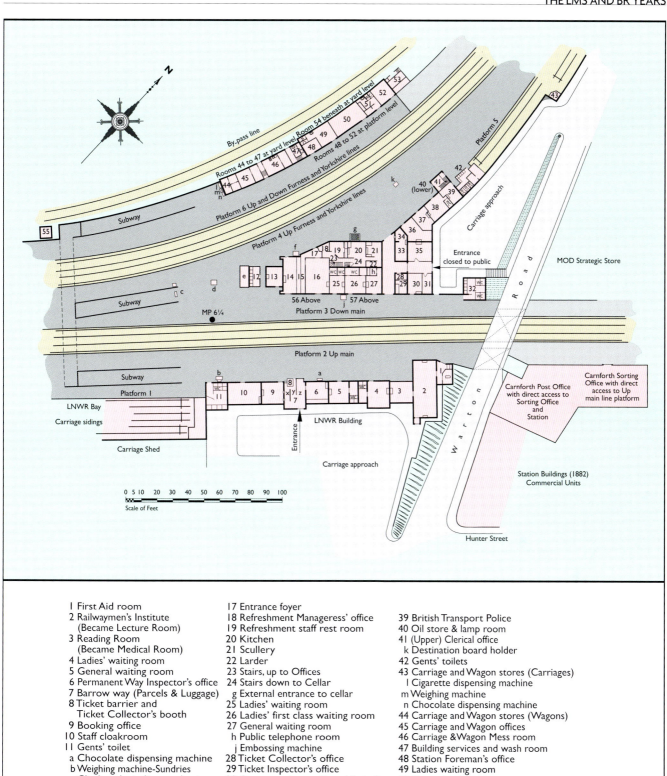

Carnforth 1950. Station Facilities. The internal layout of the railway offices and public rooms in 1950 when the station was classed as a main line station and was still fully manned. (Drawn by author from a L.M.R Civil Engineering Drawing dated 1950)

CHAPTER NINE

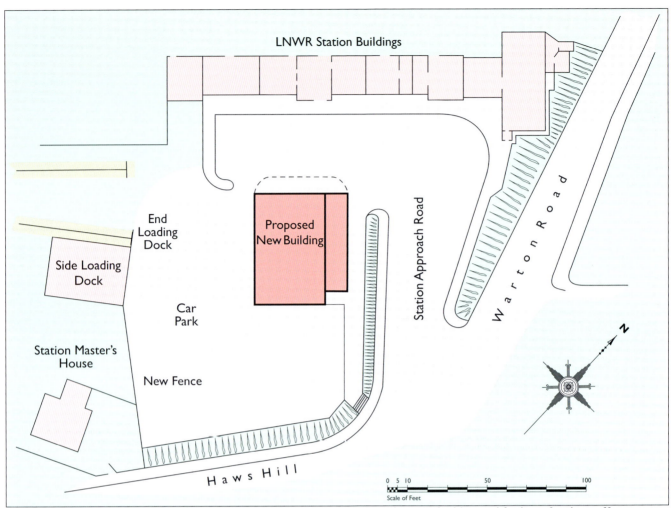

Carnforth 1965. Proposed New Social Centre. This proposal was made to provide a new building and facilities for the Staff Association (Carnforth Branch). It was one of two proposals on the same site and would have had an impact on the station approach road and car park. (Drawn by author from Architect's plan)

Carnforth 16th July 1955. 2P 4-4-0 number 40654 of Barrow shed is on the 4.16pm Leeds-Barrow train and is proceeding along the F&M direct line between East Junction and F&M junction. East Junction sidings are on the right and the Midland Middle sidings are on the left. (CRA Collection Ref. PEJ179)

THE LMS AND BR YEARS

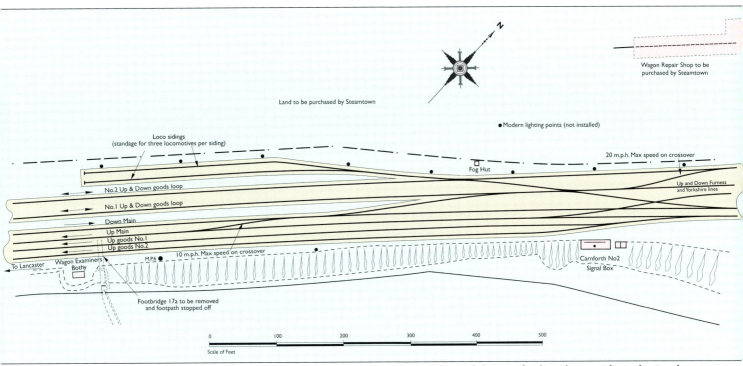

Carnforth 1970. Proposed changes to the southern loops and sidings. With the lifting of the Carnforth exchange sidings the Southern goods loops were made bi-directional and the two adjacent through lines converted into sidings. Footbridge 17a was demolished and the footpath stopped off when the WCML was electrified. (Drawn by author from a plan prepared by BRB Civil Engineering, Stephenson House, Euston 1970)

Carnforth 22nd March 1957. SR mainline diesel engine1-Co-Co-1 number 10203 at the head of the Down 'Royal Scot' at Crag Bank overbridge. The coaches are all in the new maroon livery. The train is framed by the semaphore signals controlling the Down mainline and the Down southern loops and sidings at the LNWR end of the Carnforth exchange sidings. (CRA Collection Ref. PEJ742)

CHAPTER NINE

Carnforth 16th August 1955. The Lancaster Bay with the roofless carriage shed and the 1939 LMS roof on the Up main platform 2. The subway runs from platform 2 to platform 6 and commences where the train spotters are congregated. (CRA Collection Ref. PEJ236)

Carnforth 1965. Platform 4 the island platform buildings with the clock, bookstall and telephone booth, to the left is 1939 Furness and Yorkshire line platform 6. (Douglas Fisher)

THE LMS AND BR YEARS

office for the Station Foreman. The whole of the first floor of the island platform building was closed off, the bottom three stairs being removed and sealed up with a door. New staff toilets were installed in the area previously occupied by the GGC and correspondence clerk in the Furness & Midland building and the trainmen's mess room was taken over by the Permanent Way staff.

In July 1969 the 'Carnforth Trainmen's Depot' came into use in the converted refreshment rooms and the enginemen's signing-on point and pay-out station was moved back from the engine shed to the station. The passenger guards also had a staff room and signing-on point upstairs in the main island platform building, in one of the rooms which had last been used by the catering staff in 1950. With the closure of the station upper floor they also transferred to the Carnforth Trainmen's Depot. The new joint signing-on point for drivers, second men and passenger and goods guards had an allocation of just under 250 staff, included in this number were station staff, signalmen, and permanent way staff.

On 5th March 1969 the Assistant General Manager of the LMR division confirmed that the closure of the Carnforth wagon repair shop and the exchange yard as a marshalling yard was to

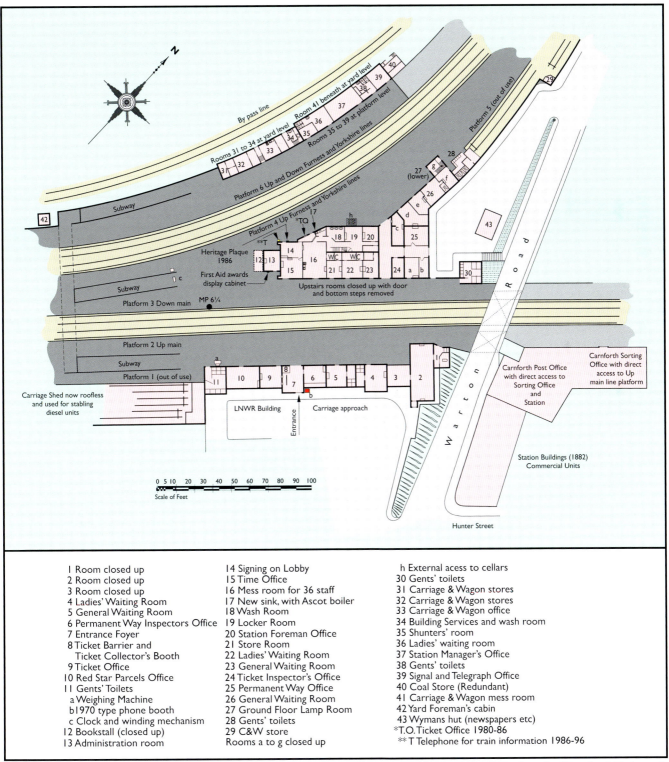

1 Room closed up	14 Signing on Lobby	h External acess to cellars
2 Room closed up	15 Time Office	30 Gents' toilets
3 Room closed up	16 Mess room for 36 staff	31 Carriage & Wagon stores
4 Ladies' Waiting Room	17 New sink, with Ascot boiler	32 Carriage & Wagon stores
5 General Waiting Room	18 Wash Room	33 Carriage & Wagon office
6 Permanent Way Inspectors Office	19 Locker Room	34 Building Services and wash room
7 Entrance Foyer	20 Station Foreman Office	35 Shunters' room
8 Ticket Barrier and Ticket Collector's Booth	21 Store Room	36 Ladies' waiting room
	22 Ladies' Waiting Room	37 Station Manager's Office
9 Ticket Office	23 General Waiting Room	38 Gents' toilets
10 Red Star Parcels Office	24 Ticket Inspector's Office	39 Signal and Telegraph Office
11 Gents' Toilets	25 Permanent Way Office	40 Coal Store (Redundant)
a Weighing Machine	26 General Waiting Room	41 Carriage & Wagon mess room
b 1970 type phone booth	27 Ground Floor Lamp Room	42 Yard Foreman's cabin
c Clock and winding mechanism	28 Gents' toilets	43 Wymans hut (newspapers etc)
12 Bookstall (closed up)	29 C&W store	*T.O. Ticket Office 1980-86
13 Administration room	Rooms a to g closed up	**T Telephone for train information 1986-96

Carnforth 1969. Station Facilities. The internal layout of the railway offices and public rooms in 1969 when the 'Carnforth Trainmen's Depot' was established in the closed refreshment room and other rooms were changed over to other uses. (Drawn by author from a BRB Civil Engineering Drawing dated 1969)

CHAPTER NINE

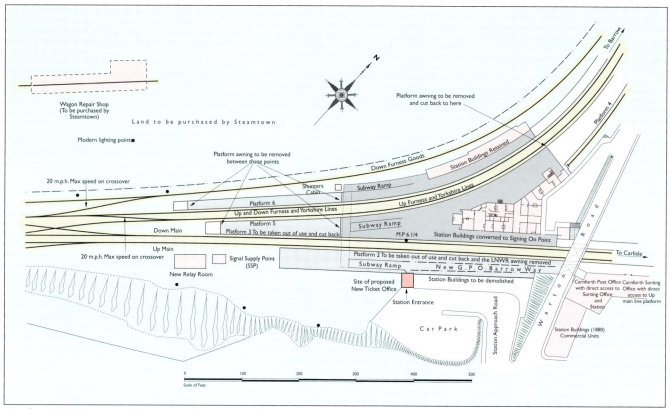

Carnforth 1970. Proposed changes to the station. The LNWR station buildings were to be demolished and replaced by a new ticket office. The Up and Down mainline platforms were to be taken out of use and some of the platform awnings were to be removed. A relay room and a signal supply point were to be installed as part of the re-signalling of the WCML. (Drawn by author from a plan prepared by BRB Civil Engineering, Stephenson House, Euston 1970)

take place and a further fifty men would be made redundant. By this time wagon load traffic and local trip work had reduced considerably and were being replaced with company and block train which ran between fixed destinations. The Carnforth train-crews still retained work on WCML where they relieved train-crews from Carlisle, Wigan and Crewe and with Workington and Barrow train-crews on the Furness line and Skipton train-crews on the Yorkshire lines. The exchange yards were lifted and by 1972 the land had been sold to Steamtown.

In 1972, British Rail announced that the Carnforth Trainmen's Depot would close in May 1974 and would affect around two hundred train crews and a further twenty clerical and supervisory staff. A meeting was held with the Preston Divisional Manager, and a request was made through the ASLEF union representative for the remaining drivers and second-men to be given training on the new electric traction which would be used on the West Coast Main Line, wiring-up of which was now well under way between Weaver junction, Carlisle, and Glasgow.

The Carnforth ASLEF representative had this to say:

Carnforth has always been a class A depot in the past but we must forget the past. Those days have gone and we must get on to the new traction. When we've gone, there will be no more depot because there will be no more recruits.

Training schools for electric traction training were set up at Preston, Carnforth and Carlisle Citadel D.M.D commencing in May 1973. A school had already been set up in Carlisle Kingmoor in May 1972. Training was given on the new 25kV AC locomotives of classes AL1, AL2, AL5, AL6, classes AL3, and AL4 were being refurbished and training was to be given later. Training on Class AL7 was not considered necessary as the driving techniques were similar to the modified AL6s.

The Carnforth Trainmen's Depot did not close up in May 1974; instead it became part of the Preston Area Depot. By 1984 all the passenger work had gone to the Preston and Wigan Depots and Carnforth had become a freight only depot for 'Freightliner' and infrastructure trains on the WCML between Crewe and Carlisle, and the nuclear flask trains which on privatisation were taken over by Direct Rail Services (DRS). The Carnforth Trainmen's Depot became part of Transrail and at privatisation was subsumed into EWS and no longer existed as such.

In line with the objective of reducing the journey times of the new electrified services that were to commence running on the West Coast Main Line in 1974, BR decided to remove the main line platforms and make alternative connections at Lancaster which is only 6¼ miles away. During 1969 the Up platform awning and supporting pillars were removed from the LNWR station building and the Lancaster Bay line and the two carriage sidings together with the loading dock sidings were lifted and the junction to the Up loops removed. The outer wall of the carriage shed was demolished, but the end wall was left standing as it was an integral part of the LNWR station building end wall. The whole area occupied by the carriage siding was filled in, and made level with the top of the platform, and surfaced for use as a staff car park. On 4th May 1970 the Up and Down main line platforms, were taken out of use and the platform edges were cut back and given a sloped face to the track and covered with flagstones; a wire mesh safety fence was placed along the cut-back edge of the platforms. The Down platform awing was cut back to the centre roof supporting girder. The closed Up platform was truncated at the north end in line with Warton Road Bridge but access to the sorting office remained, at the south end it was truncated in line with the subway. The subway ramp was roofed over and enclosed with wooden framed side screens containing high level glass side windows. The Down platform was truncated at the north end in line with Warton Road Bridge and, extended glass screens were built alongside the subway ramp on the Down platform.

Following the closure of the main line platforms, the station was downgraded to secondary status and entered a period of gradual run-down which was to last 18 years. All passengers from the Furness area and from Yorkshire who were travelling north were now inconvenienced by having to travel south to Lancaster to change trains, and within a short time, find themselves speeding back north through Carnforth's closed platforms. For this, they had to pay for an extra 12½ miles of travel, a practice which has continued to the present day.

With the closure of the mainline platforms the number of people using the station reduced and as a result other facilities were rationalised. There were two public telephones on the station one in a wooden booth on platform 4 adjacent to the refreshment room and one in a separate cubicle in the General Waiting Room on platform 3. In 1970 both were removed from within the station and replaced by a modern style flat-roof booth outside the station entrance. The 'Ladies' waiting room on the Down main line platform 3 was closed as it was now redundant and became a general storage area for the Carnforth Trainmen's Depot. The 'Ladies' first-class waiting room on platform 4 (Up Furness and Yorkshire lines) was downgraded to a general waiting room, the main item of furniture was a large oval wooden table which was still there at the time the station became an open station.

As there was insufficient headroom for the 25kV AC overhead line equipment, at both Crag Bank Bridge and Warton Road Bridge the bridges had to be rebuilt. At Crag Bank a prefabricated cast concrete flat arch was installed directly on to the lower existing two side walls of the bridge and concrete parapets erected at road level as was standard practice for minor roads. Warton Road Bridge however was totally rebuilt with new foundations as the Lancashire County Surveyor of Highways had taken the opportunity to widen the carriage way and provide a footpath on the south side. Three new substantial side walls were made from reinforced poured concrete and topped with a flat concrete road deck, the work taking place during December 1971 and January 1972. The blue brick arch giving access to the Carnforth sorting office was subsumed into the new structure and left in situ.

As a consequence of the road widening, the two northernmost bays of the LNWR station buildings on the Up platform which had become surplus were demolished. Likewise the building containing the gentlemen's toilets at the north end of the Down platform adjacent to Warton Road Bridge were also demolished. New low boundary walls were built on both platforms to fill in the gap between the end of the main station buildings and Warton Road Bridge. The chimney-stack at the east end of the Furness & Midland Railway building was also removed as it was no longer needed.

In 1970 BR prepared a plan for a new ticket office which was to be built on the cut-back LNWR Up platform, close to the subway, with an entrance from the car park. The LNWR station building was to be demolished and the platform walled off from the car park, with a mail-trolley clear-way for the GPO from the Carnforth sorting office to the subway. Following the closure of the main line platforms and the Midland Bay to passengers, the Furness and Yorkshire Lines platforms 4 and 6 were subsequently re-numbered as platforms 1 and 2. The island platform building on platform 1 was being used as a signing-on point (as previously mentioned) and was to remain in situ, as were the station buildings on platform 2 (Down Furness and Yorkshire lines).

The infrastructure work and the electrification and MAS re-signalling of the WCML over the period 1970 to 1974 often meant complete closure of sections of the line so as to give the engineers full occupation to enable them to carry out the work. For the diesel locomotive drivers and second men at Carnforth this resulted in working over diversionary routes such as the S&C and around Chorley, Wigan and Warrington accompanied by a pilot man who was familiar the route. The extra mileage more often resulted in a slow journey for the passengers and a long day for the train crew. An alternative was a motor coach service, often in rather cramped seats and sometimes of a long duration, this has now become the accepted method of transport when line closure occurs during engineering work. The car park at the station is frequently used by coaches during weekend when the WCML or the Cumbrian Coast Line is closed for engineering work. (This happened during the WCML upgrade in 2002.)

By 1973 the overhead line equipment had been erected along the West Coast Main Line from Weaver Junction to Glasgow, and the full new Inter City electric services commenced running through Carnforth on 6th May 1974. At Carnforth, the overhead line equipment was erected over the Up main line No.1 and No.2 goods loops (the No.2 goods loop was lifted during the WCML upgrade and the wires subsequently removed) and the No.1 and No.2 Up and Down (formerly Down only) goods loops and adjacent Down sidings No.1 and No.2.

The overhead line equipment was laid all the way through platform 2 (Up and Down Furness and Yorkshire) and the Roundabout Road at the rear of platform 2 and as far as north sidings No.1 and No.2 which terminated near to the F&M junction signal box. Platform 1 (Up Furness and Yorkshire) however was only wired part way. The reason for this wiring was to allow a changeover of traction from electric to diesel on the through Euston-Barrow service, but the changeover was never implemented instead changeover took place at Preston. The wires have been cutback in recent years and now terminate just beyond the Carnforth Station Junction signal box. The Roundabout Road has been used to stable empty electric trains workings off London Euston-Lancaster services which continue to Carnforth to allow the driver a personal break and for the train to reverse and return to Lancaster to form a Lancaster-London Euston service

Despite the platforms being wired-up, only a few electric trains have used either platform to changeover on charter and special trains travelling onwards over (pre 1974) North Lancs, Westmorland and Cumberland lines or the S&C line (usually behind steam). From the mid-1980s all charter and special trains have used the No.1 and No.2 Up and Down goods loops to change over from electric traction thereby keeping platforms 1 and 2 clear for service trains. The transfer is made possible as the 1974 MAS scheme allows access between the Furness and Yorkshire lines passing through platforms 1 and 2, and the No.1 and No.2 Up and Down goods loops and vice-versa.

The station clock had to be wound regularly by station staff to keep it working. However, with the complete de-staffing of the station, winding ceased and the circular clock case and winding mechanism were removed from the station. The 1895 clock mechanism was sold at a railway auction to a clock dealer who lived in Twickenham. Following local protests the clock case was reinstated with two electric motors, one driving each face, but the modifications were not a success as within a few

CHAPTER NINE

Carnforth 23rd April 1955. BR 7MT Britannia 4-6-2 70042 'Lord Roberts' pulls out of the 1939 platform No. 6 on the 3.53pm Manchester-Barrow passenger train. The sharply curved platform and the back of the 1939 offices can been seen behind the wagons .The rows of terraced houses in the centre of the picture show how the town developed outwards from the station. (CRA Collection PEJ104)

years both electric motors had become unreliable. BR had tenders submitted by a number of clock makers to replace the electric motors but this never happened and the clock was decommissioned, although the circular clock case was left *in situ*.

In October 1985 the British Railways Property Board decided that the LNWR station building was to be demolished. Very quickly, various schemes were put forward for alternative uses of the building: initially a restaurant with a garden centre, then a supermarket and finally small retail units. However none of these came to fruition and at the start of 1986 the Property Board had decided to demolish the building and to extend and upgrade the existing car park into a park-and-ride area. However, the Carnforth Chamber of Trade, together with a small group of local conservationists, voiced their opposition to this scheme, and in 1987 arranged a local petition and lobbied their Member of Parliament who gave much needed support to the case. The eventual 3000-signature petition led the British Railways Property Board to withdraw its plans. A spokesman for BR said there were now two options for the future of the site: to demolish the existing building and resurrect the proposed scheme of 1970 for a new booking office, or raise sufficient funding to preserve the whole site and restore the existing buildings. The latter option was accepted by the local conservationists as the way forwards but the lack of funding prevented further action. Over the next seven years it became a regular topic for discussion at the meetings of the Carnforth Chamber of Trade. For the local conservationists there was, however, an element of comic

Carnforth circa 1955. There was an evening train for Wennington which departed at 19.00hrs from the Midland Bay, platform 5. The coaching stock for the morning Leeds train is in the adjacent carriage siding. The 1939 LMS water tower is in the centre and a goods train has been marshalled on the by-pass line which passed around the back of platform 6. (CRA Collection Ref MO0937)

THE LMS AND BR YEARS

Carnforth 3rd June 1955. Introduced in 1954, two 'Derby Lightweight' two-car units have been coupled together for a service from Preston to Workington. This is an unusual working as these units were allocated to the Whitehaven-Carlisle services and it was not until 1960 they ran south from Whitehaven to Barrow-in-Furness. The train is running on the sixth day of the 1955 national rail strike and is passing over Carnforth Station Junction; the line curving to the left is the Carnforth Curve of 1880. (CRA Collection Ref PEJ139)

Carnforth May 1961. Jubilee 6P 4-6-0 number 45553 'Canada' of Crewe South shed is passing under Warton Road with an Up fast fitted freight. The bridge was fitted with safety screens on both sides but there was no footpath on this side of the bridge and the carriage way finished at the bridge parapet. To the right of the engine is the archway giving direct access to the Carnforth sorting office. (CRA Collection Ref. SBW029)

CHAPTER NINE

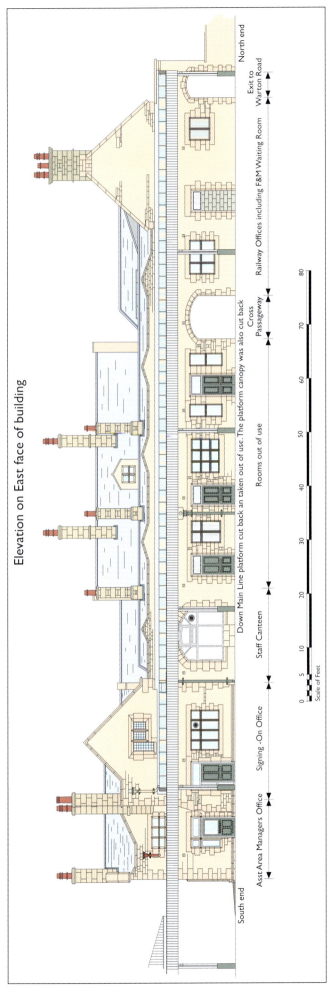

relief as in early 1987 the Lancashire comedy duo Little and Large made a sketch and musical number on the island platform of the station, and this was broadcast on BBC One TV on 14th March.

At the beginning of 1990, the area once occupied by the end and side loading dock was filled in and raised up to the level of the existing car park; the car park was then extended southwards to join up to this area and the periphery of the car park bordering Haws Hill was landscaped. By 1992 new lighting had been installed within the car park and the whole area had been re-surfaced and laid out with designated parking bays for a park and ride facility and to assist the travelling public new timetable and travel information boards were placed at the car park entrance. Concurrently a new-two storey administration building was built by Trainload Freight to replace the Carnforth Trainmen's Depot signing on point at the station. The new building which was alongside the Up WCML and to the south of the station car park had a large forecourt which provided parking for the staff and Railtrack maintenance vehicles, it was segregated from the car park by a wall which contained an entrance gate. On the ground floor of the building was a traincrew supervisor's office, a messroom, toilets and showers and on the first floor were offices which were allocated to the area permanent way staff.

On 4th November 1992 the Carnforth Trainmen's Depot was moved out of the station into the new administrative building, it became a Transrail office and subsequently on privatisation part of English, Welsh and Scottish railway (EWS), one of the privatised railfreight companies. The signing-on point closed in March 2008 and the building and offices have been taken over by Network Rail, track renewal and maintenance staff. When the Carnforth Trainmen's Depot moved out, the station buildings finally became empty. The windows and doors on all the buildings and the cross-passageway on the island platform were boarded up to prevent access to the inside of the building, and the buildings themselves rapidly fell into a state of neglect. The travelling public found Carnforth station an uninviting place to wait for a train, particularly in the dark evening hours, and consequently passenger numbers declined and the level of vandalism increased. Following rail privatisation, Railtrack became the new owners of the former BR infrastructure on 1st April 1994; again there was speculation about the future of Carnforth station.

Carnforth 1969. LNWR & FR Joint station building. At the end of 1969 the 'Carnforth Trainmen's Depot' occupied the closed refreshment and dining room areas and the adjacent waiting room and the bookstall had gone. There was no longer a station.

THE LMS AND BR YEARS

Carnforth 31st December 1971. Reconstruction work is under way on Wharton Road Bridge looking north along Down main platform. Three new side walls have been made from poured concrete and the road deck is in place. The north end of both the Up and Down platforms have been removed and the point for the northern loops taken out. (CRA Collection DUF005)

Carnforth 1962. A BR Class 40 D326 on a Down passenger train 1S53 enters south end of Down main platform No. 3 Behind the engine are two horseboxes, another source of traffic that turned over to road haulage. The 1939 LMS water tower and LNWR water crane are at the end of the Up platform. (CRA Collection Ref. WAR 371)

CHAPTER NINE

Carnforth 20th June 1968. Looking north from Grosvenor Road footbridge a class 47 Brush diesel engine passes on the Down mainline with a train of 45ton fuel oil/bitumen tanks. The lattice post signal in front of the engine controls the passenger junction. To the left is a stacked array of four shunting signals. A class 5MT 4-6-0 engine stands on the 'back road' behind platform No. 6. (CRA Collection Ref. 092g12)

Carnforth 1969. A Brush class 47 diesel engine on an Up passenger train passes under the original L&C Crag Bank Bridge. It was rebuilt at the time of the WCML electrification with a flat arch. The steps to the right of the bracket signal were used by the post office staff to take mail bags to the pickup point for the travelling post office. (Keith Lauderdale)

Carnforth 1971. The rationalised goods junction at Crag Bank. The two loops would remain but the farthest line to the left would become a dead end siding. A class 25 diesel engine stands on the loop with an engineer's train. Another class 25 diesel stands on the Up loop alongside Carnforth No. 1 signal box with a ballast train. A class 47 diesel engine is on a passenger train and is about to pass under the lattice post bracket signal. (Keith Lauderdale)

Carnforth 29th July 1969. A BR Class 50 D448, on an Up passenger train 1M18, it is passing the closed exchange sidings. The building on the left is the wagon repair shop and outside is the wagon hoist. At the north end of the station a class 47 awaits its next rostered duty. (CRA Collection Ref. A69_22_3)

Carnforth 1971. A Barrow-London train headed by a class 50 diesel engine is about to cross Keer Bridge. The yellow wagons are part of the CMEE concrete train and are standing on the goods yard line. The cantilevered bracket signal has had one signal arm removed as the connection to the exchange sidings has been severed. (Keith Lauderdale)

CHAPTER TEN

LOCOMOTIVE SHEDS AND "STEAMTOWN"

The three railway companies originally erect their own locomotive sheds, but with the formation of the London Midland & Scottish Railway, they are rationalised and eventually closed. In 1944 the LMS builds a new engine shed based upon its 'standard depot layout'. It becomes one of the last working sheds in the North West and, following closure by British Rail in 1969 it becomes 'Steamtown', housing preserved steam locomotives. The depot-museum closes its gates for the last time in October 1996 and has been re-branded as 'West Coast Railways', a private undertaking specialising in the charter trains market.

The first Ulverstone and Lancaster engine shed was built alongside Warton Road at the west end of the Joint station in 1857 as a three-road dead-end shed. When the Furness Railway took over the Ulverstone & Lancaster Railway in 1862, its layout was modified as a through shed with a coal stage and turntable at the rear. The turntable was transferred from the exchange sidings when the yard was extended in 1862. The shed at this time would have housed an assortment of 0-4-0 tender locomotives, with bar frames and 'haystack' fireboxes, and 2-2-2WTs, the latter mainly from Sharp, Stewart & Co. Connection to the shed was from the single Up and Down passenger line into Carnforth station, as the FR had not commenced doubling its mainline west from Carnforth. The shed remained in use in this modified form until 1879 when it was demolished to make way for the Carnforth Curve and the station enlargements.

The second Furness Railway shed was built in red brick in 1882 on the west side of the Carnforth exchange yard at the foot of Hunting Hill. The layout of this Furness shed was quite different to a traditional shed, with six roads entering from the north end and four exiting at the south end. The centre of the shed contained two roads where minor running repairs could be carried out; alongside them was a foreman's office, a small machine shop, and a blacksmith's forge with a tall chimney. Outside the shed were a sand and oil store and a coaling stage with a manually-operated winch. Tubs of 10cwt capacity were filled and lifted by the winch, and the coal deposited directly into the locomotives' tenders. A turntable of 42 feet diameter was installed at the north-west end of the shed. Access to the shed was from the Up and Down through goods lines controlled by Carnforth F&M Junction signal box.

The Furness Railway shed provided motive power for all Furness line passenger and goods trains, and for yard shunting – probably the most prestigious workings were the Midland Railway's boat trains to and from Barrow, where the loco changeover took place at Carnforth East Junction. The goods workings included handling the Furness line mileage of the coke trains originating at Tebay on the LNWR main line, which were routed via the Carnforth exchange sidings. At its opening the shed had an allocation of the FR's various types of 2-4-0 passenger engines and 0-6-0 freight engines and 0-4-0 tank engines for shunting duties, Carnforth and Barrow sheds always being allocated the latest motive power. After the 1923 Grouping, the

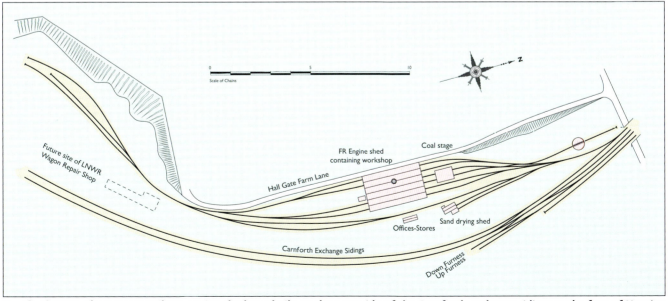

Carnforth 1882. The Furness Railway engine shed was built on the west side of the Carnforth exchange sidings at the foot of Hunting Hill. Six roads entered at the north end and four exited at the south end. The centre of the shed contained a two road workshop for engine repairs, a machine shop, stores and foreman's office. (Drawn by author based upon an Ordnance Survey Map)

CHAPTER TEN

Carnforth circa 1935. FR (1882) Engine Shed. The shed closed in 1925 and this photograph is taken at the south end where the four shed lines converged. The sand and oil store and the coaling stage are to the right of the shed and the two workshop lines terminated in the centre of the shed which is obscured by the trees. (CRA Collection Ref. FR001B-08)

Carnforth circa 1882. The FR workshop at Carnforth in the centre of the Engine Shed, the artisan staff is posed and the two FR 0-6-0 engines built by Sharp Stewart are undergoing repair. The inspection pits give access to the inside valve gear and there are a number of machine tools for manufacturing replacement parts. (Mrs Pat Jackson Collection Ref. TR46)

LOCOMOTIVE SHEDS AND "STEAMTOWN"

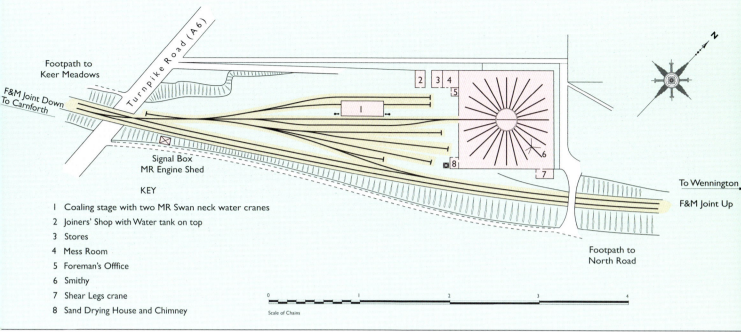

Carnforth 1874. The second Midland Railway engine shed was a square round house having twenty three roads radiating from a central 42 feet turntable. The longest road was 75 feet and contained a set of shear legs for lifting the ends of locomotives to facilitate wheel repairs. (Drawn by author from a plan in the CRA collection)

London Midland & Scottish Railway laid a link line west of the former LNWR wagon repair workshop (as mentioned in chapter 8) to facilitate the movement of locomotives between the former Furness Railway shed and the former LNWR shed. Rationalisation carried out by the LMS resulted in the Furness Railway shed being closed in 1925, with the locomotives, enginemen and shed staff being distributed between the LNWR shed and the Midland Railway shed. The passenger duties officially went to the LNWR shed and the goods duties to the Midland shed, although photographs taken at the time show the large Furness Railway 0-6-0 goods locomotives at both sheds. The FR shed remained out of use until it was demolished in 1939 to make way for the LMS 'New Shed'.

The first Midland Railway engine shed was a two-road dead-end shed, with a small turntable and a water tower on adjacent sidings; it opened at the same time as the FMJR in 1867. It was of sufficient length to hold four early MR type single wheel 2-2-2 or 2-4-0 passenger engines or 0-6-0 freight locomotives. It was built on elevated ground alongside the River Keer just beyond the viaduct over the river and was connected to the direct line of the Furness & Midland Joint Railway and east of its junction with the Furness Railway. It remained in use as an engine shed until 1874 when the Midland Railway opened its new shed one mile further to the east and on the north side of the FMJR.

The first MR shed was not demolished but was found an alternative use as a wagon examination and repairs workshop, but the MR turntable and water tower were soon demolished. Following the Grouping and subsequent rationalisation, the LMS centralised all wagon examination and repairs at the LNWR wagon repair workshop adjacent to the Carnforth exchange sidings. Following the transfer the MR shed was also demolished.

Staff access to the second MR shed was from the 1820

Carnforth circa 1932. MR (1874) Engine Shed. An LMS 3MT 2-6-2 tank engine stands on the coaling stage line with a 4F 0-6-0 engine on the shed entrance and exit line. On one of the dead end sidings is an ex-LNWR 0-8-0 goods engine and to the right is the sand drying house and chimney. (CRA Collection Ref. BOcln25)

CHAPTER TEN

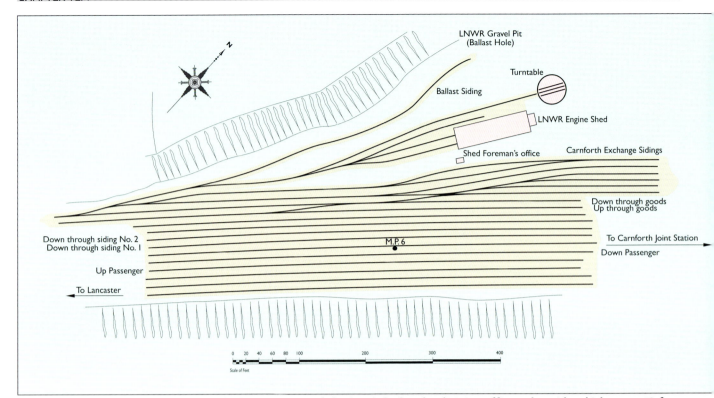

Carnforth 1873. The first LNWR engine shed was a two road dead-end shed with adjoining offices, alongside which was a 42-foot turntable. A single line known as the 'ballast siding' led to the LNWR gravel pit where in 1884 a labourer was killed by a fall of earth and sand. (Drawn by author from a plan in the CRA collection)

Garstang and Heron Syke Turnpike road (the present A6) at a point where the Furness & Midland Joint Railway crossed the road on a skew bridge. The shed was a traditional Midland Railway 'square' roundhouse, having 24 roads radiating from a central 42-foot diameter turntable within a conventional square building (a surviving example is Barrow Hill roundhouse near Chesterfield, Derbyshire). The shed and other ancillary buildings were substantially constructed in red brick. Each road was designed to hold one large or two small locomotives. A set of shear legs was installed on one of the longest roads (of 75 feet) for lifting one end of a locomotive for maintenance and repair. A smithy, sand drying house with a chimney, stores, mess room and shed foreman's office were conveniently placed around the outside walls. A tank house with a large water tank and a joiner's shop beneath was sited near to the shed. A through-road covered coal stage was installed on the line leading into and out of the shed.

The shed was connected at its western end with both Up and

Carnforth circa 1926. LNWR (1892) Engine Shed. The south end of the LNWR six-road dead end engine shed with a good selection of ex-LNWR 4-4-0 passenger and 0-8-0 goods engines. (CRA Collection Ref. BOcln21)

LOCOMOTIVE SHEDS AND "STEAMTOWN"

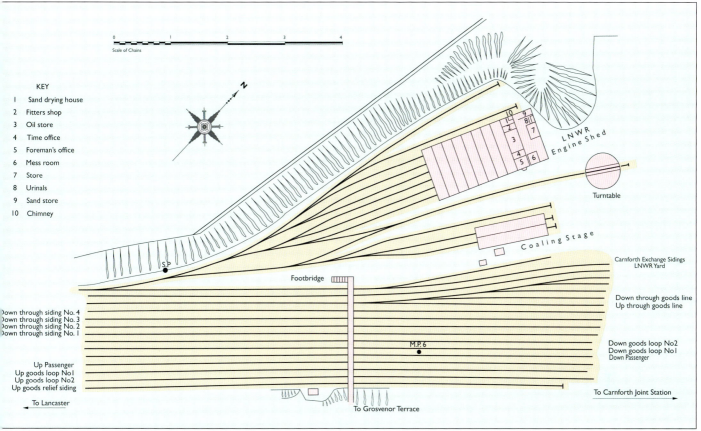

Carnforth 1892. The second LNWR shed was a was a six road dead-end shed with a north light roof and adjoining offices, workshops and sand drying house. The 1873 shed was converted into a coal facility and a new 55-foot turntable was installed on the site of the previous one. (Drawn by author from a plan in the CRA collection)

Carnforth mid 1950s. LMS 4MT Fowler 2-6-4 tank engines 42378 and 42319 stand at the ash tower. These engines were well liked by the drivers and firemen for their comfortable ride and good acceleration and for many years handled the Furness line semi-fast passenger trains. (CRA Collection Ref. BO0310)

CHAPTER TEN

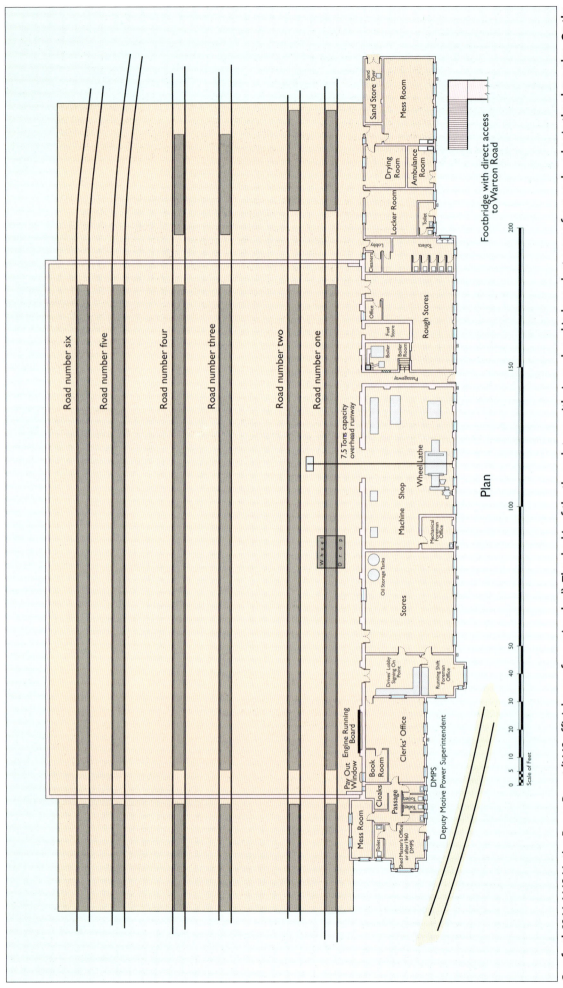

Carnforth 1944. LMS Motive Power Depot (LMS official name for engine shed). The shed is of the through type with six roads and independent access from each end as in the above plan. On the east face are offices, mess rooms, stores and a comprehensive machine shop. The shed masters' office has a good view of the shed yard. The two external elevations opposite show the south end and the east side of the shed. (Drawn by author from an LMS CES plan dated 1944)

LOCOMOTIVE SHEDS AND "STEAMTOWN"

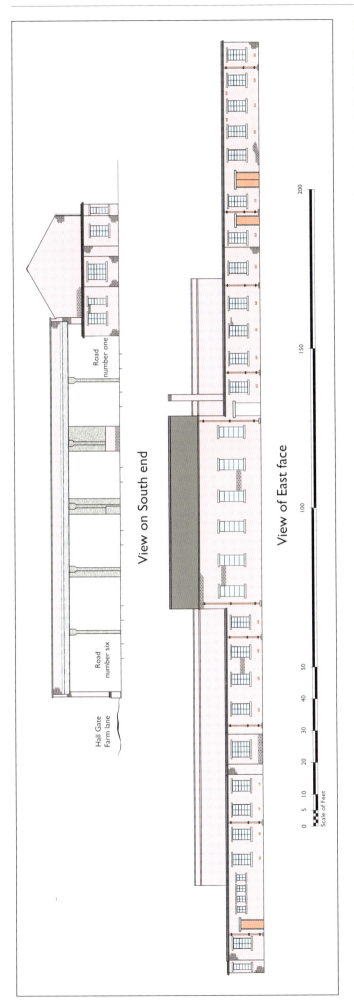

Down lines of the Furness & Midland Joint Railway, and controlled by the Midland Railway's Engine Shed Sidings signal box. The shed provided locomotives for the Midland Railway's boat trains to and from Barrow east of Carnforth, having changed over to and from FR locomotives at East Junction; it also provided motive power for passenger and goods trains over the 'little' North Western to Hellifield and Skipton, the iron ore trains from Heysham Harbour via the LNW line, and yard working. In 1920 sixty-one locomotives were allocated to the shed all of Midland origin, nearly half of these were Johnson 2F 0-6-0 goods engines and a few Deeley 3F 0-6-0 goods engines, together with Johnson 0-4-4 and 0-6-0 tank and a small number of Johnson 1P 2-4-0 passenger engines. In October 1925 the LMS Chief Mechanical Engineers Department at Derby prepared a plan for replacing the existing 42- foot diameter turntable with one of 55-foot diameter, however, this was not acted upon as rationalisation of the locomotive facilities at Carnforth was already under discussion. The MR shed closed in 1944, with the locomotives, enginemen and shed staff transferring to the LMS 'New Shed'. The signal box was 'switched out' until it too was demolished in 1949, but the shed and tank house still exist and are now in use as industrial units.

The first shed erected by the LNWR in 1873 was on the west side of the Lancaster & Carlisle mainline at Crag Bank, south of the Joint station. It was a two-road dead-end building, and had a 'Ramsbottom' standard hipped roof. It could hold four locomotives, and had an adjoining turntable road with a turntable of 42-foot diameter and a rudimentary coal stage. A much larger six-road dead-end shed was built in 1893 in red brick, with panelled walls and a standard LNWR Webb 'Northlight' roof. The shed was designed to hold twelve locomotives and each shed road contained an examination pit. The stores, fitting shop and foreman's office occupied the back wall of the shed, along with a separate sand-drying room. The 42-foot diameter turntable was replaced with a 60-foot diameter turntable on the same site, and the 1873 shed converted into an inclined LNWR-pattern 'coal hole' (or coaling stage). Being the owners of the Lancaster Canal, the LNWR had a guaranteed supply of water for the engine shed, and laid in a six-inch main feed to the shed from the canal turning basin. The main ran under Lancaster Road and Hewthwaite Terrace and across the adjacent fields to the LNWR Up sidings and under the main-lines to the engine shed. A spur feed was made to a new water tank built alongside the Up siding No.2, later the LMS installed a water softening plant alongside the tank.

Following the building of Grosvenor Terrace (as described in chapter 7), a lattice girder footbridge was built from Grosvenor Terrace across the LNWR main line and goods loops to allow staff access to the 1893 shed and the LNWR end of the exchange sidings. The footbridge was a casualty of the West Coast Main Line electrification work, being taken down during June 1971, but it has since been re-erected across the carriage sidings at Goathland on the North Yorkshire Moors Railway (see also chapter 12).

The shed connections faced south off the Up and Down goods loops, and were controlled by the LNWR Carnforth No1 signal box. It was known as the 'Wessie' shed by the enginemen and was a sub-shed of Preston with an allocation of twenty locomotives. In 1923, at the grouping, the LNWR shed foreman became responsible for the working of all three Carnforth sheds. The LNWR shed allocation was entirely of LNWR origin and was made up of 0-8-0 goods engines, 4-4-0 passenger engines, '17 inch' 0-6-0 goods engines 0-6-2 and 4-4-2 tank engines and

CHAPTER TEN

Carnforth 1967. LMS 5MT 4-6-0s 45342, 45017 and others at ash and coaling plants. The LMS 1944 ash plant is in the fore-ground with an ash tub and behind it is the LMS 1944 Cenotaph type coaling tower which had both centre and side loading chutes and is unique to Carnforth. A Riddles 5MT 4-6-0 stands under the side loading chute. (CRA Collection Ref. BO0310a)

saddle tank 0-6-0s for yard shunting. The shed provided locomotives for main line goods and passenger trains, as well as local trains and yard working. Both pre- and post-grouping the Lancashire & Yorkshire Railway rostered one of their large 0-8-0 goods engines from Rose Grove shed for the trains of locomotive coal which came from pits in the Burnley coalfield, the locomotive being serviced on the LNWR shed before returning to Rose Grove. After 1929, Fowler 0-8-0s also appeared on these workings. By 1935 the shed had five new Fowler 4MT 2-6-4 tank engines which were well-regarded by the ex-LNWR drivers and firemen for their comfortable ride and good acceleration.

In 1932 the LNWR shed became responsible for manning the *Ulster Express* boat train from Morecambe Promenade to Crewe; the 'top link' passenger duty at Carnforth LNWR shed from 1932 was the 'Ulster Link'. For this work, the shed initially received eight LMS Class 4P Compound 4-4-0 engines, but as train loads increased they were replaced first with LNWR rebuilt 'Claughton' class 4-6-0s and then with new LMS Stanier 'Jubilee' class 4-6-0 locomotives. Finally with Stanier 'Princess Royal' and 'Coronation' class 4-6-2s, which were from Camden shed and from 1962 they too were replaced by new diesels, initially of class 44 and later classes 40 and 47.

By the mid-1930s the structural condition of the LNWR shed had deteriorated to such a degree that the local railway union representatives put pressure on the regional management to bring forward the work for an LMS 'New-Shed'. Colonel Harold Rudgard, the LMS Motive Power Superintendent, travelled from LMS headquarters at Euston to be shown the waterlogged pits and worn-out drains in the old building. In 1938, the LMS announced that the modernisation work then taking place at the station would be extended to include a new locomotive depot. The locomotives, enginemen and shed staff finally transferred to the LMS 'New-Shed' in 1944, and in 1945 the LNWR shed and coaling stage were demolished, the turntable removed and its pit filled in.

Carnforth LMS 'New-Shed' was laid out to deal with a large number of engines in an efficient manner; its layout being based upon the standard depot layout developed by the LMS in 1933 for all future depots. In this layout engines coming in from duty can pass forwards continuously through a series of operations before disposal on shed or be returned to duty. Engines are able to move on and off shed at either Carnforth No.1 signal box at Crag Bank or at Carnforth F&M Junction signal box at Keer Bank. From the Crag Bank end, an engine would take the back road behind the wagon repair shop to pass under the coaling tower or to go alongside it. From F&M Junction, the engine would pass alongside the turntable and enter either the ash plant or the coaling tower roads via the three-way point adjacent to the shed offices.

Following the demolition of the Furness Railway shed in 1939, work commenced on the mechanical coaling plant and ash plant, both of which were constructed in reinforced concrete. The cenotaph-type LMS 75-ton coaling plant was unique to Carnforth, because, as well as having two centre-loading chutes there were also two side chutes on its west face. This allowed engines to be coaled at the same time, from underneath and from the side. The coaling plant was worked from a console housed in a small concrete shed on the east side of the tower. Coal wagons were positioned on the east face, then lifted and tipped sideways to discharge their contents into one of the two 75-ton hoppers. One hopper held classes 1 and 2 coal for passenger and fitted freight locomotives, and the other hopper classes 3 and 4 coal for freight locos. Water sprays could be activated to suppress airborne particles of fine coal. The majority of coal came from the east Lancashire coalfields, with some from Yorkshire, and some from as far as South Wales.

The ash plant was a 25-ton LMS standard design and ash disposal was carried out on a separate road. An engine which had been coaled under the coaling plant had to move forwards and pass through the three-way point adjacent to the shed offices, and then reverse to the ash pit. If the engine had been coaled from the side of the coaling plant, it only had to move forwards to the ash pit. Ash was removed from the smokebox by shovelling it out into small rail-mounted tubs which sat in the ash pit. When the tubs were full, they were lifted and tipped into an ash hopper which discharged into an open wagon. Full wagons were taken on a trip working to Heysham Harbour where there was an ash tip.

A 70-foot diameter turntable was supplied by Cowans Sheldon of Carlisle, and was installed at the north end of the site and was operated by an articulated vacuum motor. The civil engineering works included the provision of a new water main and improvements to the watering arrangements for locomotives. Water continued to be drawn from the Lancaster Canal but could be boosted by a mains supply. A new six-inch main was laid in from Warton Road to a new 75,000-gallon water tank which was installed at the south west end of the new shed alongside the lane leading to Hall Gate Farm. Water was pumped from this header tank to two new high-level water tanks erected at the ends of the Midland bay, platform 5 and the Lancaster bay platform 1, and to the two existing tanks beside the Up siding No.2 and on the Down mainline platform 3 at Warton Road Bridge. The latter was in use until the mid-1950s being taken out of use and removed during 1960 to coincide with the rundown of mainline steam-hauled trains. New water columns were erected at the shed, the goods loops at Crag Bank, and on the ends of the LNWR and Furness line platforms. All these facilities were completed and in use by April 1940.

During the latter part of 1940, the shed floor and inspection pits were built, using substantial amounts of concrete, but further work was held up until 1942 when work commenced in earnest on the new shed building itself. The contractor employed Italian prisoners of war from the Bela camp, near Milnthorpe, as general labourers. The shed had six through roads with inspection pits on each road. The red-brick shed was 119 feet long with a louvered-pattern concrete roof, along the eastern face were mess rooms, stores and offices. Access for staff was *via* a new footbridge which ran directly to the shed from Warton Road, across the Furness line and Carnforth exchange sidings.

The shed opened on 18th December 1944 and had an allocation of 46 locomotives, being a mixture of pre-grouping LNWR 7F 0-8-0 goods engines, early LMS Fowler 4F 0-6-0 goods engines and 2MT 2-6-2 and 3F 0-6-0 tank engines, more modern locomotives including seven Stanier Class 5MT 4-6-0s and nine Class 4MT 2-6-4 tank engines; however the express train engines for the *Ulster Express* were no longer allocated to Carnforth but to Camden shed (London). By 1962 various early type 2 diesel locomotives of classes 17, 25, and 28, could be seen on the shed. Carnforth now had an allocation of eight Stanier 'Jubilee' Class 6P5F 4-6-0s some of which had been displaced from Camden shed by new English Electric type 4 diesels (later class 40). With the end of steam approaching all the earlier LMS and LNWR engines had gone and the allocation consisted of Stanier Class 5MT 4-6-0s together with Ivatt 2MT and 4MT 2-6-0s, Stanier 8F 2-8-0s and Riddles 4MT 4-6-0 (mainly for banking duties on Shap) and some of the last Riddles 9F 2-10-0s; these were used on the fuel oil trains from the Shell distribution depot at Heysham Moss to Leeds and soda-ash trains to Marchon-Whitehaven. From 1965 yard shunting at Carnforth was gradually taken over by the ubiquitous 350bhp diesel shunters (later Class 08); Carnforth had four, one of which was out stationed to shunt at Heysham Harbour on a rotating duty.

In 1960, Carnforth shed had nine salaried staff, 230 drivers and firemen, passed firemen, passed cleaners and cleaners, together with 32 'conciliation staff' who were boiler washers, steam raisers, and fire droppers. Added to these was 30 artisan maintenance staff; mechanical fitters, machinists, a blacksmith and a boilersmith. It was a main running shed or (as defined by the LMS) a 'concentration' depot and the LMS had installed a comprehensive machine shop so that major repairs could be carried out on Carnforth's own locomotives (and of its sub-sheds). The machine shop equipment installed by the LMS in 1944 was in use up to the end of steam in 1968 and continued to be used by Steamtown.

An overhead crane of 7½ tons capacity had been installed for lifting wheel-sets from the wheel drop on road 1 and moving them through the machine shop to the wheel lathe. The wheel

Carnforth March 1964. A Metro Vickers Co-Bo diesel engine D5709 stands outside the LMS 1944 Carnforth Motive Power Depot. These engines were unreliable and the artisan staff at Carnforth found the faults hard to trace. At one time they were put to work on the Manchester boat train, but not for long, the business men soon complaining to the divisional management about their reliability. (Dr Reid / G. Nightingale collection)

CHAPTER TEN

Carnforth circa 1965. The end of steam on BR is drawing nearer and the preservation of steam locomotives is underway. Sandwiched between 5MT 4-6-0 44709 a long time Carnforth engine and an unidentified 2-8-0 8F engine (with a capped chimney) is an ex LT&S railway 4-4-2 tank engine number 80 and named 'Thundersley'. It is has been preserved and is part of the National Railway Museum collection. Two BR class 08 diesel shunters stand in the yard. (CRA Collection Ref. MAY262)

lathe was a product of Craven Brothers of Manchester in 1905; it had been brought from the closed Furness Railway workshops at Barrow and was able to machine wheels up to 6ft 9in. diameter. Also in the machine shop were a number of substantial machine tools for carrying out major repairs to the bearings of locomotives. The lifting and moving of these heavy parts was done with the aid of a 1-ton capacity radial arm hoist made by the Vaughan Crane company of Manchester. A white hearth for melting white metal for wheel bearings and a black hearth for hot blacksmithing work completed the workshop equipment.

Boiler and firebox inspections were arranged by the Boilershop Forman and were carried out in accordance with a laid down maintenance procedure, passenger engines weekly and freight engines fortnightly. Major maintenance was organised on a five-day week basis by a Mechanical Foreman, and a Chargehand fitter and was carried out by the artisan maintenance staff between the hours of 8.00am and 5.00pm. During this time the majority of locomotives were out working and all the shed roads could be used for stabling and carrying out running repairs. Road 1 of the shed was on the east side adjacent to the workshop and administration block, it was used for engines requiring heavy repairs to bearings and springs, and for those requiring wheel turning as it had a wheel-drop and crane. Road 2 was used also used for changing springs and for general repairs such as brake blocks, valve gear and injectors. Roads 3 to 6 were used for boiler washout and inspection, and for firebox and boiler repairs and for engine preparation and lighting-up following maintenance and repairs.

The Running Shift Foremen worked on a three-shift 7 days rota and with the help of a clerk organised the driver and firemen's duty roster, the allocation of locomotives and the work of the conciliation staff and turn-round drivers. Between 5.00pm and 8.00am the shed roads were re-arranged by the turn-round drivers, who were medically restricted and could only drive within the confines of the shed. They arranged the locomotives in order for their next rostered duty, or placed them on one of the shed roads ready for inspection and repair. The signing-on point was inside the shed in a separate part of the clerk's office, with the duty roster board hanging on the wall alongside road 1. Payment of wages was made from a small window in the signing-on point office (see also chapter 9).

Carnforth shed gradually absorbed duties from Oxenholme (closed on 18th June 1962), Lancaster Green Ayre (closed on 18th April 1966) and Tebay (closed on 1st January 1968), and the total number of drivers and fireman increased to 247 as some transferred from the closed sheds to cover the extra duties. During this time the shed's outer roads at Keer Bank slowly filled up with locomotives which were surplus to requirements, some of which were less than ten years old. These stored locomotives often with a full tender of coal had their chimneys covered with a bag made from sacking to prevent foreign objects from falling into the smokebox (via the blast pipe and exhaust pipe) and entering the cylinders, where damage to the moving parts would occur should the locomotive be brought back into service.

The top link at Carnforth was the number one passenger link which included the Manchester and Euston boat trains working, from the mid-1950s and through the 1960s, the Euston boat train ('Ulster Link') was a voluntary link as it involved a lodging turn. The Carnforth traincrew worked down to London on the 16.48pm Carlisle to Willesden a fast fitted freight, the motive power was generally two Stanier class 5MT 4-6-0s; this train stopped in the Up through loops at Carnforth to change crews. The Carnforth traincrew lodged at Willesden Barracks (a railway hostel) in North London and returned home the following evening on the Down 'Ulster Express' (working W141) departing 6.10pm London Euston to Morecambe Promenade, here the locomotive was uncoupled and ran light engine back to Carnforth shed.

From 1962 many of the younger drivers and passed firemen at Carnforth who intended to stay in railway service were starting to undergo training on diesel traction. The earliest training took place with instructors from English Electric on the Type 4 1-Co-Co-1 2,300 horse power Sulzer engined 'Peaks' (original allocated numbers D1 to D10 and later Class 44) as these engines were diagrammed for the 'Ulster Express'. Over the next few years' further training by trained and passed instructor drivers took place on various DMU classes and diesel classes 17, 25, 28, 40, 47 and eventually class 50. When the date for closing the depot became confirmed those enginemen nearing the age of retirement and who had not converted to diesel traction took early retirement, the remaining ninety-nine being made redundant and were helped in finding employment locally. As enginemen were used to regular shift work, some easily found employment as process operatives at Henry Cooke Ltd (now Billarud), the paper-making factory at Beetham, a few miles north on the A6, which appreciated their conscientious work ethic.

Four diagrammed steam-hauled freight workings from Carnforth took place on Saturday 3rd August, the last day of steam freight working on the national system. Two of them were the Kendal trip-working with Stanier Class 5MT 4-6-0 44709 and Standard Class 4MT 75019 on the final steam hauled freight (working 6P52), the 14.55 from Heysham Harbour to Carnforth exchange sidings.

On 4th August Carnforth engine men worked the last privately chartered steam special from Carnforth with Class 5MT 4-6-0s 45390 and 45025. The train had originated in London and had changed over to steam at Manchester Victoria and from there ran through Blackburn to Hellifield and Carnforth, the Carnforth engine men ran back over the same route to Blackburn where 45390 and 45025 were uncoupled and returned light engine to Carnforth for final disposal. Carnforth shed closed for steam maintenance on and from 4th August 1968, being one of the last three sheds in the Great Britain to operate standard-gauge steam traction.

On the Sunday 11th August 1968 the last two steam locomotives at Carnforth shed, Class 5MT 4-6-0s 44871 and 44781, were prepared for one part of the BR 'Fifteen Guinea' final steam special. They left Carnforth travelling as light engines to Carlisle via Hellifield, with Carnforth enginemen who would return later in the day as passengers on a service train. The two locomotives took over the train for its return journey from Carlisle with enginemen from Rose Grove shed. At Blackburn, another set of Carnforth enginemen accompanied by the Carnforth Traction Inspector took over the train and ran via Bolton to Manchester Victoria. At Manchester Victoria, 44871 and 44781 were uncoupled from the train which continued onto Liverpool Lime Street and journeys end behind Class 5MT 45110. This engine had worked the Liverpool Lime Street to Manchester Victoria part of the trip in the morning.

44871 and 44781 returned from Manchester to Carnforth with the Carnforth enginemen who were the last BR steam crews to 'sign off' at Carnforth. After arrival at Carnforth at 22.00, the two firemen, brothers, Malcolm and Ian Thistlethwaite were requested to leave 44871 and 44781 overnight besides the ash plant as both engines were required in steam for filming for 12th August (the following day) BBC TV North West News programme. After filming, which by then was mid-afternoon, they were moved under their own steam to storage at the south end of the shed. 44871 passed into preservation initially at 'Steamtown' but 44781 ended up masquerading as a tank engine in Columbia pictures, *The Virgin Soldiers*, and was destroyed in the making of the film.

Also on Sunday morning 11th August Britannia class 7MT 4-6-2 70013 *Oliver Cromwell* and Class 5MT 45305 were in steam at Lostock Hall shed in readiness for the BR 'Fifteen Guinea' final steam special but the later failed and was replaced by Class 5MT 45110. 'Britannia' class 7MT 4-6-2 70013 *Oliver Cromwell* was the last locomotive to undergo a heavy overhaul and was out-shopped from Crewe works on 2nd February 1967. It was allocated to Carnforth shed (10A) on the 6th January 1968 to work the end of steam rail-tours in the North West and was picked up from Preston station by a Carnforth driver and fireman. Head office at Euston House sent written correspondence to the shed-master requiring the locomotive to be kept in good working order for use on these rail-tours. During its time at Carnforth it was observed on the FR line at Grange-over-Sands on a short freight train and on the truncated Sandside branch being run-in after light maintenance had been carried out.

It was one of the four engines which worked the 11th August 'Fifteen Guinea' final steam special being used on the Manchester to Carlisle part of the trip. On the 11th August *Oliver Cromwell* went light engine from Carlisle to Lostock Hall MPD (for servicing) then left at 21.30 to Doncaster where it arrived on shed in the early hours of the 12th August. Despite the BR 'steam-ban' it left Doncaster and ran light engine to Norwich where it arrived at 13.30, it was then hauled to Diss station yard and from there taken by road on a low loader to Bressingham. It was the last BR steam locomotive to operate on the national system.

With the end of steam on 3rd August 1968 Carnforth shed did not close but continued as a signing-on point for those enginemen who had been trained on diesel locomotives and diesel multiple units prior to 1968. Schedule inspections and minor running repairs continued to be carried out by the remaining 30

Carnforth June 1971. The lattice footbridge which gave access from Grosvenor Terrace to the LNWR end of the exchange sidings and the LNWR shed is being taken down in one piece with aid of two cranes. The remains of the exchange sidings are in the foreground. (CRA Collection Ref. DUF 006)

CHAPTER TEN

'artisan staff', being twenty-nine maintenance fitters and one electrician. British Rail finally closed the shed on 31st March 1969 making the 30 artisan staff redundant. Much effort was made to find employment for them in local industry, such as with the Ribble Motor Services bus depots at Lancaster and Morecambe and with Hudsons, the heavy lifting and crane operator at Milnthorpe.

When the shed closed to steam all the diesel locomotives in use at Carnforth were transferred to Wigan Springs Branch TMD, being out stationed at Carnforth for their allocated duties, while all the DMUs were allocated to Barrow-in-Furness. A number of diesel locomotives of Classes 24,25 and 47and later class 31 were out stationed at Carnforth, initially they were stabled in the Carnforth exchange sidings Furness Yard end, on the three sidings close to the back of platform 6 (from 1972 platform 2) as these were the nearest to the signing-on point. After the Carnforth exchange sidings were lifted in 1972; they were stabled in the Midland Bay, the Midland Bottom End sidings, or the North sidings No.1 and No.2 at F&M Junction.

In 1967 a group formed jointly of enthusiasts and professional people decided to form a private company to re-open the railway from Ulverston to Lake Side, at the foot of Windermere, having purchased several steam locomotives direct from British Rail for use on the line. In May 1967, the 'Lakeside Railway Estates Company' was formed and was given permission to store two of the locomotives inside the shed. In December 1968 the company successfully negotiated the leasing two of the shed roads at Carnforth for under-cover accommodation for additional engines. When British Rail finally closed the shed on 31st March 1969, the Lakeside Railway Estates Company purchased from the British Railways Estates Board the whole of Carnforth depot, with the intention of using it as a base for operating steam locomotives on the Ulverston – Lake Side branch.

However, the planned lifting of the Plumpton Junction-Haverthwaite section (which finally took place in June 1971) would sever the Haverthwaite – Lake Side line from the national network, and persuaded the LREC to concentrate on the development of the depot as a museum 'Steamtown', leaving the Lakeside & Haverthwaite Railway Co. Ltd (which had a number of former LREC directors on its board) to re-open the upper portion of the branch in May 1973. The 1st July 1969 marked the centenary of the Ulverston to Lake Side branch, resulting in an Open Day at the shed; in brilliant sunshine, some 600 people visited the site and the pattern of future Open Days was set.

Popular locomotives at Steamtown were Class 5MT 44871, two Fairburn 2-6-4Ts 42073 and 42085 and Class 5MT 61306, a Thompson-designed B1, the latter being the last steam engine to haul the 'Yorkshire Pullman' and named *Mayflower* after preservation at Carnforth. The fleet also included Class 4MT 75029, the last Tebay banking engine, and additional Class 5MTs 44767, 44806 and 44932. They were joined by Class 2MT 46441 from Lancaster Green Ayre shed, which had been bought by Doctor Peter Beet of Hest Bank, one of the LREC's directors, and which is now a static exhibit at the Ribble Steam Railway Museum in Preston.

The collection eventually included a number of steam, diesel and electric industrial locomotives which had been owned and operated by private industry in the North-West, together with items of rolling stock. A 'Collector's Corner' selling railway artefacts, a 15-inch-gauge line 'Steamtown Museum Railway', a cafe and gift shop, plus a miniature model railway, were also set up on site. Visitors arriving by road in their own cars and gained access to 'Steamtown Railway Museum' via the Shore Road and through the Northgate where they were then directed to a designated parking area, those arriving by train had a half-mile walk from the station. A new Southgate was opened at Crag Bank for the Steamtown sub-contracting business 'Carnforth Railway Restoration and Engineering'; it provided access to road vehicles carrying heavy rolling-stock parts.

Further additions to the Steamtown collection came from both France and Germany, at a time when interest in European traction amongst UK rail enthusiasts was not as high as it is today. An ex-SNCF 4-6-2 locomotive, built in 1914 for the Paris-Lyons-Mediterranean Railway and rebuilt in 1937 by Andre Chapelon, arrived in March 1970. This arrived on a heavy haulage low loader which was directed on to the ironworks site for unloading, here the engine was re-railed and to clear the BR loading gauge, as it had to pass under the FMJR bridge, the chimney was removed. It was towed up the incline to East Junction and then to Steamtown. It was followed in spring 1973 by a German Railways (DB) 4-6-2 of the '012' Class (previously '01.10' Class of the pre-war Deutsche Reichsbahn). The 012 was followed, in 1974, by DB 0-6-0T no.80.014, a member of a class to be found shunting in German marshalling yards and which was acquired from a museum in Bochum-Dahlhausen. Less well-known was ex-DR 60 cm-gauge 0-8-0 no. 99 3462, which arrived at Steamtown in January 1971 for major repair. Built in 1934 by Orenstein & Koppel for the extensive Mecklenburg-Pommeranian system, it left Carnforth for the Festiniog Railway's Boston Lodge Works in May 1972, where it was stored until December 1978. The loco then returned to Germany and the Dampfkleinbahn Mühlenstroth at Gütersloh, where it is still based.

On Friday the 21st August 1971 Steamtown sent Class 5MT 44871 to the Morecambe Rail Day, an exhibition of locomotives which was held at Morecambe Promenade station (Saturday 22nd and Sunday 23rd August). Before leaving Steamtown, the locomotive had been put into steam to prevent damage to its moving parts, in order to comply with the then BR 'steam-ban' (which prohibited steam operations over BR lines); it was towed to Morecambe Promenade station by a Class 25 diesel locomotive D5298. The combination left Carnforth No.1 signal box at 18.12, and used the Hest Bank Bare Lane curve: it was the first time since Saturday 3rd August 1968, and just three years after the end of BR steam that a steam engine had travelled between Carnforth and Morecambe.

A much larger exhibition of locomotives and other rail vehicles including a five-inch gauge miniature steam railway which ran along platform 3 took place 19th and 20th August 1972. This time Steamtown sent Class 5MT 44932 which had been painted green and Ivatt 2-6-0 6441 in LMS maroon. BR sent a class 40 English Electric mainline diesel-engine, a 'Cartic' Car carrier and two coaches from the electrification train. The penultimate exhibition took place 11th and 12th August 1973 and Steamtown again sent two engines, the National Collection's Gresley V2 4771 and also Gresley A4 4498. On this occasion they travelled on the 11th August under their own steam as light engines from Carnforth to Morecambe.

British Railways lifted its 'steam-ban' in 1972, allowing approved preserved locomotives to work over designated routes. One such authorised route was the Furness line around the North Lancashire, Westmorland and Cumberland coast as far as Sellafield, and 'Steamtown' was admirably sited to provide servicing facilities for locomotives (its own and visiting) and for the handover of the charters between the different forms of traction. On 23rd September 1972, and following earlier test

LOCOMOTIVE SHEDS AND "STEAMTOWN"

Carnforth August 1985. Ex SR Lord Nelson engine number 850 in SR green livery stands under the ash plant at Steamtown museum. This was one of a number of engines passed for mainline steam and was often seen on the Cumbrian Mountain Express. (CRA Collection Ref. PWR-C3812)

trips, Class 5MT 44871 headed a nine-coach special train of BR Mk1 stock on the 12.42 Carnforth to Barrow-in-Furness and return, with sister locomotive 44932 handling the 16.10 working from Carnforth: both trains carried the 1L29 reporting number. The train was organised by the combined efforts of Steamtown and local railway staff, and was operated with the full support of London Midland Region headquarters at Euston and the Preston Division management. In the early 1970s it was a matter of finding volunteer drivers and firemen to run the increasing number of steam special, however in 1987 eight ex-Carnforth and Lancaster Green Ayre depot drivers and firemen, together with a local Traction Inspector, formed a steam panel or 'volunteer's link' to provided crews for these and future steam specials.

In late 1972 Sir William McAlpine rescued the A3 locomotive 4472 *Flying Scotsman* from its exile in America. It returned aboard the Blue Star lines' *California Star* to Liverpool Dock where in February 1973 it was swung by the docks floating crane to rest one more on British tracks. The loco travelled under its own steam to British Rail's Derby Works for an overhaul and a repaint and the removal of the American bell cowcatcher and whistle. After a season working on the Torbay Steam Railway *Flying Scotsman* was stored during the winter at a rail-connected industrial site at Market Overton, which jointly owned by Sir William McAlpine and the Hon John Gretton, owner of GWR 4-6-0 4079 *Pendennis Castle*. In early 1974 *Flying Scotsman* was exhibited at the Kensington Olympia Exhibition before moving permanently to Carnforth. To commemorate its move back to Carnforth in 1974 a major exhibition was held at Steamtown. During 1978 a heavy overhaul was carried out by Vickers Engineering Ltd at Barrow-in-Furness where a reconditioned spare boiler was fitted. This gave *Flying Scotsman* a further seven years of service before the boiler certificate expired.

As an A1 Pacific 4-6-2 it entered service on the LNER on 24th February 1923 and it was a year later in 1924 that the engine was given the number 4472 and named *Flying Scotsman* – remarkably she was still at work in her 60th year during her time at Steamtown. On 24th February 1983 a Diamond Jubilee celebration was held at Steamtown for *Flying Scotsman*, it was hosted by Russell Harty, a teacher at Giggleswick Grammar School and TV presenter of arts programmes and chat shows. The main guests were Tim West CBE, stage, TV and film actor, Joe Brown MBE, entertainer and singer who started work as a railway fireman at Plaistow engine shed and Ray Milland an American film actor and director, but what connection had he with *Flying Scotsman*?

Ray Milland (1907-1986) was the stage name for Alfred Reginald Jones who was born in Wales; he first appeared as an extra in the films *Piccadilly* and *The Informer* which were made in 1929. He was hired by Castleton Knight for his first acting role as Jim Edwards the fireman in the thriller film *Flying Scotsman*. It was one of the first British films with both a sound track and recorded voices. The filming took place in real time on the Hertford Loop with Pauline Johnston the heroine walking along the outside of the carriage in 1930-style high heel shoes whilst the train ran at high speed. When Sir Nigel Gresley saw the film he was so appalled that he never let any films be made again whilst he was employed by the LNER. His role in the film brought Ray Milland to the attention of the vice president of MGM films and in 1930 he emigrated to America where he became one of MGM films main star. From 1955 he concentrated on directing for both TV and films and appeared on CBS television in the American sitcom meet *Mr McNutley*. Many of the people who attended the celebration event were leading personalities from the Steam Locomotive Operators Association (SLOA), Lancaster Railway Circle, Steamtown and Flying Scotsman Services together with national and local personalities involved in the preservation movement.

Carnforth 21st August 1971. Class 5MT 44871 is in steam and is being towed by an EE type 2 diesel engine D5298. The combination is passing Carnforth No. 1 signal box at 18.12 hours en-route to the Morecambe Rail Days, which was held at Morecambe Promenade station on August 22nd 23rd and 24th Bank Holiday weekend. (R. Herbert collection A3162)

CHAPTER TEN

Carnforth 31st May 1975. Steamtown open day. German Railways (DB) 4-6-2 number 01.01104 stands alongside BR 9F 2-10-0 number 92220 on road number 1 at the south end of the ex LMS motive power depot. (R. Herbert collection A4037)

'Flying Scotsman Services' (FSS) was formed in 1976 with its main offices at Steamtown Carnforth to promote market and sell private rail charter throughout the United Kingdom. Flying Scotsman Services owned its own passenger rolling stock such as the 'Scotsman Pullman' train and the Maroon MK1 stock both of which included at-seat catering services. *Flying Scotsman* itself was the flagship steam locomotive and could only be booked through FSS for use on approved routes. In addition FSS dealt with private rail charter bookings, in conjunction with the Steam Locomotive Operator Association and BR using other preserved locomotives to work private charters, BR summer season specials and SLOA weekend steam tours. After 1990 FSS moved from Carnforth to Lichfield to the office of the SLOA.

Steamtown played host to other famous engines such as the Southern Railway 4-6-0 No. 850 *Lord Nelson* and Merchant Navy 4-6-2 No. 35028 *Clan Line*. The 'Cumbrian Coast Express' to Sellafield and the weekly Carnforth-Grange-Skipton-Carnforth trains were popular trains in the North West as these lines were among the first to be approved for steam use following the lifting of the 'steam-ban' in 1972. In 1977 the S&C line Leeds to Carlisle was approved and the 'Cumbrian Mountains Express' began running to Appleby. The 'Cumbrian Coast Express' and 'Cumbrian Mountains Express' started at Crewe and through bookings could be made from London, Birmingham, Manchester, Liverpool and Preston. The train was electrically hauled to Carnforth where a change to a Carnforth based steam engine took place. The name Cumbria came into use in 1974 when the Furness area of North Lancashire and the counties of Westmorland and Cumberland were amalgamated under the 1972 Local Government Act.

In the early 1970s, a mixed-gauge miniature line (3½ and 5 inches) was constructed on the west side of the site, it ran from the north end of the shed to Keer Bank, a more substantial 15-inch-gauge line, was laid down in 1975 on the west side of the site at the south end of the shed, using a Bassett-Lowke 4-4-2 steam locomotive *Princess Elizabeth* hauling two coaches on 200 yards of track. (This locomotive was of great historic interest, having been constructed as long ago as 1911 by the Northampton company, for use on Southport's Lakeside Miniature Railway). This line rapidly expanded into a more permanent route, running from the south end of the shed, to the site of the 1895 LNWR shed, where a wooden platform was later built. Both the 15-inch gauge line and the standard gauge line terminated on each side of the platform enabling a round trip to be made on them. The standard gauge line ran a shuttle service from the north end of the site using a variety of engines and either goods brake vans or coaches.

In 1978, motive power on the 15-inch gauge line was boosted with the arrival of an additional Bassett-Lowke 4-4-2 *King George V* (also built for the Southport line in 1911) and a Bo-Bo diesel-hydraulic locomotive *Royal Anchor*, the latter having been purchased from the Ravenglass & Eskdale Railway. In 1980, the line was extended north to pass through the engine shed to a new station at Keer Bank, and a Pacific 4-6-2 locomotive (built by G & S Light Engineering, Stourbridge, in 1946) was acquired. Christopher Hughes winner of *Mastermind* and *International Mastermind* in 1983, and a quiz contestant on *Eggheads* was invited during that year to the 'Steamtown Museum Railway' to name the 15-inch gauge Pacific 4-6-2 *Prince William*. The engine was painted in LMS crimson lake and was named after Prince William, Duke of Cambridge who was born on the 21st June 1982. At the time of the ceremony Christopher Hughes was employed by BR as a train driver but is now retired.

In the early 1980s, there was a proposal to extend the 15-inch-gauge line to Happy Mount Park in Morecambe, a route via Bolton-le-Sands and Hest Bank having been surveyed. The line would have been just less than five miles long, but for a variety of reasons, the scheme was not proceeded with.

In 1991, following the conclusion of the deal between David Smith and Sir William McAlpine (mentioned later), it became uneconomic to continue operation of the line, the track was dismantled and together with locomotives and rolling stock shipped to California, excluding *Prince William* (which went to the Evesham Vale Light Railway in Worcestershire).

Early in 1984 the Lancaster & Morecambe Model Engineering Society was invited to Steamtown and built a new 3½, 5 and 7¼ inch-gauge line (not to be confused with the early 1970s track), on the site of the 1895 LNWR shed which was now known as the 'Desert'. This area, and the land to the south which was allocated

LOCOMOTIVE SHEDS AND "STEAMTOWN"

Morecambe Promenade Station 20th August 1972. A second Morecambe Rail Days took place on the 19th and 20th August 1972. Steamtown sent Class 5MT 44932 in green livery and Ivatt 2-6-0 6441in LMS crimson lake and BR sent a class 40 English Electric mainline diesel-engines. (R. Herbert collection A3357)

for housing development as far as Crag Bank, had been levelled during the extraction of sand and gravel. The site was an ideal location for the venture and was somewhat idyllic with wild flowers and bushes that had taken root in the limestone rich soil. The L&MMES left Steamtown in 1995, and moved at the request of the LCC, who wished to regenerate as a tourist attraction, to a redundant road maintenance depot at Cinderbarrow, near Yealand three miles to the north of Carnforth where L&MMES still operate in 2014.

In 1985 Steamtown class 5MT 5407 resplendent in LMS black livery appeared in the media when it was used to haul a special train from Carnforth to Hellifield. The train stopped at Arkholme station where Jim Bowen, compare of the TV game show *Bullseye*, lived. Arkholme once an intermediary station on the FMJR had closed in 1966, and the station building had been converted into a dwelling house. On board the train was Eamonn Andrews (1922-1987) of *This Is Your Life* fame along with the BBC film crew. The interview was broadcast on 10th April 1985 as programme number 409 series 16 by the BBC.

The comprehensive machine shop which BR left in the shed in 1969 was now operated by Steamtown, who were carrying out contracting work for other steam preservation societies and even for BR. Throughout the 1970s up to the mid-1980s, Steamtown was one of the major leisure attractions in the North West but then visitor numbers steadily declined, and by 1988 Steamtown was in financial difficulties. Discussions took place with the volunteers of the 10A Association (10A being the old Carnforth shed code) to see if they could take over the management and running of the depot. Although there was a majority in favour, this plan did not go ahead, despite Steamtown being one of the first successful railway preservation ventures, having attracted thousands of visitors to the town during its lifetime.

The preservation world was stunned at the announcement

Carnforth 27th July 2008. The Railway Magazine-West Coast Railways open day. This line up of engines at the south end of the 1944 LMS Carnforth Motive Power Depot are from left to right, 70013 Oliver Cromwell, 46115 Scots Guardsman, 5690 Leander and 48151. (Alan Johnstone)

CHAPTER TEN

that a local wealthy property dealer David Cadman was taking over control at the end of January 1989 from principal shareholder and company chairman Sir William McAlpine for a reputed sum of £250,000. At that time Carnforth Railway Restoration and Engineering Services which employed 25 full-time staff was said to have an annual turnover of £750,000 and the museum a £70,000 overdraft. For a number of reasons this deal did not proceed.

In 1991, however, David Smith, owner of Stanier 8F 2-8-0 48151, took control of the loss-making Steamtown Railway Museum following a six-figure deal with Sir William McAlpine. The new owner took over as chairman of both the ailing museum and its associated sub-contracting business Carnforth Railway Restoration and Engineering Services. At the end of October 1996, Steamtown Railway Museum closed to the public never to reopen, it was officially closed on and from 1st May 1997 when the high cost of meeting Health and Safety requirements made it unviable. Re-branded as West Coast Railways, the site is now home to both steam and diesel locomotives and coaching stock, which are used on the business of charter trains together with the maintenance and restoration of the fleet. New buildings have been erected on the site, the diesel shed, an addition at the north end of the LMS shed, in 2006 and a carriage restoration in 2010 close to the ex-LNWR wagon repair shop.

In October 1995, fifty years after *Brief Encounter*, the previously-mentioned German Pacific No.012-104 took part in the film *Brief and Sinister Encounter* which was shot at Steamtown. The film was a Shakespearean drama set in the 1930s with Sir Ian McKellen in the title role as King Richard III, together with Annette Bening and Maggie Smith in supporting roles. Steamtown volunteers who offered their services as engine drivers and as extras, on arriving at 07-30 for the day's filming, were shocked to find that they had to have a very "short back and sides" haircut in order to portray black-shirted storm-troopers. The film was directed by Richard Loncraine, who also directed the Michael Palin film *The Missionary* in 1982 and the TV series *Band of Brothers* in 2001.

In mid-1998, the three European engines (the French and German Pacifics, and the 0-6-0T) which formed part of the early Steamtown collection were sold, and are now (Summer 2011) in the Sud Deutschses Eisenbahnmuseum (SEH) at Heilbronn, Germany. The French and German Pacifics both left Steamtown in mid-1998, on heavy haulage low loaders, they were taken out of the South gate at Crag Bank to the A6. Under a police escort they were taken via major trunk roads to Immingham docks where they remained for nearly six months whilst the required documents were processed for their onward journey across the North Sea to Europe. The Pacifics went initially to Nordlingen, where they remained until the SEH was completed, moving there in August 2001. The 0-6-0T took a more circuitous route, having been first moved to the Nene Valley Railway in the UK in 1980, where it was dismantled in 1985 for examination and eventual restoration. The frames went first to Holland, then to France, with new components being commissioned from a variety of manufacturers. The dismantled loco was moved to Stuttgart around 1998 for preliminary restoration work, before being transferred to the SEH in 2002; it remains there, following cosmetic restoration, as unfortunately many components were lost during the 1998 move to Stuttgart.

The *Railway Magazine*, in conjunction with West Coast Railways, organised a public opening to the site, on a one-off basis, during 26th and 27th July 2008 to commemorate 40 years from the end of BR steam in August 1968. As well as 'West Coast Railways' own steam and diesel locomotives, there were many other exhibits including Class 7MT 4-6-2 70013 *Oliver Cromwell* which was delivered on a low loader. The locomotive later hauled a commemoration of the 1968 'Fifteen Guinea Special' over the Settle & Carlisle line.

On the Carnforth skyline, the public can still see the concrete coaling tower and ash plant, now the only such structures left in the United Kingdom. The condition of the coaling plant is slowly deteriorating, and how much longer it will dominate views of Carnforth is unclear, as public funding for conservation is unlikely.

Carnforth 27th July 2008. The Railway Magazine – West Coast Railways open day. A line of DRS Ltd diesel engines stand alongside the Carnforth Coaling and Ash Plant. The engines are 37229 Jonty Jarvis, 47802 Pride of Cumbria, 57010 and 66429. (Alan Johnstone)

CHAPTER ELEVEN

RAILWAY TRAFFIC

With the growth of Victorian industry within Carnforth and the Furness peninsula, extensive goods sidings were laid down by the three railway companies for the interchange of traffic, and for a time Carnforth had its own local Control Office to deal with the large amount of inter-district goods traffic.

Freight facilities at Carnforth were commissioned in 1857 when the Ulverstone & Lancaster Railway laid down the first three exchange sidings for the pig iron and iron ore traffic passing south on to the Lancaster & Carlisle Railway. In the first year of opening approximately 592,000 tons of iron ore had passed through the sidings, but by 1864 this had reduced to 450,000 tons with the erection and blowing-in of three blast furnaces at Messrs Schneider, Hannay & Co's ironworks at Hindpool, Barrow-in-Furness.

In 1863 and 1864, the exchange sidings were enlarged to deal with the increased coke traffic now coming into Carnforth from County Durham *via* Tebay and the South Durham & Lancashire Union Railway for Barrow ironworks. In 1870, only 270,000 tons of iron ore were exchanged through the sidings travelling south to other ironworks, this was compensated by a steady increase in coke traffic with the opening of Askam and Millom ironworks in 1867, and again in 1874 when the North Lonsdale ironworks opened at Ulverston. By 1877 most iron ore coming into Carnforth via the Furness Railway was being taken directly into the Carnforth ironworks itself, and little was passing southwards through Carnforth exchange sidings to other destinations. In 1887 eight coke trains per week were passing through the sidings for Barrow alone, and a further nine for the other ironworks, the increased coke traffic had more than compensated for the loss of iron ore traffic.

In July 1866 Mill Lane had been diverted further east by the Carnforth Haematite Iron Company, leaving the Furness Railway with a plot of land alongside the ironworks branch, upon which the first goods yard sidings were laid down. The goods yard entrance utilised part of Mill Lane at the north end of Carnforth joint station and opened in 1867.

By 1880, Carnforth had become an exchange point for freight traffic passing between the Furness Railway, the Midland Railway and the London & North Western Railway. Each company had built its own yards where wagons could be re-marshalled for their final destination, and in some cases the wagons would be moved between the various companies' yards for this purpose. The Carnforth yards

Carnforth August 1927. Two ex LNWR passenger engines a 'Precursor' 4-4-0 number 5294 (pilot engine) and a Claughton 4-6-0 are re-starting the Up (south-bound) 'Royal Scot' after an engine change at the north end of the station. The 'Ramsbottom' type platform roof and the Lancaster Bay are to the right of the train. (CRA Collection Ref BOcln07)

Carnforth 31st May 1955. Class 5MT 45257 on a passenger train on the Down Furness mainline approaching F&M Junction. On the right is the Up and Down goods lines and the siding to Watsons Wool Warehouse. In the left distance are the Midland Middle End sidings (CRA Collection Ref PEJ 134)

Carnforth 23rd April 1955. On the Carnforth Curve is LMS 4MT single chimney 2-6-0 43117 on the 4.50pm Carnforth-Leeds passenger train. On the left is the Railway Club and the wagons over the wall are in the goods yard. The train is passing a good example of a wooden post signal with home and distant arms on one post. (CRA Collection PEJ103)

Carnforth 25th June 1958. An LMS 7P rebuilt Scot 4-6-0 46106 'Gordon Highlander' (with straight sided smoke deflectors) approaches the station on the Down mainline with the 3.50pm FO Crewe-Glasgow passenger train. A train of Shell-BP tank wagons were often seen in the exchange sidings en route to various destinations from Heysham Moss sidings. (CRA Collection PEK395)

Carnforth 1st September 1962. A Class 5 MT 4-6-0 no 44904 heads the 9.10am Barrow train for Leeds out of Carnforth on the FMJL. It is crossing over the WCML upon which stands some ballast wagons and a ballast plough van. (CRA Collection Ref A62_14-7)

covered an extensive area alongside the main line of each company.

To manage the local and inter-district goods traffic being handled through the Carnforth exchange yard, the LNWR & FR Joint Goods Committee was set up, *circa* 1865 with the Midland Railway being included in 1881. The Joint Goods Committee consisted of the LNWR, FR, and later MR goods managers and was set up to co-ordinate and arrange for the transfer of goods traffic between the five yards of the three companies, each goods manager acted as chairman on an annual basis. In 1903, Mr Unsworth of the MR was the chairman of the Joint Goods Committee. In 1923 goods traffic provided employment for around 100 staff such as foremen shunters, shunters, clerks, goods guards, and carriage and wagon staff. For revenue apportionment purposes, Railway Clearing House staff worked alongside employees of the local companies and later LMS, so that the identification numbers of individual vehicles could be correctly recorded.

In 1880 further sidings were laid down between Crag Bank and Carnforth F&M Junction, to the west of the original ULR Carnforth exchange sidings, and the FR goods shed at Keer Bank was demolished. Carnforth exchange yard eventually totalled twenty-three sidings, most of them being through sidings, but for operational purposes they were divided at a nominated point between the LNWR and the Furness Railway. The Up and Down through goods line were used by the coke trains which were collected at Tebay from the North Eastern Railway, although after 1917 (as previously mentioned) FR coke traffic was re routed between Hincaster and Arnside, via the Sandside line. In 1922 there were six FR-line trips in each direction, split equally between the LNWR and the FR. Those worked by the LNWR terminated at Lindal sidings and those by the FR ran directly to Barrow.

The LNWR end of the yard sorted traffic to and from the NER at Tebay and handled local traffic from LCR-line stations, Lancaster Yard, and Kendal Yard and the Morecambe and Windermere branches, and Heysham Harbour after its opening in 1904. Traffic to and from Manchester, Liverpool, Crewe and the south, as well as the Lancashire & Yorkshire Railway's lines in East Lancashire, was also sorted and re-marshalled here. After 1940 petroleum traffic from the Trimpell refinery and chemicals from ICI on the Middleton estate near Heysham together with fuel oil from the Shell-BP storage depot at Heysham Moss, were handled through the yard. The LNWR end of the yard also dealt with all the incoming coal traffic, locomotive coal, and household coal from the South Lancashire pits.

The Furness end of the yard sorted traffic to and from Workington, Whitehaven, Millom, Barrow, Lindal Ore Sidings, Ulverston including North Lonsdale sidings, and traffic from FR-line stations. In 1900, one siding at Carnforth was allocated to the Anglo-American Oil company traffic, mainly kerosene from the new oil tanker discharge facility and tank farm which had been built at Ramsden Dock in Barrow-in-Furness. Nine freight trains daily were booked to leave the Furness end of the yard for Barrow, Millom and Whitehaven, in addition to which there were two pick-up goods one which shunted at all stations as far as Lindal before returning to Carnforth and another for Ulverston Yard and North Lonsdale.

The Midland Railway managed its freight traffic through the Midland Top End, Middle End, Bottom End and East Junction sidings, all of which were connected into the Furness & Midland Joint line. The Midland Top end sidings ran down on an incline from Carnforth East Junction and were the exchange sidings for full and empty wagons going into and out of the ironworks. The Midland Middle End sidings were for sorting and re-marshalling traffic between the Furness Railway and the Midland Railway for the Great Northern Railway and Great Central Railway's South Yorkshire traffic; the ironworks pig iron was despatched from these sidings for the steel making centres around Sheffield.

The main purpose of the Midland Bottom End sidings was to exchange traffic between the Furness Railway and the Midland Railway, and to sort and re-marshal wagons for the goods yard and goods warehouse at Warton Road. These sidings held traffic destined for West Yorkshire and Sheffield and, in the opposite direction, coal coming in from the South Yorkshire and Nottinghamshire pits. The Midland Bottom End sidings connected into both the F&M main line and a single line which crossed the Up and Down F&M main line and goods lines, to enter the goods yard and warehouse at Warton Road on a separate bridge over the River Keer.

The goods yard had nine sidings (designated roads 1 to 9) all of them fanning out from the single line as soon as it passed over the River Keer. By 1882 the Furness Railway had built an eight-bay two-road goods warehouse with adjoining offices for the goods manager and his clerks on the new Warton Road goods yard to replace the one at Keer Bank. A third siding ran down the outside of the west face of the warehouse. Inside the warehouse was a long wooden platform, the top of which was level with the floor of a wagon. Four one-ton cranes were mounted upon the platform for handling general merchandise from open wagons. Around the mid-1930s, the LMS erected a wooden extension over the west siding to increase its handling capacity, as more merchandise was being transported in vans. On the east face was a loading bay where a cart or trailer could be parked and loaded with merchandise for delivery to the surrounding commercial outlets.

As Carnforth was situated in a predominately agricultural area, the goods yard had a large three-bay cattle pen and holding area. Up to the late 1960s, cattle on the hoof were regularly brought over by ferry from Ireland to Heysham Harbour where they were loaded into cattle wagons. Cattle destined for the southern markets were taken from Heysham to Carnforth Exchange yard and then to the Warton Road goods yard. Here the cattle were unloaded from the wagons and placed in the cattle pens where they were fed and watered. The cattle wagons were cleaned out and the cattle then reloaded to continued their journey to a cattle market and abattoir.

The local coal factor, Reese, had offices on the Warton Road goods yard with a small coaling stage for unloading, weighing and bagging household coal which they supplied to Carnforth and the surrounding villages. Two cranes, one of 3 tons and one of 10 tons capacity, were sited on separate sidings; alongside each was a hard-standing area for vehicular traffic. They were used for lifting to and from rail wagons such loads as felled timber, cast iron gas-pipes and the occasional road-rail container. A Pooley weigh bridge was located in the far corner of the yard, for weighing goods coming into or going out of the yard. Stables for cart horses were provided; the latter were displaced during the 1930s by two petrol-engined tractor units. An end-loading dock for loading and unloading horse-drawn carriages and (later) motor vehicles was sited close to the LNWR carriage siding, with access from the station forecourt. Between 1940 and 1960 crushed limestone from the adjacent Haws Hill quarry was also loaded here.

The telegraph was used on the railway to transmit both routine and urgent messages along the line. The LNWR telegraph office was set up in 1880 in the LNWR station buildings behind

RAILWAY TRAFFIC

Carnforth 1960. Heavy passenger trains would sometimes require two engines to keep time over the Northern Fells. An afternoon train is running into Platform 2 Up mainline with a 2P 4-4-0 40657 as pilot to 'Britannia' 4-6-2 70054. The Nissen huts on the left remain from the WW2 MoD strategic store. The Carnforth Sorting Office is on the right and the mailman waits to transfer parcels to the rear guards van of the train. (CRA Collection Ref. WOR030)

Carnforth 5th May 1964. Metro-Vickers Co-Bo diesel engines D5711 and D5700 are approaching F&M junction on the Up mainline on the 1.45pm Barrow-Carnforth parcels. The train is made up of BR Mk1 full brakes and a variety of four-wheeled parcels vans and has been signalled for the Up mainline to Carnforth Station. Sands Lane is to the left. (CRA Collection Ref. HER-218)

CHAPTER ELEVEN

Carnforth 1966. A railway in 'transition' from steam to diesel. A Brush type 4 D1858 in two-tone green livery departs Carnforth with passenger train 1S53 whilst Britannia 4-6-2 70013 'Oliver Cromwell' arrives with a passenger train from Carlisle. It is passing the banner repeater signal, the left hand banner is for the Up mainline and the right hand banner for the Up goods loops. (CRA Collection Ref. WAR206)

the booking office and the Furness Railway's in the Furness & Midland station building and probably at the same time. The telephone was only installed at Carnforth prior to 1914 and at key locations, including the offices of the station master, station inspector, and station foreman: the signal boxes and the engine shed foreman's office a total of nine extensions. In 1920, two additional extensions had been added for the LNWR Control Office.

At the 1923 Grouping, the Joint Goods Committee was disbanded, and the LMS set up the Carnforth Control Area to control the goods traffic being handled through the five yards. The yards were described according to their pre-grouping ownership as the 'LNWR Section', the 'Furness Section' and the 'Midland Section'. In each yard, every siding was allocated a number, its wagon capacity, and a destination for its traffic. In 1931, Carnforth Control (Midland Division section) was closed and transferred to Lancaster Castle station.

Control allocated two shunting engines to Carnforth exchange yard and three other shunting engines covering the Midland yards, all to be manned continuously, Sundays excepted. A further shunting engine was allocated to the Warton Road goods yard and warehouse shunt and the transferring of wagons between the various yards and the goods yard. Pre-Grouping, the LNWR had allocated a shunting engine for train marshalling duties, attaching and detaching through coaches at the south end of the station to and from Furness Railway trains, but this duty ceased with the running of through trains.

British Railways allocated four shunting engines on a three-shift-7days roster covering all the yards. The goods warehouse and yard at Warton Road was a five-day Monday-to-Friday day turn from 7.45am to 4.00pm. Carnforth yard was at its busiest during the evening and early night time between 7.00pm and midnight, sorting and making up the early morning departures which started at 00.30am and continued until 7.30am. There was another busy period between 9.30am and 2.45pm, sorting and breaking up early morning arrivals. Shunting loco drivers were normally medically unfit for mainline duties and were given this less demanding and more restricted task, while the shed locomotive cleaners were given the opportunity to learn the art of firing an engine. Change-over of the train crews was done in the yard at the end of each shift, and the engines returned on a rotational basis to the shed for coal during the early afternoon. This pattern of operations continued up to the early 1960s when the Fowler 3F 0-6-0T shunting engines were replaced by 350bhp 0-6-0 diesel shunting locos (later Class 08); by this time, three diesel shunters were able to carry out all the yard duties. After 1968 the diesel shunting locos were transferred to the Birmingham Division, by this time the amount of shunting had reduced considerably and the train engine then carried out this duty.

Around 1890 a corrugated iron shed was erected on a narrow piece of land hard alongside the banks of the River Keer, and close to the Furness Railway Keer Bridge. The shed was painted black and was known locally as *Watson's Wool Warehouse*. With the advent of steam-powered mills, woollen manufacture had centred on the West Riding of Yorkshire, the first wool market being established in Rochdale in 1863, to be followed by Huddersfield and Leeds in 1865. The latter became the main wool exchange for the Yorkshire woollen trades. The 1884 trade directory for North Lancashire lists the business as 'Watson and Hartley, wool staplers (sorting and grading), Furness sidings, Carnforth', and in 1901 as 'Watson and Company, sheep dip and cattle food manufacturers, Carnforth, with offices in Warton', the partnership having been dissolved in June 1888.

The shed was rail connected to the Furness Railway's Down goods line by a trailing connection a few yards east of the F&M Junction signal box. Bales of sheared wool were brought in by rail from the agricultural areas of South Cumberland, Westmorland, West Yorkshire and North Lancashire. It was unloaded, sorted and graded before being taken out by rail to either Bradford or Huddersfield, the principal centres of the Yorkshire woollen industry, or to an east coast port for export to Europe. The warehouse was sited away from the main goods yard to provide good security for the wool and to reduce the risk of fire. As there was no road access, its employees had permission to enter the railway yard at Keer Bank and cross over the Keer Bridge under the watchful eye of the Carnforth F&M signalman. In 1958, the Watson Wool Company was taken over by Wool Growers, part of Scottish, English & Welsh Wool Growers Ltd with branches through the country. Anecdotal evidence from railway staff states that, in the BR era, the traffic was moved in covered vans to Yorkshire and the ports on the East coast in order to protect the wool.

In May 1959 a new purpose-built warehouse was opened on the ironworks site on Warton Road, with modern baling, sorting and weighing facilities. Loading and unloading was done under cover to and from road vehicles using mechanical handling equipment, thus making Watson's railway warehouse redundant. One of the end products which could be purchased locally from the warehouse was good quality woollen blankets. The Wool Growers warehouse closed in 2002 as a consequence of the foot-and-mouth epidemic, and the contraction of local farming. The business has now transferred to Dumfries in Scotland and 2005 was still part of Scottish, English & Welsh Wool Growers Ltd.

After the closure of the ironworks in 1929, the LNWR ironworks sidings were used as refuge sidings for holding and sorting traffic from Merseyside until 1942, when they were converted into the Northern goods loops. At the end of the Second World War, a slag crusher was set up on the middle of the 1860 Keer Marsh slag tip to replace the one on the Warton Sands slag tip. This tip contained only the harder slag from the manually charged blast furnaces, and was operated on behalf of Lancashire County Council. The slag from the slag boxes contained a high proportion of iron, and quantities of slag were crushed and taken for reprocessing to recover this metal. The crusher was rail-connected to the ironworks' north headshunt, alongside the West Coast Main Line, and wagons of crushed slag were propelled up to Carnforth East Junction: they were then transferred to the relevant sidings to be re-marshalled. The rail connection was removed in the mid-1950s, after which all slag was taken out by road *via* the ironworks site until crushing ceased around 1960.

In 1970 the Midland Middle End sidings and all but a run-round loop, of the Midland Top End sidings, were lifted, but the Up and Down F&M direct goods lines connecting the Midland Top End and Midland Bottom End sidings remained in place at East Junction. With the closure and lifting of the north sidings the ironworks industrial site was still rail

Carnforth 30th July 1968. A class 40 diesel engine D318 comes round the curve at F&M Junction with the 10.49am Preston-Barrow passenger train composed of MK1 stock. Sands Lane terminates here and a steel decked bridge crosses the River Keer just beyond where the Ford Anglia is parked. (CRA Collection Ref A68_27-1)

CHAPTER ELEVEN

Carnforth 1945. An 8F 2-8-0 8012 passes the recently closed MR shed with a train of wooden bodied hoppers containing coke for the Barrow Haematite Steel Company at Hindpool. The coke has originated from the Barnsley area coalfield and the train has joined the FMJL at Wennington. It will pass along the direct line to F&M Junction and join the FR mainline. (CRA Collection BOcln01)

connected from the run round loop at the Midland Top End sidings for use by Boddy Industries Ltd. Withers Limestone were also using the remains of the ironworks mineral bank as a loading bay to tip crushed limestone into open railway wagons, the limestone was brought in by road vehicles from their quarries at Burton-in-Kendal and Kellet. The empty wagons were left on the Up or Down goods lines at East Junction for transfer to the ironworks industrial site. The full wagons were worked up to Carnforth East Junction and from there taken by BR to Liverpool. Boddy Industries owned a Hudswell-Clarke 0-6-0 diesel-mechanical-locomotive (works number D761/1951), formerly owned by the Port of Bristol Authority where it was numbered 23 and carried the name *Merlin*. The loco handled all rail traffic to and from the ironworks industrial estate up to 1981, when rail traffic ceased; it was removed from the site sometime after this date.

On the WCML, the Up and Down south goods loops and lay-by sidings were regularly occupied by freight trains, stopping for train crew changes or for water, or for allowing faster traffic to pass on the main line. At Carnforth the LNWR stopped all live cattle trains and meat specials conveying carcasses for examination; many of these had originated in Scotland and were bound for London, this continued into LMS and BR days, only ceasing when this traffic transferred to road haulage. The wagon examiners had a hut alongside the Up through siding No.1 and close to the Grosvenor Road footbridge, they reported to the Carriage & Wagon foreman who had an office in the 1939 building on platform 6. The examiner checked for hot boxes and binding brakes as he walked alongside the train from the engine to the brake van.

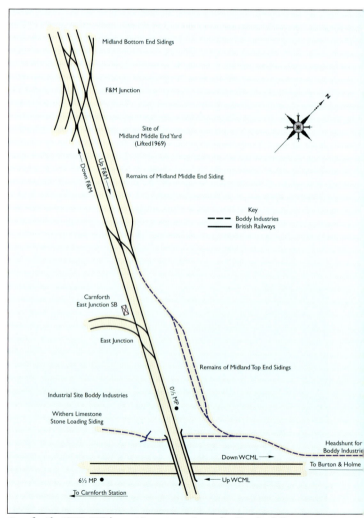

Carnforth 1970. Withers Limestone Branch. Crushed limestone was moved to the truncated remains of the Midland sidings where they were collected by British Railways. (Drawn by Author from LMR DCES Plan August 1970)

The freight traffic over the Furness & Midland Joint line was quite heavy, and from 1880 up to the 1923 Grouping, all through goods trains to and from Furness and Cumberland for destinations in Yorkshire (and vice-versa if originating from Yorkshire) changed engines at East Junction. With the formation of the LMSR, locomotive changes ceased and instead engine crews changed over at East Junction, a practice which continued into British Railways days. From the mid-1970s the few freight trains originating from Furness and West Cumbria for Yorkshire no longer used the direct F&M line between F&M Junction and East Junction. They now took the Up mainline through F&M junction to pass through the station and into the No.1 and No.2 Up and Down goods loops at the south end of the station. Here the engine uncoupled and ran round its train and having coupled up now passed through the station on the Down mainline and over Station Junction to East Junction to regain the F&M line (and vice-versa if originating from Yorkshire).

Freight operations in and through the yards at Carnforth had changed very little over the succeeding years since 1923 and Carnforth remained a busy junction for freight traffic until the mid-1960s, when road haulage started taking over from the railways with the gradual expansion of the national Motorway network. According to anecdotal statements, around 300 wagons were shunted in the yards during a 24-hour period each day in 1960, but in the following years, the number gradually declined. Extracts from the Working Timetable for freight traffic for years 1964/65 have been selected as being representative of the goods traffic being handled at Carnforth, and show the arrivals and departures in all the yards at Carnforth.

On 5th March 1969 the Assistant General Manger BR LMR confirmed that the closure of the Carnforth exchange yard as a marshalling yard, along with the goods yard and warehouse on Warton Road and the wagon repair shop was to take place, and a further fifty men would be made redundant. By 1970 the points from the Up goods line to the Up mainline had been taken out and replaced with a new crossover on the south side of Crag Bank Bridge, further points had also been removed at the south end of the exchange yard closing off some of the through sidings. The Civil Mechanical and Electrical Engineers who were working on the WCML electrification and re-signalling programme used the remaining sidings to hold their wagons and mess and tool vans and cranes. Out-stationed diesel engines of classes 24, 25, 47 and 50 were stabled at the Furness end close to platform 6 as these were the nearest sidings to the signing on point. By the beginning of 1973 the Carnforth exchange sidings had been completely lifted leaving a large area of land which was purchased by 'Steamtown'.

In mid-1969 the goods warehouse was demolished but not the associated goods office building and the warehouse sidings roads No.1 and No.2 were lifted but the sidings in the goods yard were not. In 1972 Carnforth goods yard was taken over by the Civil Mechanical and Electrical Engineers' department as a construction site for the WCML electrification project and roads No.1 and No.2 were re-laid. The goods office building was taken over by the CM&EE. A mineral loading plant was installed alongside the re-laid roads for loading the CM&EE concrete mixing train, each wagon of the consist was placed under the hopper for loading the minerals directly into the mixer. British Insulated Callender's Company (now Balfour Beatty) electrical

Carnforth 28th October 1950. A LNWR G2 0-8-0 49241 is leaving the LNWR end of the exchange sidings on an Up goods train and is crossing from the goods line to Up main line. Looking north from Crag Bank overbridge Carnforth No. 1 signal box and up goods loops are on the right. In the next decade the limestone workings on the left would remove the hill completely. (CRA Collection PEO054)

CHAPTER ELEVEN

Working Timetable 7/9/1964 to 13/6/1965

Carnforth Exchange Yard via WCML

Carnforth Exchange Yard Departures Down (To North via WCML)

Target	Departure time	Frequency	Working
6L21	05.37	DLY	Carnforth-Carlisle
6L25	06.25	SX	Carnforth-Windermere
6L25	07.20	SO	Carnforth-Oxenholme
7T82	08.45	SX	Carnforth-Milnthorpe
6L24	12.58	SX	Carnforth-Burneside

Carnforth Exchange Yard Arrivals Up (From North via WCML)

Target	Working	Frequency	Arrival time
6P50	04.28 Carlisle Yard-Carnforth	DLY	08.42 SX
6P50	04.28 Carlisle Yard-Carnforth	DLY	09.12 SO
6P56	12.55 Kendal-Carnforth	SO	14.27
6P56	11.38 Windermere-Carnforth	SX	15.58
6P58	16.40 Burneside-Carnforth	SX	16.52

Carnforth Exchange Yard Departures Up (To South via WCML)

Target	Departure time	Frequency	Working
6P77	00.05	MX	Carnforth-Colne
4F05	03.05	MO	Carnforth-Edge Hill
4K04	03.30	DLY	Carnforth-Crewe Gresty Lane
4F05	03.40	MX	Carnforth-Edge Hill
6P75	03.55	SO	Carnforth-Lostock Hall
6P75	03.55	MSX	Carnforth-Farington Junction
6G02	04.45	DLY	Carnforth-Bescot
9T83	05.00	MX	Carnforth-Lancaster Castle
9T83	05.10	MO	Carnforth-Lancaster Castle
9T81	06.25	SX	Carnforth-Morecambe Promenade
9T79	06.33	SX	Carnforth-Heysham Harbour
9T76	06.55	SO	Carnforth-Heysham Harbour
5F32	07.40	DLY	Carnforth-Warrington
9T76	07.50	SX	Carnforth-Heysham Harbour
6F35	09.00	DLY	Carnforth-Ince Moss Junction
9T84	09.20	DLY	Carnforth-Heysham Harbour
9T84	14.25	DLY	Carnforth-Heysham Harbour
9T79	14.47	SX	Carnforth-Heysham Harbour
7P81	15.00	SXQ	Carnforth-Farington Junction
6K03	21.15	SX	Carnforth-Basford Hall
6J82	22.20	SO	Carnforth-Liverpool Road
5J82	23.35	SX	Carnforth-Liverpool Road

Carnforth Exchange Yard Arrivals Down (From South via WCML)

Target	Working	Frequency	Arrival time
5P12	22.52 Liverpool Road-Carnforth	SX	00.20
7P30	22.50 Lostock Hall-Carnforth	SX	00.30
5P17	23.00 Edge Hill-Carnforth	MX	03.01
7P24	02.15 Springs Branch-Carnforth	MOQ	04.13
4P10	23.00 Crewe-Carnforth	MX	04.25
7P04	02.15 Rose Grove-Carnforth	SO	05.47
6P04	04.15 Crewe-Carnforth	MO	08.20
5P07	07.00 Warrington Old Jnc-Carnforth	MO	09.34
9T83	12.25 Morecambe Promenade-Carnforth	SX	12.49
9T84	11.30 Heysham Harbour-Carnforth	SO	12.49
9T83	12.40 Lancaster Castle-Carnforth	SO	13.00
9T79	12.28 Heysham Moss-Carnforth	SX	13.42
9T76	13.15 Heysham Moss-Carnforth	SO	14.15
6T82	15.38 Lancaster Castle-Carnforth	SX	15.55
6P13	14.30 Springs Branch-Carnforth	DLY	16.35
9T84	16.20 Heysham Harbour-Carnforth	SX	17.28
9T81	19.02 Lancaster Castle-Carnforth	SX	19.22
9T84	19.20 Heysham Harbour-Carnforth	SO	20.10
9T76	19.55 Lancaster Castle-Carnforth	SX	20.15
9T79	19.55 Morecambe Promenade-Carnforth	SX	20.20
9T83	20.15 Heysham Moss-Carnforth	SX	21.05

cable manufacturer and Construction Company was the main contractor and shared the depot at Carnforth. They also had depots at Wigan (L&Y) shed, and Carlisle Upperby, a specially adapted overhead cable train being used for wiring up operations. BICC had the contract for wiring the WCML from just south of Bolton-le-Sands to Carlisle Upperby. When the work was finished the yard was cleared except for roads No.1 and No.2, on the latter a new building was erected for the Permanent Way Department workshop.

In 1972, the track layout at the south end of Carnforth station was rationalised in readiness for the electrification of the Crewe to Carlisle section of the WCML. The two Down goods loops were converted into No.1 and No.2 Up and Down goods loops, and two through sidings surviving from the exchange yard were shortened into dead-end sidings. All were wired up for use by electric traction. Through the 1970s and 1980s, coal trains from Lakeland Colliery Maryport (for Fiddlers Ferry power station), rail trains from British Steel Corporation Workington, Albright & Wilson (Marchon) chemical trains from Whitehaven, and some long-distance West Coast Main Line Freightliner trains stopped at Carnforth for crew changes. The relieving train crews on the Up trains from West Cumberland trains either changed over in platform 1, or in the No.1 and No.2 Up and Down goods loops, and in the Down direction at the No.1 and No.2 Up and Down goods loops. All Down WCML train crews change over at the No.1 and No.2 Up and Down Loops and all Up WCML trains crews changed over at the Up loops on the east side of the mainline.

With the gradual decline of heavy industry in West Cumbria during the 1980s, and also of the fuel oil and chemical traffic from Heysham Moss sidings, the traffic using the No.1 and No.2 Up and Down loops continued to decline. The final block coal trains still using HAA wagons to and from Hunterston and hauled by EWS Class 66 were the last freight trains in 2006 to regularly use both the loops on each side of the WCML, these workings stopped for crew changes at Carnforth the crews signing on and off in the EWS building. The Class 57 diesel locomotives, nicknamed 'Thunderbirds' for their role as recov-

Working Timetable 7/9/1964 to 13/6/1965

Carnforth Midland Yards via F&M Joint line and Yorkshire

Carnforth Midland Yard Departures
Up (To East via F&M Joint line

Target	Departure time	Frequency	Working
6E03	00.15	DLY	Carnforth-Firth Sidings
8N83	02.44	MO	Carnforth-Carlton
6E86	06.30	DLY	Carnforth-Roundwood
7P83	12.40	SX	Carnforth-Skipton
7N56	17.18	SO	Carnforth-Neville Hill
6N56	19.40	SX	Carnforth-Neville Hill
8P25	21.00	MSX	Carnforth-Skipton
6N18	21.35	SX	Carnforth-Stourton

Other Departures (stopping at East Junction for train crew change)

Target	Departure time	Frequency	Working
8N83	Arr 00.24 Dep 02.22	SX	18.40 Workington-Carlton
7N62	Arr 10.41 Dep 10.53	TFO	09.30 Barrow-Monkton Main
7E56	Arr 16.41 Dep 18.15	MO	13.42 Whitehaven Corkickle-Ripple Lane

Carnforth Midland Yard Arrivals
Down (From West via F&M Joint line)

Target	Working	Frequency	Arrival time
8M33	22.05 Carlton-Carnforth	MX	02.09
7P35	01.00 Skipton-Carnforth	MO	02.29
9P10	01.15 Skipton-Carnforth	MX	04.00
8M93	0.05 Stourton-Carnforth	MX	04.33
7P39	05.47 Skipton-Carnforth	MX	07.21
5M32	05.30 Hunslet-Carnforth	MX	08.25
8M94	04.55 Hunslet-Carnforth	MO	09.24
7P37	07.50 Skipton-Carnforth	MO	09.47
7P37	07.50 Skipton-Carnforth	MX	09.28
7P38	08.37 Skipton-Carnforth	DLY	11.45
7P41	15.15 Skipton-Carnforth	SO	16.45
8M92	15.30 Stourton-Carnforth	SO	19.54
8M37	17.35 Hunslet-Carnforth	SO	21.20
8M37	17.35 Hunslet-Carnforth	SX	22.02
8M85	19.15 Stourton-Carnforth	SO	22.42

Carnforth Exchange Yard via Furness lines

Carnforth Exchange Yard Departures
Down (To Furness line)

Target	Departure time	Frequency	Working
6L40	03.30	MO	Carnforth-Barrow Yard
6L40	03.40	MX	Carnforth-Barrow Yard
6L41	05.00	MO	Carnforth-Workington Main
6L41	05.15	MX	Carnforth-Workington Main
6L42	06.05	DLY	Carnforth-Barrow Yard
7L27	06.15	SX	Carnforth-Ulverston
6L43	09.25	MX	Carnforth-Workington Main
6L45	10.03	DLY	Carnforth-Barrow Yard
6L46	14.30	DLY	Carnforth-Workington Main
6L47	14.45	SX	Carnforth-Barrow Yard
6L49	20.05	SX	Carnforth-Barrow Yard

Other Departures (stopping at Carnforth Exchange for train crew change)

Target	Time	Frequency	Working
7L48	Arr 17.11 Dep 17.16	WSX	13.10 Fleetwood Burn Naze-Corkickle No.1
4L25	Arr 19.50 Dep 19.52	MWFO	18.50 Heysham Moss-Corkickle No. 1
4L25	Arr 19.50 Dep 19.52	THO	18.50 Heysham Moss-Plumpton Jct (Glaxo)

Carnforth Exchange Yard Arrivals
Up (From Furness line)

Target	Working	Frequency	Arrival time
7P18	09.30 Barrow Yard-Carnforth	TFX	10.38
7P17	09.30 Ulverston-Carnforth via Sandside)	SX	12.30
8P80	07.25 Derwent Ironworks (Workington)-Carnforth	MX	12.56
8P78	14.28 Barrow Yard-Carnforth	DLY	16.05
8P92	13.25 Workington Main-Carnforth	FX	19.13
8P92	13.25 Workington Main-Carnforth	FO	19.23
8P81	19.00 Barrow Yard-Carnforth	SX	21.01
8P94	20.37 Barrow Yard-Carnforth	DLY	22.42
7P19	22.00 Barrow Yard-Carnforth	SX	23.20
7P19	18.40 Workington Main-Carnforth	SO	00.05

Other Departures (stopping at Carnforth Exchange Yard for train crew change)

Target	Time	Working
6F14	Ar 11.05 Dep 11.28	07.25 Whitehaven Corkickle-St Helens

DLY Daily
SO Saturdays Only
SX Saturdays Excepted
MO Mondays Only
MX Mondays Excepted
FO Fridays Only
FX Fridays Excepted

MSX Mondays and Saturdays Excepted
TFX Tuesdays and Fridays Excepted
WSX Wednesdays and Saturdays Excepted
MWFO Mondays, Wednesday, and Fridays Only
THO Thursdays Only
Q Runs when required

ery locomotives for any 'Pendolino' failures, also spent much of each day sat in the No.1 and No.2 Up and Down loops. Presently only West Coast Railways charter specials arrive and depart from the Up and Down loops and occasionally infrastructure trains use them when work is being carried out on the WCML.

The working of passenger and non-passenger traffic through Carnforth Station gradually increased after 1880 as a result of the station enlargement. The Joint station had staff from three companies, the LNWR, FR and MR, but the LNWR always appointed the Station Master, and the MR only ever used the station as a tenant, the owners being jointly the LNWR and the FR. To complicate matters, the whole station was not joint, the Up LNWR main platform and its bay remaining wholly LNWR owned, being maintained by that company.

The first LCR timetable for December 1846 shows only one train daily each way starting from Lancaster and Carlisle respectively and non on Sundays. The 1847 LCR timetable shows that three trains now called at Carnforth for the South (Up direction)

CHAPTER ELEVEN

Carnforth June 1965. Rebuilt Royal Scot 4-6-0 No 46140 'The Kings Royal Rifle Corps' is approaching Carnforth on a fitted freight on the No.1 Up goods loop. Carnforth No. 2 signal box and the Down goods loops are to the right and the coal and ash plant of Carnforth shed are partially obscured by the engine's exhaust. (CRA Collection Ref BO 0305)

during the day and non on Sundays. These started at Kendal, Carlisle and Edinburgh respectively for London, whilst two trains (Down direction) called *en-route* to Carlisle, these being a Liverpool and Manchester working, which combined at Preston, and a Birmingham train.

By December 1848, the passenger train service on the Lancaster & Carlisle Railway consisted of six trains a day, Monday to Saturday and two on Sunday in each direction between Lancaster and the Border City (see chapter 1). With the opening of the Ulverstone and Lancaster Railway in August 1857, Carnforth became a junction. The four ULR passenger trains per day each way terminated at Carnforth, and all passengers travelling to and from the south had to change trains there. Until the opening of the Furness & Midland Joint Railway, all traffic to and from the Furness district and Yorkshire travelled by way of Lancaster and the 'little' North Western Railway. All passengers had to change at Lancaster Castle into a 'little' North Western Railway connecting working to Lancaster Green Ayre for a further change into an eastbound train.

In the early 1900s, very few LNWR express trains to and from London to Carlisle and Glasgow stopped at Carnforth during the day but most of the semi-fast trains to and from Carlisle and Windermere stopped in both directions. All local southbound LNWR trains from Carnforth started from the Lancaster Bay, LNWR platform 1, the services running directly to Morecambe Euston Road, or to Lancaster and Preston. Northbound terminating services all used the Down mainline LNWR platform 3 as there was no connection from the south into the Lancaster Bay. The local trains to Morecambe Euston Road were withdrawn at the start of winter timetable in 1952 when BR started to rationalise local workings and made Lancaster Castle the interchange for Morecambe services. The last regular passenger train to use the Lancaster Bay was the 6.35am which ran from Carnforth to Lancaster, appearing for the last time in the WTT on the 16th June 1957, after which the bay platform was used for stabling coaches and from around 1960 DMUs awaiting their next rostered duty.

In July 1927 the 10.00am from Euston and the 10.00am from Glasgow Central received the title 'Royal Scot' and the LMS arranged for the named train to stop at both Carnforth and Symington. The arrangement was for Glasgow Polmadie shed to provide two of their new LMS compound 4-4-0 engines to work the up train to Carnforth and to return with the corresponding down train on the same day. The down train from Euston was worked to Carnforth by ex-LNWR engines and was usually a Claughton class 4-6-0 piloted by a George the Fifth class 4-4-0. They also returned with the corresponding down train on the same day. At Carnforth engine changes took place in both North and South directions with the train clear of the station and stopped on the main line. This practice ceased in September 1927 with the introduction of sufficient and the more powerful LMS 'Royal Scot' class 4-6-0 locomotives as they could run non-stop from London to Carlisle.

By 1930 rail services at Carnforth were facing competition from the Ribble Motors Services Ltd bus company (formed in 1919) which had regular services from Carnforth to Lancaster via Bolton-le-Sands and Slyne, and from Carnforth through Hest Bank to Poulton Square and Morecambe Euston Road (terminating at the new bus station there). In 1930, a limited stop service was running between Lancaster and Kendal, later extended to Ambleside, calling at Carnforth in each direction. All these bus services made inroads into railway passenger traffic. By this time, however, the LMS had become a major shareholder in Ribble Motor Services, and was happy to balance declining railway

Passenger Trains To and From Carnforth
Over F&M Joint Line: 7 September 1964 to 13 June 1965

Carnforth Station Departures
F&M Joint (Up :Carnforth to Wennington and Leeds)

Target	Working	Frequency	Arrive, depart or pass at Wennington
2N79	08.05 Carnforth to Wennington Arr 08.20. Combines with 2N71 08.05 Lancaster Green Ayre to Leeds City	Daily	2N71 arr 08.25/ dep 8.30
1N53	10.35 Carnforth to Leeds City	Daily	Pass 10.52
2N79	12.20 Carnforth to Wennington Arr 12 38. Combines with 2N71 12.30 Morecambe Promenade to Leeds City	Daily	2N71 arr 12.59/ dep 13.06
1N56	DMU 14.43 Carnforth to Wennington Combines with 1N55 14.40 SX DMU Morecambe Promenade to Leeds City	SX	Arr 15.11/ dep 15.16
1N56	14.43 Carnforth to Wennington Combines with 1N55 14.40 SO Morecambe Promenade to Leeds City	SO	Arr 15.11/ dep 15.16
2N79	16.55 Carnforth to Leeds City	Daily	Arrive 17.15/ dep.17.17
2N79	19.18 Carnforth to Wennington Arr 19.36. Combines with 2N71 19.17 Morecambe Promenade to Leeds City	Daily	2N71 arr 19.43/ dep 19.50

Wennington Station Departures
F&M Joint (Down: Leeds and Wennington to Carnforth)

Target	Working	Frequency	Arrive, depart or pass at Wennington
2M79	08.31 Wennington to Carnforth. Detaches from 2M71 06.04 Leeds City to Morecambe Promenade	Daily	Arr 08.16/ dep 08.21
2M79	DMU 12.40 Wennington to Carnforth. Detaches from 2M71 10.48 Leeds City to Morecambe Promenade	SX	Arr 12.36/ dep 12.43
2M79	12.48 Wennington to Carnforth. Portion of 10.48 Leeds City to Morecambe Promenade, but detached at Skipton and forwarded on 2P73 11.41 Skipton to Morecambe Promenade	SO	Arr 12.39/ dep 12.44
2M79	13.15 Leeds City to Morecambe Promenade	Daily	Pass 14.54
1M46	13.52 Leeds City to Carnforth Detaches to form 1M46 15.49 Wennington to Morecambe Promenade	Daily	Arr 15.37/ dep 15.42
2M79	17.22 Wennington to Carnforth. Detaches from 2M71 15.18 Leeds City to Morecambe Promenade	Daily	Arr 17.12/ dep 17.17
2M79	19.59 Wennington to Carnforth. Detaches from 2M71 17.43 Leeds City to Morecambe Promenade	Daily	Arr 19.48/ dep19.53

CHAPTER ELEVEN

Carnforth 6th June 1968. Metro Vickers Co-Bo diesel engine D5716 brings the Plumpton Junction(Glaxo)-Heysham Moss sidings train of empty 45-ton fuel oil tanks through the Up Furness and Yorkshire lines platform 4 watched by a solitary train spotter. A DMU is parked up in the now roofless carriage shed and on each platform are water cranes and fire devils. (CRA Collection Ref A68_17-6)

revenues (through station and line closures) with the increased income from the profitable bus routes.

The Furness Railway had a total of seventeen arrivals and nineteen departures daily during the summer of 1903. By the early 1900s, through LNWR and L&Y coaches were running over the Furness Railway from Whitehaven and Barrow, destined for Preston, Manchester, and other destinations. The attaching or detaching of these through carriages on the Up or Down LNWR main line south of the station was an on-going operational problem until the formation of the LMS, when through working commenced. After the Grouping, the LMS arranged for joining or splitting of portions to take place at Lancaster Castle or Preston, as the layout at both these stations was more convenient than was the case at Carnforth.

From 1867, the Midland Railway had commenced running its boat train traffic to the Isle of Man and Belfast from Leeds to Wennington, and then along the Furness & Midland Joint line to Carnforth F&M Junction where an engine change took place. The Isle of Man down boat train left Leeds at 10.32am and arrived at East Junction at 12.30pm to change engines. For this service, the Midland Railway provided the coaching stock, all six wheelers; they were taken forward by a Furness Railway locomotive to the deep water berth at Piel Pier arriving at 1.40pm. According to the author W. McGowan Gradon BA (author of the 1946 book *The Furness Railway: Its Rise and Development*), W.F. Pettigrew, the Furness Railway's Locomotive, Carriage, and Wagon Superintendent, introduced a number of semi-corridor bogie coaches to this service in 1897. By this time the two boat trains from London St Pancras ran to the new terminus at Barrow Island Ramsden Dock which was alongside the ship's berth. In addition there were four through trains between Leeds and Barrow in each direction during each day.

When the Carnforth Curve (East Junction to Station Junction) was opened in 1880, all engine changes took place at East Junction. In 1892, the Midland Railway obtained powers for a branch from Morecambe to Heysham, together with a large new harbour to handle Irish and Isle of Man traffic. Construction of the harbour took much longer than anticipated, and the new Heysham Harbour station did not open until 11th July 1904 (for public viewing purposes only), with the Belfast and Douglas sailings transferring from Barrow on 1st September 1904. On this date, the boat trains ceased running over the F&M Joint line, instead travelling on from Wennington down the Lune Valley, then via Lancaster Green Ayre to the new harbour station.

Up to the time of the 1923 Grouping, the Midland Railway ran through carriages from Leeds to terminate at Carnforth. On these workings, the Midland Railway engine brought the train from Leeds with the through carriages for Carnforth marshalled at the front of the train. These were detached at Carnforth East Junction and worked around the Carnforth curve by an MR locomotive to the Joint station. A Furness Railway engine then coupled up to the train at Carnforth East Junction and the remaining portion left for Barrow-in-Furness, and in the case of some workings, for Whitehaven Bransty. The same joining manoeuvre was performed in the reverse direction.

After 1923, the newly-formed London Midland & Scottish Railway ran through trains from Carnforth to Leeds, and also through carriages, the latter being attached to the main Morecambe Promenade-Leeds City portion at the junction station of Wennington and detached in the reverse direction. The direct FMJ line continued to be used for seasonal workings

RAILWAY TRAFFIC

Carnforth 30th July 1968. 75048 approaching F&M Junction on the Ulverston trip freight. The train is passing alongside the Midland Bottom End sidings and has been signalled for the F&M direct line. The 'out of position' signal has been placed on the right hand side of the line for sighting purposes. The Carnforth (Furness & Midland Junction) station which opened on the 1st July 1868 occupied the site where the outer signal stands. (CRA Collection Ref. A68_27-2)

CHAPTER ELEVEN

Carnforth 23rd April 1955. A MR 3F 0-6-0 43428 is starting out with a Carnforth-Skipton goods from the Midland Middle Sidings. The engine has just passed over Warton Road Bridge where on the left is the gas meter house. A further goods train is standing on the direct F&M Up mainline. Carnforth train crews often changed over here. (CRA Collection PEF 999)

to and from the Furness line and the Lake District, the July 1938 timetable showing scheduled Summer Saturday trains, such as the 1.50pm Barrow-Manchester Victoria, via Hellifield, and nearly a quarter of a century later the 1962 LMR Summer Timetable showed an 11.14am SSO Leeds City-Barrow/Windermere, also avoiding Carnforth station. This working appeared for the final time the following year, the last scheduled passenger working between Carnforth East and F&M Junctions taking place in August 1963. Copies of the Working Timetable for passenger traffic to and from Leeds via Wennington have been included on page 121, showing the arrivals and departures at Carnforth for 1964/65.

The 1960 LMR Summer Timetable shows six Down trains originating in London or Birmingham and six Up trains originating in Glasgow or Carlisle stopping at Carnforth, and in addition there was a Down London-Windermere and an Up Windermere-London. Five local trains started and terminated at Carnforth for Windermere, Carlisle and Preston making the station a busy place to operate at arrival and departure times. In 1960 a number of the second batch of 'Derby Lightweight' two-car diesel multiple units (with yellow diamond coupling code) were diagrammed to work from Carnforth on the services to Carlisle, Windermere, and Preston. In 1964 a number of Cravens two-car DMUs (with blue square coupling code) were also diagramed to work from Carnforth and were much preferred on the Carlisle workings with their extra power. These units were described as

'power twin' sets (class 112/113) as each coach was motorised with a more powerful Rolls-Royce engine of 238bhp with hydraulic transmission and torque convertors. The drivers said that these units were easy to drive, and that the passenger accommodation and ride was as good as any passenger stock then running on BR.

With the establishment of the Carnforth letter and parcels sorting office in 1879, with its direct connection to the LNWR Up platform 1, Carnforth became a busy station during the night hours. In 1881, postal work commenced at 9.45pm with the arrival of the Furness mails from Whitehaven and Barrow, followed by the LNWR Up mail from Carlisle at 10.00pm. At midnight, the Midland Railway mails departed for Leeds and Bradford with a corresponding arrival from Leeds and Bradford at 12.35am. The West Coast Down postal arrived at 1.34am, being the fastest booked timing on the LNWR at the time and running from Preston to Carnforth (27¼ miles) in 29 minutes. The final Down mail working over the LNWR arrived at 3-51am, and transferred mail for Barrow and Whitehaven. Leaving Carnforth at 4.40am the Down Furness mail train took 1 hour 45 minutes for the 28½ miles to Barrow-in-Furness. The final exchange of mail at Carnforth took place on platform No.1 on 28th September 1991 with the Whitehaven-Huddersfield TPO. The door leading directly from the Carnforth sorting office to the station was finally closed up and from then the GPO mail traffic passed over to road haulage.

RAILWAY TRAFFIC

19th March 1955. Crossing East Junction is LMS 4F 0-6-0 44562 on the 10.15am Stourton-Carnforth goods and it is taking the direct F&M Down mainline to the Midland Bottom End sidings. The wagons on the left are held on the Midland Top End sidings which descend to meet the sidings at Carnforth North Frame. The old Northern turnpike road passed over the hill on the right. (CRA Collection PEF978)

Mail had been carried by the railways from November 1830 and a manual means of dropping and collecting mails without stopping came into use in 1852, but it was not until 1880 that a mechanised method of collecting and dropping mail at speed became practical. Lineside equipment for the collection and dropping of mail was installed to the south of Crag Bank Bridge and Carnforth was one of the last collecting and dropping off points in use on the WCML.

Express Parcels and Special Delivery Parcels were given priority, and were forwarded from the Carnforth sorting office by the next available passenger train throughout the day and evening, with standard-rate parcels usually loaded on to scheduled parcels trains. The station had busy periods during the night when bags of mail and parcels were loaded or unloaded and transferred via the subway to and from the Carnforth sorting office and adjoining platforms. This was a task which required much muscle power and skill, as often three trolleys would be coupled together, with three postal employees moving them up and down the subway ramps.

One retired GPO staff described how the trolleys were worked:

We would put the trolley with the best brake on the front of a train of three trolleys, the maximum that could be handled when full of mail bags or parcels etc. Then we would set off and go down the subway ramp as fast as possible so that the momentum helped us go up the next subway ramp.

In BR days a battery-powered trolley was made available to assist these manoeuvres, with one man at the front driving and two pushing at the back. The battery-powered trolley was registered for road use, and was allocated the number RMK 360. Additionally, some outward carpet traffic from nearby Holme Mill left for the south on evening parcels trains – small livestock, such as locally-reared chickens in boxes, was also handled. New motor cycles and pedal cycles arrived on parcels trains and were collected in the early morning by the local retailers.

In the early hours of the morning (from around 4.00am), fish and newspaper trains arrived at the Down main LNWR platform 3, with the local tradesmen meeting the trains to collect their goods. From the late 1960s, newspapers and magazines were transferred from platform 3 to the 'Wymans' hut which was placed on the forecourt near to the former Furness & Midland Warton Road station entrance, and collected from there by the newsagents or wholesalers. The station bookstall always had the first edition of the morning papers on sale before the newsagents' shop opened in town.

Carnforth was also a popular receiving station for racing pigeon traffic, with the station porters releasing the birds at an agreed time of day, so that the owners could time the birds' flight home. Eventually this traffic was lost to road haulage.

CHAPTER ELEVEN

Carnforth 9th July 1972. An EE type 2 diesel engine D7545 at Carnforth No.1 signal box on the BICC overhead wiring train 9L21 (R. Herbert collection A3352)

Carnforth 9th July 1972. On the roof of the overhead wiring train 9L21. The overhead wires are being run out under the new flat arch of Crag Bank Bridge. The signal arms on the semaphore signal have been re-arranged for the final time and would soon be replaced by MAS colour light signals. (R. Herbert collection A3355)

Carnforth 11th April 1972. The CM&EE concrete mixing train and the wiring train stand on the goods yard re-laid siding No1. The mineral plant and associated conveyor has been installed for loading the cement mixers. Thompson B1 number 1306 has yet to be named *Mayflower*. It is powering the brake-van ride which ran to and from north end of the site. (R. Herbert collection A3126)

Carnforth 16th July 1956. The Carnforth portion of the 15.16 Leeds City-Morecambe Promenade has been detached at Wennington. The train is made up of one van and three coaches and is headed by LMS 3MT 2-6-2T 40041 of Carnforth shed. The train is approaching East Junction on the F&M line and is passing over the WCML; to the left are the Midland Top End sidings. (CRA Collection PEG745)

A Carnforth-Wennington-Carnforth Passenger Train Working through lovely Lonsdale

Carnforth was the starting and finishing point of passenger services to and from Leeds City (North) via the F&M joint railway to Wennington. At Wennington Junction the F&M joint line from Carnforth joined with the 'little' North Western line from Morecambe Promenade which ran via Lancaster Green Ayre and the Lune valley. In 1960 five trains per day departed and arrived at Carnforth daily two of these were through trains which generally consisted of seven carriages and started from platform 6 with limited stops to Leeds City.

The remaining three trains were described in the timetable as conveying through carriages to Leeds City as far as Wennington where they were combined with the Morecambe Promenade train, only one of these trains running on Sunday. They generally consisted of three or four carriages sometimes reduced to two in winter; they started from the Midland bay at the north end of Carnforth Station. Over successive years until its closure in 1944 Carnforth MR Shed provided the engine these were MR 4-2-2, singles, 2-4-0 tender engines and 0-4-4 tank engines. The new LMS shed opened in 1944 and Fowler 2-6-2 3MT tank engines were allocated to these trains; Carnforth had 40011 and 40070 in 1955 and later 40041 as a replacement for 40011 which went to Tebay for banking duties. From around 1960 4MT 2-6-4 tanks were used and later class 5MT 4-6-0 these were more than adequate for the task. A retired driver who started work at the MR shed in 1935 recollected that one of the last Johnson 1P 2-4-0 was used on these trains. The train crew consisting of driver, fireman and guard signed on at Carnforth for these workings.

The Fowler 2-6-2 3P tanks had small grates and were not good steamers so the fireman would build up a hot fire to get a good head of steam when leaving Carnforth as the line to Wennington Junction, although undulating, was generally uphill with a climb at the end through Melling Tunnel. To keep up the steam pressure the firemen fired little and often in order to maintain a steady steam output. There were three intermediate station stops at Borwick, Arkholme and Melling until the stations closed in 1960. The outer distant signal for Wennington Junction was just beyond the east end of Melling tunnel and had been placed on the opposite side of the line for sighting purposes as the line curved round to the left. The drivers said it was hard to see because of the curve and the drifting steam and smoke created by the engine as it left the tunnel mouth.

Wennington Station was just east of the junction and had a bay platform on the up side in the Leeds direction. The Carnforth train was the first to arrive at Wennington Junction about ten minutes before the Morecambe portion; it ran through the Up platform of the station and then reversed into the bay platform which could only hold four carriages. The Carnforth engine uncoupled and ran forwards and crossed over to the Down line and went over the junction to stand on the Down F&M joint line to await the next down train from Leeds City. The exception being the engine for the 13.52 departure from Leeds City – in this case the engine ran forwards past the junction to stand on the Down line of the Lancaster branch to await the next down train from Leeds City.

The main portion of usually six coaches for Leeds City departed from Morecambe Promenade and travelled via Lancaster Green Ayre and the 'little' North Western line to

CHAPTER ELEVEN

Wennington and typically arrived seven minutes after the Carnforth train. Passengers for local destinations would alight at Wennington station Up platform, then the train would draw forwards before reversing into the bay platform to collect the Carnforth portion and after coupling up the combined train departed for Leeds City.

In the reverse direction three down trains from Leeds City divided at Wennington station. One, the 13.52 departure from Leeds City, was operated differently to the other two which were operated identically. For these two the combined train on arrival at Wennington station Down platform was divided at the station platform where the Morecambe and Carnforth portions were uncoupled. The Morecambe portion which was at the front of the train would then depart with the train engine and pass onto the Lancaster branch at Wennington Junction for Morecambe Promenade. The Carnforth engine which had been waiting on the F&M joint line beyond the junction then reversed over the junction onto the rear portion of the train and after coupling up departed for Carnforth via the F&M joint line. The Carnforth train would leave Wennington station typical four minutes after the Morecambe train. Whilst waiting the Carnforth fireman would tend to the fire to ensure that there was a good head of steam on leaving Wennington and being gradually downhill little extra firing effort was needed.

The 13.52 departure from Leeds City for Morecambe Promenade with through coaches for Carnforth and on arrival at Wennington station Down platform was divided at the station platform where the Morecambe and Carnforth portions were uncoupled. The train engine uncoupled and ran forwards over the junction on to the F&M joint line. The Carnforth engine which had been waiting on the Lancaster branch then reversed onto the front portion of the train and worked the train to Morecambe Promenade via Lancaster Green Ayre. The Carnforth engine later returned from Morecambe Promenade light engine back to Wennington via Lancaster Green Ayre. The train engine had reversed back over the junction on to the rear portion of the train and departed for Carnforth via the F&M joint line.

On Saturday a passenger guard from Barrow accompanied the 19.18 which was the last train to leave Carnforth riding on the cushions as far as Wennington, he then returned with the 19.59 Wennington – Carnforth. There was a wait of around 20 minutes for the Leeds City train so there was time to chat with the station staff or the signalman at Wennington and on a summers evening to take a short stroll around the station forecourt. The service ceased on 1st January 1966 as part of the Beeching cuts; it remained a steam-hauled passenger train to the end and finally with Mk1 passenger coaches.

A typical connection at Wennington as extracted from the 1962 timetable is as follows. Through Coaches for Leeds City – Carnforth portion, Depart Carnforth 19.00 arrive Wennington 19.18. Through carriages for Leeds City – Morecambe portion, Depart Morecambe Promenade 18.56 arrive Wennington 19.25. The combined train – Depart Wennington 19.30 for Leeds City.

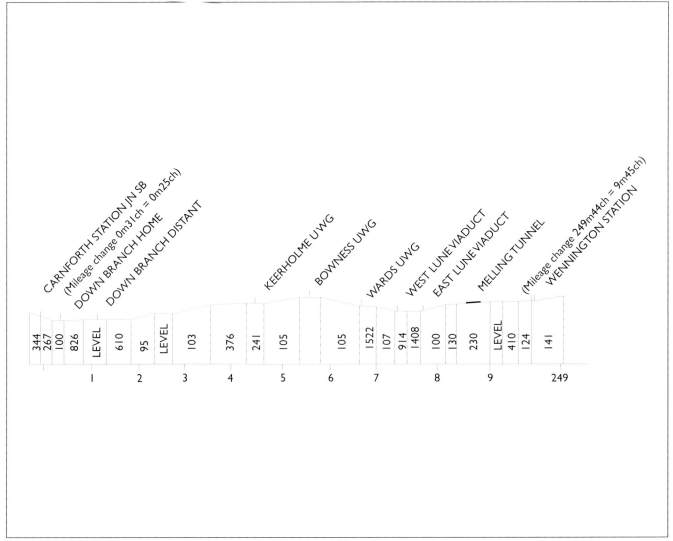

Gradient profile for the section Carnforth to Wennington.

CHAPTER TWELVE

SIGNALLING AND OPERATIONS

Each of the three railway companies had its own style of signal box and semaphore signalling equipment. The LMS modernisation scheme of 1939 replaced all the pre-grouping signals and some signal boxes with LMS standard equipment. At Carnforth, modernisation, rationalisation, and operational changes have swept away the semaphore signals, and only one ex-Furness Railway signal box now remains in use.

When the Lancaster and Carlisle Railway opened in 1846, Carnforth was classed as a wayside halt and with only six passenger trains each way per day in 1850 signalling was worked on the 'time interval system'. Thus, when a train passed the signal, the signal arm was returned to the 'Stop' position, and then, after a fixed interval of time, usually around ten minutes, the signal arm was moved to the 'Proceed' position. Signalling at Carnforth would have been simple, with only one or two signal posts and the station staff working the signals by hand.

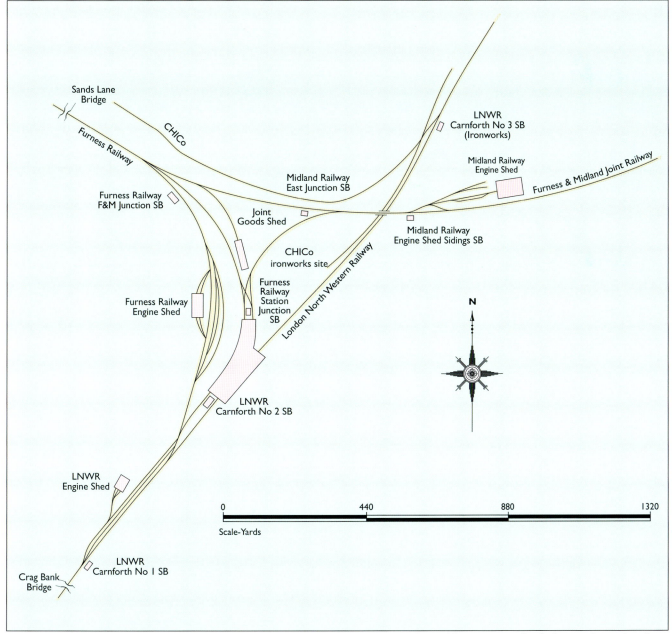

Carnforth 1882. The plan shows the relative positions of the mainline companies' signal boxes at Carnforth. (Drawn by author from Midland Railway Diagram Book)

CHAPTER TWELVE

In 1857 the first signal box Carnforth Station Yard was erected at the north end of the Ulverstone & Lancaster Railway's exchange sidings to control the junction between the U&LR main line and the sidings. At the same time, an additional signal box Carnforth Station Junction was erected at the south end of the station alongside the Up LCR main line to control the passenger junction and the separate southern junction to the exchange sidings. These early signal boxes tended to be small and the signals that they controlled fairly basic, as the railways still operated on the 'time interval' system.

With the increasing density of traffic, the time interval system was no longer adequate or safe, and the railways adopted the 'block' system in which trains were separated by distance. The system relied on the signalman who, through the use of bell codes and telegraph instruments, controlled the movement of trains through the block section. At Carnforth, each signal box controlled a so-called 'block section' between that box and the adjoining signal box. In 1880 the Board of Trade required that mechanically worked points should not be more than 150 yards from the signal box, although this was relaxed to 200 yards in 1900. However all the signal boxes at Carnforth were built besides the junction or loops they controlled, and the points and signals were in sight of the signalman.

By 1880, Carnforth had become an intensive area to operate, with three main routes, four junctions, and seven signal boxes dealing with local and long-distance passenger and goods trains, together with the transfer of traffic between the various yards and the light engine movements on and off the three companies' engine sheds. Eventually, the three railway companies in Carnforth, the London & North Western Railway, Midland Railway, and Furness Railway developed their own distinctive style of signal box and semaphore signals.

With the increase in coke traffic from South Durham now passing through Carnforth to the ironworks around the Furness and West Cumberland coast, the existing ULR sidings were becoming inadequate. In 1863 the LNWR jointly with the FR extended these siding southwards along the west side of the LNWR main line, and a new goods junction was made just north of Crag Bank Bridge. To control this new junction, the LNWR erected a signal box Carnforth Goods Junction alongside the Up LNWR main line. This goods junction must have created operational problems as all coke trains destined for the Furness and West Cumberland ironworks as well as local goods trains from the north, had to run past the signal box and the junction before coming to a stand beyond Crag Bank Bridge. They then had to reverse and cross over the LNWR Down mainline to gain access to the LNWR end of the Carnforth exchange sidings.

For the opening of the Carnforth Haematite & Iron Co's ironworks in 1864 the LNWR laid down two parallel sidings alongside the ironworks east boundary wall, for holding full and empty wagons for the ironworks. They also erected a new signal box Carnforth North alongside the Up LNWR main line, just north of the Furness and Midland Joint Railway Bridge then under construction. This box controlled the Up and Down main lines to the north of the station, the trailing connection from the ironworks sidings to the Down mainline and the crossover from the Down main line to the Up mainline for working empty wagons or light engines back to the Carnforth Exchange sidings.

The Furness Railway built the first Carnforth F&M signal box in 1867 on land just to the west of the junction with the Furness & Midland Joint Railway and a third of a mile north of the Joint station, the box upper being wood framed and panelled, with a base made out of white limestone blocks. The box controlled the junction between the Furness & Midland Joint Railway line, and the Furness Railway main line and goods lines and the new Furness Railway ironworks branch.

The second Midland Railway engine shed opened in 1874 on land to the east of the turnpike road (the present A6), and a small signal box Carnforth Engine Shed with ten levers was erected alongside the F&M Joint Down line and within sight of the road. This box controlled all the engine movements on and off shed, as well as the Up and Down main line signals on the approach to the shed. It was renewed in 1890 with a similar box of Midland design, which was in use until the shed closed in 1944, after which it was switched out. Once the connections to the shed had been taken out and lifted, and the associated signals removed, the box was officially closed and demolished in 1949.

When the station was enlarged in 1880 a new LNWR signal box, of a long and low profile Carnforth No.2 Junction was erected at the south end of the station between the Down LNWR main line and the FR passenger line. It controlled the FR to the LNWR passenger junction, the Up and Down LNWR mainline at both the south and north ends of the station and the south exit from the exchange sidings to the LNWR Down mainline. Also the north end of the Down goods loop No.1 and No.2, and the Up goods sidings No.1 and No.2, as well as the Lancaster bay platform (LNWR platform1), carriage sidings and end loading dock sidings. This was the busiest signal box at Carnforth and as well as the signalman there was a 'signal box lad' who job was to record the train movements in the signal box register. When through working of passenger trains commenced following the Grouping of the railways in 1923 a speed restriction of 20mph was brought into use on the curve through the Furness Railway's reversible platform and across the passenger junction.

The Carnforth Curve (East Junction to Station Junction) was opened in 1880, giving the MR access to the enlarged Joint station and new bay platform and adjacent carriage siding at the north end of the station. The double-track sharp curve of nine chains radius commenced at the end of the platform and ran round to East Junction where it made a junction with the direct F&M Joint line, and a permanent speed restriction of 20mph was brought into use. To control traffic at the new station junction, the Furness Railway built a tall signal box Carnforth Station Junction in brown sandstone to blend in with the station architecture. On its north face and inset in a panel is the Furness Railway's coat of arms carved in stone, whilst the south face contained a clock also in an inset panel. An internal staircase gave access to the first floor which contained the lever frame. Carnforth Station Junction signal box came into use on 30th January 1882, initially it had thirty-one levers but to comply with the 'Regulation of Railways Act' 1889 the lever frame was extended to thirty-six levers to comply with the interlocking of points on railway lines.

In 1884 a new LNWR signal box, Carnforth No.1 Junction, this time of tall and long profile was erected at Crag Bank. It replaced the first Carnforth Goods Junction signal box which was now closed and dismantled, all new signal boxes being much longer to accommodate the extra levers required for the locking of points and the operation of more subsidiary signals for shunting movements. This new box controlled the Up and Down Mainline to and from Carnforth No.2 Junction signal box, and the south junction from the Up and Down LNWR main line to the enlarged Carnforth exchange sidings. (There were now six relief sidings and through goods lines to Carnforth Station Junction). The box also controlled the new LNWR engine shed

SIGNALLING AND OPERATIONS

Carnforth 1882. Station Junction signal box. This unusual signal box was built in brown sandstone to match the enlarged station buildings, and was brought into use in 1882. The operating levers were situated on a high level floor which was reached by an internal staircase. (Drawn by author from a site survey carried out by author in 2005)

CHAPTER TWELVE

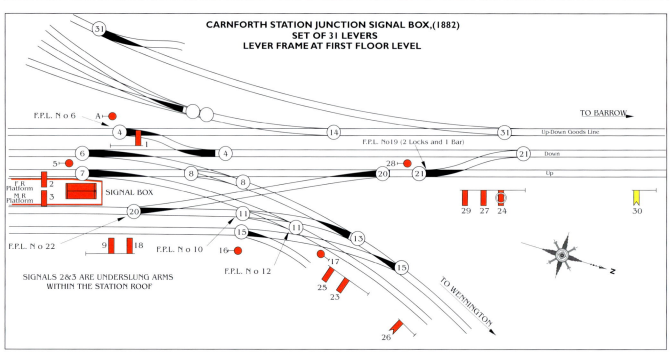

Carnforth 1882. Signal Plan. Station Junction signal box controlled the Carnforth Station Junction. Signal Arm 24 had a ring attached to it and acted as a shunting signal allowing an engine to access either platform No. 1 or No. 2 when occupied by a train. The original signal box diagram was prepared by the signalling contractor and it has been reproduced to show the style adopted by the contractor. (Drawn by Alan Johnstone from a plan in the National Archives at Kew)

lines, the southern entrance to the Down goods loops No.1 and No.2, the exit from the southern Up goods sidings No.1 and No.2 and the Up and Down mainline south to Detron Gate up to 1937.

To the south of Carnforth, Bolton-le-Sands signal box was demolished sometime after 1910, although the distant signals (apparently interlocked with the level-crossing gates) were retained and worked by the station staff. In 1937 the semaphore signals on both the Up and Down lines between Hest Bank signal box and Carnforth No.1 signal box were replaced by two-aspect 'searchlight' colour light signals. The Up signals becoming intermediate block signals (IBS) and brought under the control of Carnforth No.1 Junction signal box and the Down signals becoming intermediate block signals (IBS) and brought under the control of Hest Bank signal box. The crossing gates continued to be worked by the station staff but the gate locks were now released from Hest Bank signal box. In 1938 the 1884 LNWR Carnforth No.1 Junction signal box was closed and replaced by a new LMS type E box. This new box was sited slightly further south nearer to Crag Bank bridge and was named Carnforth No.1.

From 1944 a light engine arriving from the south on the Down mainline and destined for the new LMS engine shed would be directed from the Down main line to the Down through sidings, and from there it would go around the west side of the LNWR wagon repair shop to the shed. Before moving off the shed in a southerly direction, the driver had to obtain permission from the signalman at Carnforth No.1 signal box. The fireman would telephone the signalman and tell him the locomotive's destination and the signal man would set up the route and clear the points for the movement on to the Up mainline.

In 1898 the first Carnforth F&M signal box was closed, dismantled and rebuilt at Coniston as the new station signal box. The new Furness Railway Carnforth F&M signal box was a much larger box, being was constructed in red brick with a panelled base and an external wooden staircase. It cost £400 to build and equip, and had a Railway Signal Company lever frame containing sixty-five levers. The new box controlled the junction between the direct Furness and Midland Joint Railway line from East Junction and the Furness Railway's main line and through goods lines to Carnforth Station Junction, together with the line to the joint goods yard and warehouse and the Midland Bottom End sidings. The box controlled the Up junction splitting home signals for the Furness Up goods line and Up main line, and the direct Furness and Midland Joint line. The junction signal had fixed distant signals (on the same bracket) for the Furness Up main and goods lines as there was a speed restriction of 20mph through the junction and around the curve leading onto the Keer Bridge and Carnforth station.

Between 1880 and 1927 an engine entering the Furness Railway engine shed from the north would have the route set up by Carnforth F&M signalman for the engine to reverse from either the Down goods line or the Down passenger line into the shed entrance line. From 1944 the Carnforth Station Junction signalman set up the route for the engine to enter the LMS new shed by either the Up or Down goods line into the shed entrance line. The driver of an engine before moving off the shed had to obtain permission from the signal man at Carnforth Station Junction signal box. The fireman would telephone the signalman and tell him the locomotives destination and the signal man would set up the route. Upon receiving clearance, the locomotive if going north would pass onto the Down goods line and move over the Keer Bridge towards F&M Junction, or reverse from the Down goods line and cross onto the Up goods line if going south.

Carnforth F&M Junction signal box also controlled the Furness Railway main line to Silverdale, the next block post. To the south of Silverdale station the line crossed Silverdale Road where a FR crossing keeper's house and gate box controlled operations. The signals were locked with the gates and the crossing gates were manually opened and closed by the crossing keeper. In June 1966 the crossing was fitted with automatic half-barriers (AHB) and came under the control of Silverdale signal box; the gate box, signals and the FR house were demolished. When Silverdale signal box closed on 14th February 1969 the block section then extended from Carnforth F&M Junction to

SIGNALLING AND OPERATIONS

Arnside and the crossing came under the control of Carnforth F&M signal box and when that was switched out to Carnforth Station Junction signal box. The level crossing controls default to 'stopping train' mode unless 'non-stopping train' mode is selected by the signalman. For passenger trains stopping at Silverdale there is an override 'ready to start' switch (RTS) installed on the Up platform which is operated by the guard when the train is ready to leave and this closes the AHBs.

The 1882 Carnforth Station Junction signal box was taken out of use in 1903 and replaced by a new Furness Railway signal box, also named Carnforth Station Junction. The new signal box contained more levers to operate additional signals and point locks and was sited further north in the vee of the Furness Railway lines and the Carnforth Curve to East Junction, the signalman now having better visibility of train movements around the Carnforth Curve and the station junction itself. The signal box was constructed in red brick with a panelled base and integral staircase, and a Railway Signal Company lever frame was installed. The box controlled the junction between the FR mainline and the Carnforth Curve to East Junction, the FR reversible platform line and run-round loop, and the Midland bay and carriage siding; it also controlled the FR main line, the through goods line from the Furness end of the enlarged Carnforth exchange sidings and the goods lines to and from F&M Junction and the Furness Railway engine shed. This signal box is a listed building; however the 1882 signal box has never been listed but should been as it is the oldest ex-FR signal box still standing.

In 1905 the Furness Railway Engineers Office prepared a scheme for improving the handling of traffic at the north end of the station just beyond Carnforth Station Junction signal box. The proposals were for a new crossover to be put in from the exchange sidings so called 'roundabout road' (running along the back of the screen wall) to the Down goods line and a further crossover from the Up FR goods line to the Down FR mainline. The changes (including signalling) were carried out at a cost of £250, and the crossovers remain in use in the current rationalised layout.

On the 7th September 1907 a FR passenger train collided with a light engine standing on the FR Down line within the confines of the station. The passenger train had just left the FR long curved platform and crossed over onto the Down line to leave the station when it ran into the light engine which was standing on the Down line. The LNWR signalman in Carnforth No.2 signal box had cleared the train to proceed onto the Down line, as the signal and points were under his control, they were about 200yards from the signal box and being under the station roof not very visible to him. The light engine was waiting for the FR signalman in Carnforth Station Junction signal box to clear the signal so it could proceed out of the station. As the train was travelling at a low speed no passengers were injured and each engine suffered only minor damage. The Inspecting Officer laid the blame on both signalmen.

The first Carnforth East Junction signal box was renewed in 1902, this new box being of wooden MR design and with a Midland Railway tumbler frame containing twenty-four levers. The Carnforth East Junction signal box controlled the junction and between Carnforth East Junction to Station Junction and the direct Furness and Midland Joint Railway line to F&M Junction, as well as the connections to the Midland Middle End and Top End sidings. The Down bracket signal at East Junction had splitting home and distant signals for controlling the junction to Carnforth station and the F&M direct line to F&M Junction. There was a permanent speed restriction of 10mph around the Carnforth Curve into the station and less than the stipulated braking distance, to the next signal on the Down FMJR direct line to F&M Junction so BR fixed the distant signals for each route.

The Carnforth Station Junction signal box and the Carnforth East Junction signal box were only 300 yards apart and for operating purposes, Carnforth Station Junction Up distant signal was placed below the Carnforth East Junction Up home signal on the same post and operated by a slotting device on the post, meaning the distant signal could only be pulled off when the

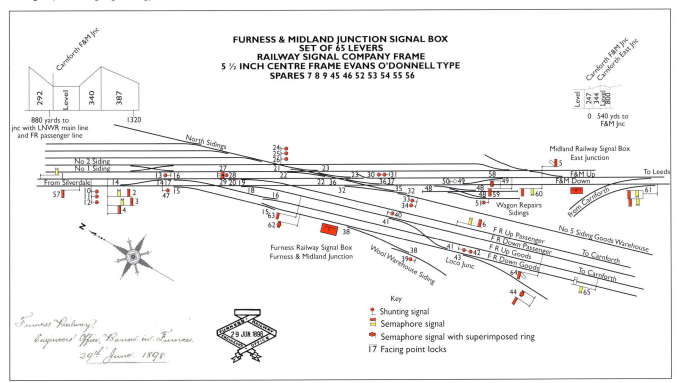

Carnforth 1898. Signal Plan. Carnforth Furness & Midland Junction signal box controlled the Furness & Midland Junction. The Furness Railway's preferred practice was to place ground signals in line rather than stack them except those in confined locations; the diagram accurately depicts both conditions. (Drawn by author from a plan in the National Archives at Kew)

CHAPTER TWELVE

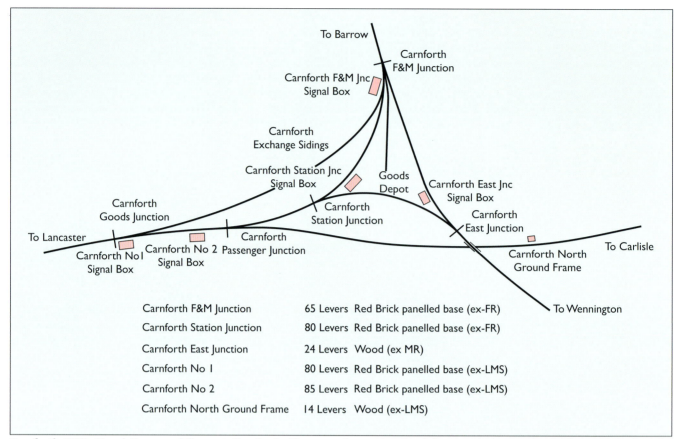

Carnforth 1940. Signal Boxes and lines at Carnforth. The map shows the signal boxes existing at Carnforth in 1940 after the modernisation of the station and before the onset of rationalisation and the electrification of the WCML. (Drawn by author)

home signal had also been pulled off, in line with normal signalling practice.

The LNWR had systematically renamed its signal boxes (generally at renewal time) at Carnforth and added a suffix to the title in line with company practice, thus Carnforth Goods Junction became Carnforth No.1 and Carnforth LNW Station Junction became Carnforth No.2 Junction. In 1899 Carnforth North signal box was replaced on the same site by a new LNWR signal box Carnforth Ironworks No.3. Following the closure of the ironworks the box was renamed Carnforth No.3 in 1930.

Between 1880 and 1900 the three companies had made only minor changes to their signal boxes and signalling equipment, and operating practices altered little until 1938 when the station was modernised by the LMS (as previously mentioned in chapter 9). When the independent Furness and Yorkshire line platform (LMS platform 6) was built a new junction was created from the Down LNWR main line to the new platform. The new layout allowed the platform to be signalled as a reversible platform.

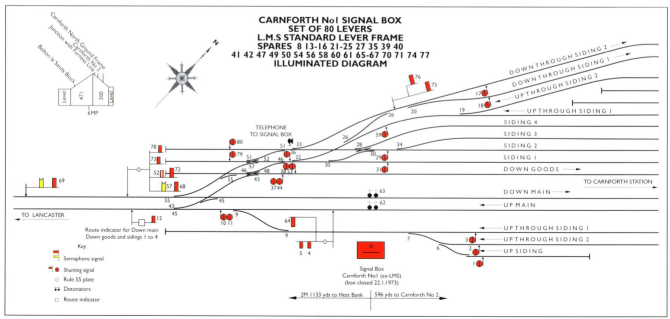

Carnforth 1960. Signal Plan. Carnforth No. 1 signal box controlled the south junction to and from the LNWR end of the Carnforth exchange sidings and the south entrance and exit to the LMS motive power depot as well as the Up and Down south goods loops and sidings. When the Preston power signal box was commissioned Carnforth No. 1 signal box was closed in January 1973 and demolished. (Drawn by author from a BR LMR S&T diagram)

134

SIGNALLING AND OPERATIONS

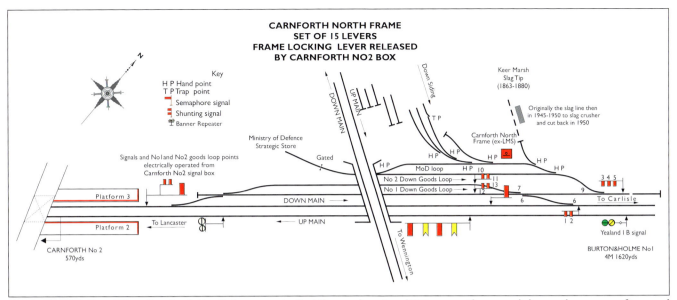

Carnforth 1954. Signal Plan. Carnforth North Frame controlled the numbers 1 and 2 Down northern goods loops; these were often used by slow goods trains and sometimes when an engine change was needed or when a relief crew was required. The North Frame closed in 1969 and was demolished. (Drawn by author from a BR LMR S&T diagram)

The construction of the new junction brought about the demolition of the 1880-built LNWR Carnforth No.2 Junction signal box, being replaced on 6th November 1938 by a standard E type LMS-designed signal box named Carnforth No.2. This was built on the east side of the Up mainline, with a standard LMS frame containing 85 levers. At the south end of the station on the LNWR side, the track and points from the Lancaster bay (LMS platform 1 Bay 1) were realigned to connect directly into the LNWR Up mainline. A new facing connection was also made from the LNWR Up mainline to the Up goods relief sidings No.1 and No.2 using a double-slip point, this simplified the 1880 LNWR layout and improved the handling of the Lancaster bay traffic and mainline goods traffic at the south end of the station.

At the south end of the station on the Furness side, a further new junction was made from the LNWR Down goods loops and both the Up and Down Furness and Yorkshire lines, and with the new 'by-pass' line which ran around the back of the new platform 6. On official plans this line has been variously described as the 'by-pass line', the 'avoiding line' or 'roundabout road', and 'up and down Furness goods' and local railwaymen knew it as 'back-of- the-wall line'. The line connected with the Furness Down main and Up and Down goods lines opposite Carnforth Station Junction signal box. It enabled a movement to be made between the north and south ends of the station without having to pass through the Down platform. Carnforth Station Junction signal box lever frame instruments and signal diagram were modified for operating this new independent Down line and its connections to the goods lines, the box now having eighty levers.

In the 1950s and 60s this line was often used for train crew changes on through goods trains passing from the West Coast Mainline (WCML) to the Furness line, the relief train crews would wait in the shunters' room adjacent to the line. It was also used for marshalling goods wagons that were to be added to long distance goods trains, often a fast fitted freight that had been put in one of the Up or Down loops.

Carnforth No.1 Junction LNWR signal box was replaced on the 17th September 1938 by a standard E type LMS-design box named Carnforth No.1, it was sited further south beside the LNWR Up mainline and contained a standard LMS frame with 80 levers. There were detonator placers on both the Up and Down mainlines, these being worked in conjunction with their respective home signals as was national practice. When the respective home signals were 'on' the device automatically placed a number of detonators on the running lines and automatically removed them in the 'all-clear' position. This new box controlled the same signals and points as its predecessor.

As part of the modernisation scheme some of the pre-grouping wooden post semaphore signals were replaced with standard LMS designs particularly on the ex-LNWR mainline. These were all of steel construction with upper quadrant arms, which A.F. Bound, the Chief S&T Engineer for the LMS, had decided would be standard for all new and replacement signalling schemes. The replacement signals had main posts of lattice steel construction as this method of construction had been initially chosen by the LMS for tall signals and bracket signals; later this was superseded by an H-section broad flange beam or a heavy section tubular post. Tubular posts with upper quadrant arms were fitted to the tops of the bracket. Tubular posts with upper quadrant arms were also used for a single-post application with one or more arms, and the standard LMS ground disc signal for subsidiary moves was installed in a single or multiple-stack array.

Further modernisation replaced multiple arms on one post with one arm and route indicators and one location where this was applied was at the LNWR goods junction. Here the LMS replaced the LNWR signals and installed a new tubular post signal just beyond Crag Bank Bridge on the Up main line, with a stacked array of five route indicator boxes mounted below a short shunting arm. The signal was operated from Carnforth No.1, signal box and as the signal faced in the opposite direction of travel it was used as a 'backing signal' to control the reversing of goods trains into the LNWR end of the Carnforth exchange sidings. With the shunt signal in the 'clear' position, one of the indicators would display a number for either the Down goods loop, or sidings 1 to 4. The train would then reverse on the Up main line for a short distance, cross on to the Down main line, and then finally reverse into the selected siding. This method of operating ended in 1970 with the rationalisation of track and the closure and lifting of LNWR end of the Carnforth exchange sidings. On the Down mainline a bracket signal with an H-section broad flange beam main post and an array of signals for controlling the Down mainline, the Down goods loop, and sidings 1 to 4

CHAPTER TWELVE

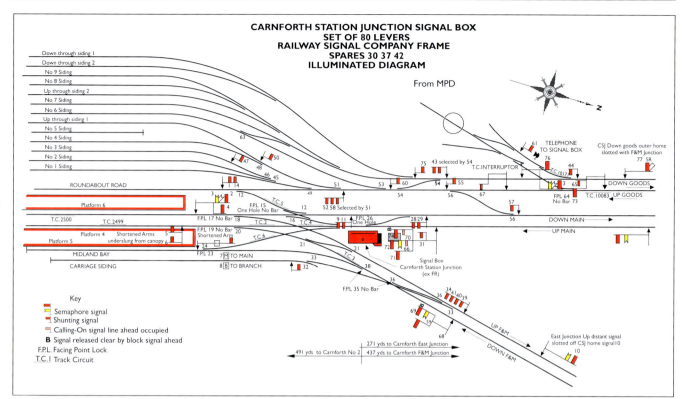

Carnforth 1960. Signal Plan. Carnforth Station Junction signal box controlled the Furness and Yorkshire lines station junction, the northern end of the 'roundabout road' and the FR end of the exchange sidings, the Up and Down goods lines and the north entrance and exit to the LMS motive power depot. (Drawn by author from a BR LMR S&T diagram)

were placed on the south side of Crag Bank overbridge. One of the signals (called a calling on signal) allowed a second engine or train to enter the selected Down goods loop when it was already occupied by a train.

The Down inner home mainline signal operated by Carnforth No1 signal box was placed on the south face of the lattice footbridge to avoid slewing the lines for loading gauge clearance purposes. To ensure it was clearly visible from its mounted position, a substantial white sight-screen or sight-board was fastened on to the footbridge behind the signal. Concurrently the LMS Signal & Telegraph department took over the responsibility of maintaining the footbridge from the Civil Engineering department. In 1971 rationalisation of track and signalling took place in readiness for the WCML electrification and the footbridge was taken down.

Limited replacement was carried out on the Furness main line. The Up main line outer splitting distant of FR origin for the F&M junction at Sands Lane was replaced by an all wooden bracket signal of early LMS design (with both MR and LNWR fittings) being controlled by Carnforth F&M signal box. The Furness and Midland direct line and the Carnforth Curve line continued to operate with wooden post signals of Midland Railway design but with replacement upper quadrant arm, the majority lasting until they were replaced in the mid-1950s by BR with tubular steel posts. When the station was rebuilt in 1939 the LMS under hung four semaphore home signals on a wooden beam beneath the new platform awning at the end of platforms 4 and 5 the Midland bay, the signals having shortened arms to clear the underside of the awning when in the 'off' position. They controlled the exit from platforms 4 and 5 to the Furness Down mainline and the Up Carnforth Curve to East Junction line.

Around 1960 BR replaced the two Midland bay signals on platform 5 with a tubular post signal which was sited beyond the platform end; it had a short arm to clear the edges of the adjoining 1882 signal box and still remain within gauge clearance, it was fitted with a stacked array of two route indicators, this was second location where route indicators were used. It controlled the exit from platform 5 and the route indicators displayed which route had been selected, the Midland bay to the Down Furness line (M) and the Midland Bay to the Up F&M line (B) for branch.

A.F. Bound also required that all signals should be on the left-hand side of the line to which they applied, but in three cases at Carnforth this was not possible and these 'out of position' signals were designed to suit specific location. At Carnforth F&M Junction a cantilever-type lattice-post bracket signal with home and distant arms for three separate routes was placed on the right hand side of the Down Furness mainline. It was operated from Carnforth F&M signal box and controlled the direct Up FMJL to East Junction the Up passenger line to Carnforth Station Junction, and the Up goods line to the Furness end of the Carnforth exchange sidings. On the Down mainline a cantilever-type lattice-post bracket signal was placed on the right hand side of the line for sighting purposes, at the south end of the Down platform, (LMS platform 3). The signal was operated from Carnforth No.2 signal box, the home signal controlled the Up mainline, and the two subsidiary arms in stacked array controlled the entry to the Up through sidings No.1 and No.2. Also between East Junction and F&M Junction was a signal with opposite facing arms on one post, the Down main home and distant signals and the Up main outer home signal. It was arranged as such to give the driver a better view on the approaching curve at East Junction.

At the south end of the Up Furness and Yorkshire lines platform, LMS platform 4 was another signal of unique design. On the same post was the Up starter home signal controlled by Carnforth No.2 signal box and below it the Carnforth Station Junction outer distant signal, these signals controlling the movement over the junction to the Up mainline. Attached to it and

SIGNALLING AND OPERATIONS

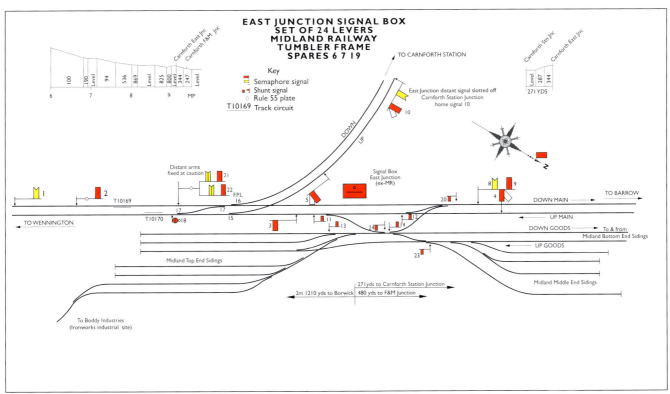

Carnforth 1968. Signal Plan. Carnforth East Junction signal box controlled the junction to Carnforth station and the direct lines to F&M junction as well as the Midland Top End and Midland Middle End sidings. The signal box was closed in November 1998 and demolished. (Drawn by author from a BR LMR S&T diagram)

suspended from it on the right hand side was an under-slung miniature shunting signal for controlling movements into the relief sidings 1 to 4, west of the mainline also controlled by Carnforth No.2 signal box. There was a similar signal at the south end of the Down and Up (reversible) Furness and Yorkshire lines platform LMS platform 6 the only difference being that the miniature shunting signal for controlling movements into the relief sidings 1 to 4, was on a conventional bracket and not under-slung.

Where signals are difficult to see special measures are taken to ensure that the driver has a clear view of them and can act in accordance with their indications. In these situations co-acting arms are provided on the same post, with one arm high up and the other low down. On the Up WCML and commencing at the 9½-mile post south of Burton & Holme, there is a continuous falling gradient of 1 in 134 for approximately 3 miles. This would allow a train to increase its speed and consequently it would require a longer braking distance should the signal be at danger. For this reason the LNWR placed a tall signal with co-acting home and distant arms on the same post close to Carnforth No.3 signal box and a few yards north of the bridge carrying the FMJL over the Up LNWR mainline. Also a tall junction signal was placed around 100 yards from the north end of the Up LNWR mainline platform 2. A further tall signal with co-acting home and distant arms on the same post was placed at the end of Down LNWR mainline platform 3, just beyond Warton Road Bridge. At this point the line curves through the platform and the lower arms of the signal were partially obscured by the platform awnings and Warton Road Bridge. Both the Up and Down line signals were operated by Carnforth No.2 signal box.

At the time of the 1939 re-signalling the tall LNWR co-acting signal close to Carnforth No.3 signal box was replaced by a tall LMS lattice steel post also with co-acting arms. The tall LNWR junction signal at the north end of the Up mainline platform, (now LMS platform 2), was replaced by a Sykes electrically-operated banner repeater signal operated from Carnforth No.2 signal box. The LMS used this type of signal display when the signal ahead was obscured, in this case by Warton Road Bridge and the station awnings. The banner repeater signal displayed splitting aspects, one for the Up main line and one for the Up through sidings No.1 and No.2.

Following the closure of the ironworks in 1929, the LNWR ironworks sidings remained in place and were renamed the No.1 and No.2 'northern refuge sidings'; they were used for holding and sorting traffic from Merseyside, any shunting being done within the confines of the sidings. At this time incoming trains had to reverse from the Down mainline into the refuge sidings. As the crossover from the Down mainline to the Up mainline had been taken out by the LMS and any engine or train leaving the sidings had to return 'wrong road' on the Up mainline to the south end of Carnforth station. This move was done by the signalman 'blocking back' to Carnforth No.2 signal box to avoid conflicting movements. This arrangement continued until the northern goods loops were taken out of use on the 23rd November 1969.

For most of the time between 1929 and 1939 Carnforth No.3 signal box was switched out. It only was manned in summer when traffic was heavy, or when the northern refuge sidings were shunted, 1939 being the last year it was regularly used. It was brought back into full use as an emergency measure in 1940 when the Ministry of Defence (MoD) strategic store opened on the former ironworks site, and the northern refuge sidings were then used for holding and sorting the MoD Store's traffic. The MoD Store line connected into the ironworks run-round loop on the west side of the northern refuge sidings, and into the remains of the ironworks' north-facing head shunt. As the head-shunt could only hold one engine and six wagons, shunting of the MoD Store was protracted. On 26th October 1941 the LMS closed Carnforth No.3 signal box and subsequently demolished it. The operation of all the Up and Down mainline signals were

CHAPTER TWELVE

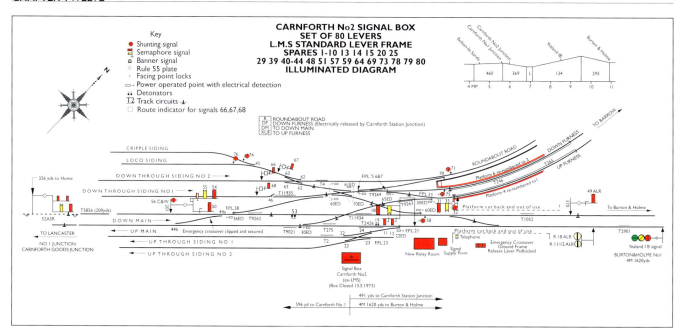

Carnforth 1972. Signal Plan. Carnforth No. 2 signal box, after rationalisation of track in readiness for the electrification of the West Coast Mainline from Weaver Junction to Carlisle. The signal box then controlled the re-modelled south junction in and out of the station and the Up and Down goods loops and the mainline to the Warton IBS. When the Carlisle power signal box was commissioned Carnforth No 2 signal box was closed in May 1973 and demolished. (Drawn by author from a BR LMR S&T diagram)

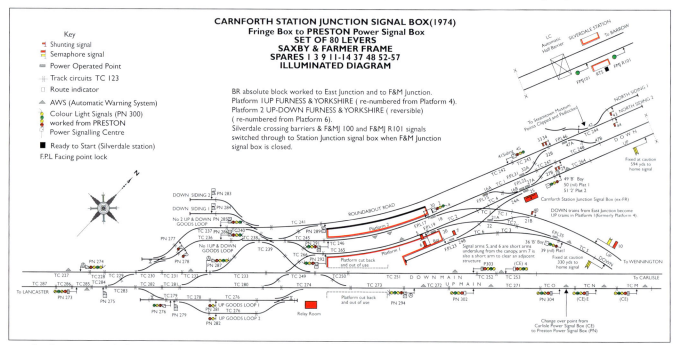

Carnforth 1974. Signal Plan. Carnforth Station Junction signal box became a fringe box of Preston power signal box in May1973. The box controlled the Furness and Yorkshire lines station junction and the lines to Silverdale and to Settle Junction when Wennington signal box was switched out. The WCML through Carnforth including loops and sidings and the entrance and exit at the southern end of the station were now controlled from the Preston power signal box. (Drawn by author from a BR LMR S&T diagram)

transferred from Carnforth No.3 signal box to Carnforth No.2 signal box. The operation of the northern refuge sidings was transferred from Carnforth No.3 signal box to a new ground frame which was out in the open on the west (or Down) side of the sidings. The ground frame could be worked (by a shunter, fireman or guard) once the train was in the northern refuge sidings and the points leading to the Up mainline had been locked by Carnforth No.2 signal box.

At Yealand a small Saxby & Farmer type signal box had been erected by the company for the LNWR, the work on the L&C section being carried out between 1867 and 1872. These intermediate signal boxes were erected to control a few signals and in the case of Yealand provide a shorter block section between Carnforth No.3 and Burton & Holme No.1 signal boxes. It was closed on 28th June 1943 and the semaphore signals were replaced by electrically controlled two-aspect colour light signals. The new Up line Yealand intermediate block signal (IBS) was controlled from Burton & Holme signal box and the Down line Yealand (IBS) was controlled from Carnforth No.2 signal box.

The large amount of Second World War goods traffic being handled through Carlisle yards caused a bottleneck on the WCML and consequently all loops and layby sidings to the south were continuously full of goods trains awaiting their allotted path. In September 1942 to provide more capacity at Carnforth, facing points were installed at the north end of the station from the LNWR Down main line, converting the 'northern refuge sidings' into 'northern goods loops' No.1 and No.2. A new tubular post bracket signal was erected on the sloping northern-end ramp of the Down mainline platform; it was fitted with a home signal for controlling the Down main line and two subsidiary arms in stacked array for controlling the entrance to the loops. The Down main home signal and the subsidiary arms for the northern goods loops were electrically operated from Carnforth No.2 signal box and the signals were placed low down for the driver to see them through the arch of Warton Road Bridge.

In 1925 the Board of Trade had laid down that mechanically worked points should not be more than 350 yards from the signal box that operated them. When the northern refuge sidings were converted into the through goods loops, the outlet points were around 1,000 yards from Carnforth No.2 signal box. The cost of providing a brand new fully equipped signal box for what was perceived by the LMS as a short-term war time measure prevented the LMS from building a replacement Carnforth No.3 signal box. Instead, the 1941-built ground frame was removed and replaced with a new fifteen lever frame and instruments all of which was housed in a small LMS-type cabin built at ground level at the outlet end of the loops. It was named Carnforth North Frame, and was brought into use on 20th September 1942. It was electrically locked and unlocked by Carnforth No.2 signal box. During the war it was fully manned but by the 1960s a relief signal man was sent 'as required'. It controlled all movements to and from the MoD store, the north headshunt and the connecting line to East Junction via the Midland Top End Sidings, the exit signals to the Down mainline from the loops and from the Midland Top End sidings and the 'backing signals' from the Down mainline. The Down mainline home signal protecting the move was locked from Carnforth No.2 signal box.

The northern goods loops played an important role in relieving the pressure on the Down goods loops at the south end of the station. If the southern goods loops were full, the slower goods train was held in the northern goods loops awaiting a suitable path north. The northern goods loops were lengthy, and depending on train-length it was possible to hold two goods trains in each loop. It was not unusual even in the 1950s during busy times for a slow goods train to take up to eight hours (and much more in war time) to travel the 78¼ miles from Crewe to Carnforth, by which time the footplate crew were ready for relief and the locomotive had probably left its home depot up to 12 hours previously. At busy times, Train Control at Lancaster Castle station (later at Preston) allocated a Carnforth driver and fireman to be on duty at the ground frame to relieve those foreign footplate crews who had already worked their rostered hours. A retired driver from Wigan-Springs Branch MPD recalled that as a fireman he and his driver were often put into the loops to be relieved by a Carnforth train crew. They then walked back to the station to sign off at the goods clerk's office, then to the mess room where they waited for an evening passenger train which took them back to Wigan.

The Carnforth fireman carried out such tasks as raking out the fire, drawing down coal in the tender, placing coal in the firebox and filling up with water. Sometimes it was necessary to change engines as the coal in the tender was either down to a low level or had been in the tender so long that it was either coal dust or solidified lumps. In recent conversations with a retired Carnforth enginemen, he said that when an engine had to be changed, the relief crew was sent to the engine shed. They then took the locomotive from the engine shed to F&M Junction before crossing over and travelling down the direct line to Carnforth East Junction. The relief loco then entered the Midland Top End sidings; from where it moved down the inclined siding into the north-facing head shunt before setting back into the goods loops. The train engine then returned 'wrong road' to Carnforth No.2 as described previously and then to the engine shed. By the late 1960s the northern goods loops saw little use and they were taken out of use on 23rd November 1969. The loops were soon lifted, and the connection to the MoD store was removed and the Carnforth North Frame demolished.

The signal gantry installed in 1942 at the north end of the northern goods loops, spanned the loops and the Down mainline. The gantry was constructed from H-section broad flanged beams, and carried both the Down mainline signal and the exit signals for No.1 and No.2 goods loops. On the Up mainline, the tall LMS lattice post with co-acting arms was replaced around 1960 with a three-aspect (red-yellow-green) colour light signal, erected around 200 yards to the north of the River Keer Bridge and controlled by Carnforth No.2 signal box.

With the closure in May 1970 of the Up and Down mainline platforms, the Lancaster bay, carriage sidings, and end-loading dock siding at the south end of the station were lifted and the connecting points from these lines to the Up through loops No.1 and No.2 and associated signals were removed. The number of levers in use in Carnforth No.2 signal box was reduced. Following closure of the Carnforth exchange sidings in 1972, the number of points and signals controlled by Carnforth No.1 signal box was also reduced. In 1972 the Furness and Yorkshire lines passenger junction with the mainline, at the station's southern end, was re-modelled as part of the electrification scheme for the Crewe-Carlisle section of the WCML.

The Down through sidings No.1 and No.2 (southern goods loops) were retained, made bi-directional and renamed No.1 and No.2 Up and Down goods loops and the two adjacent through goods lines. The remnants of the Carnforth exchange yard relief sidings were converted into sidings for stabling crippled wagons. The Civil Engineering Department prepared a plan for these two sidings to be converted to stabling sidings for diesel locomotives, but the plan was never executed as the changeover of traction from electric to diesel on the Up through Euston-Barrow services took place at Preston (see chapter 9).

At the same time, the exit from southern Down goods loops and sidings to the Down mainline, the Furness and Yorkshire lines platforms, and the 'roundabout road' (behind the newly renumbered Platform 2) were re-modelled. All the points were now power-operated with electrically detected locking and the remaining semaphore signals simplified.

With the commissioning of Preston power signal box (PSB), new multiple-aspect signalling (MAS) now controlled all movements from Preston PSB on the Down Main north of Carnforth at Dale Grove-Yealand where control passed to the Carlisle PSB and on the Up main Carlisle PSB passed control to Preston PSB at Hyning; also north of Carnforth and Carnforth No.1 signal box closed on 21st January 1973 and was soon demolished. From January 1973 Carnforth No.2 signal box remained in use as a block post linking the fully commissioned Preston PSB to Carlisle PSB which at that time was still being commissioned. The commissioning of the Carlisle PSB was completed on 13th May 1973 and at 17.00 the last electrically controlled signals were operated by miniature levers from Carnforth No.2 signal box by signalman A. Meyer. They were the Down line Yealand

CHAPTER TWELVE

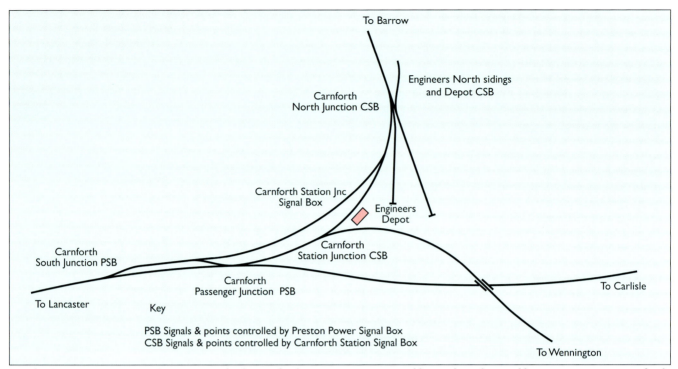

Carnforth 2000. Signal Box and lines at Carnforth. Carnforth Station Junction signal box is the only signal box in operation at Carnforth. It controls the Furness lines to and from Silverdale and the Yorkshire lines to and from Wennington. It also releases the permanent way depot sidings and ground frame for inbound and outbound movements. The plan shows the signal box and lines at Carnforth in 2000. (Drawn by author)

intermediate block signal (IBS) and the Carnforth outer colour light signal north of Keer Bridge. The box was then closed up and demolished shortly after.

The new Up Starter signals (on a large gantry) at the south end of Platforms 1 and 2 were multiple aspect colour lights and controlled access to the WCML with junction indicators. For the southern loops, the southern exit from the 'roundabout road' was a position light shunt signals and all were operated from Preston PSB. In May 1973 Carnforth Station Junction signal box became a fringe box to the Preston PSB. It retained control of the traffic at the north end of the station along the Furness Line as far as F&M Junction, from the south end of the 'roundabout line' to F&M Junction and the link into 'Steamtown' and the Carnforth Curve to East Junction, and also the Midland bay platform line.

At the north end of platform 2 the semaphore junction signal for the Down Furness line and Up Carnforth Curve was replaced by a three aspect colour light signal fitted with a junction indicator for the Carnforth Curve. The north exit from the 'roundabout road' (now described as 'Up and Down Furness Goods' on the renewed signal box diagram) to the Down Furness line was also controlled by colour light signal with a position light shunt signal for the North Siding No.1 and No.2.

At the north end of platform 1 (formerly platform 4) the two semaphore home signals under hung from the station awning, and the Midland bay platform semaphore home signal still remained, but the indicator was removed in 1974. The semaphore junction signal for the Up Furness mainline near to Carnforth Station Junction signal box was replaced with a three aspect colour light signal fitted with a miniature theatre-type route indicator for platforms 4, 6 and (B) bay. The 1972 re-signalling allowed platform 2 (Down Furness-Up Yorkshire) to continue being operated as a reversible platform and the working of the automatic warning system (AWS) ramp on the line was arranged so that it would operate only in the direction of travel. When the Midland bay was taken out of use around 1980 the lines were lifted and the points taken out and the under hung and bay signals were removed; at the same time the platform awnings were cut back to the end of the bay. A new semaphore home signal was mounted on the platform at the north end of platform 1 but does not seem to have been operational, it was shown on the Carnforth Station Junction signal box diagram as 'fixed'.

To bring the Furness lines at Carnforth station up to modern standards all the manually operated points, except the North Siding No.1 and No.2 and the 'Steamtown' connections were now power operated. However the signalling on the Furness line remained a mixture of semaphore and multiple aspect colour light signals, and there was still a fixed distant signal on the Up Furness mainline. The numbers of levers in use in the Station Junction signal box was reduced to 45 and the signal box diagram was renewed at this time to reflect these changes.

In 1974 semaphore signals still remained on the F&M Joint line along with the Midland Railway-design signal box at East Junction and there was still a fixed distant signal on the Down Carnforth Curve line. To reduce operating costs the outer distant and home signal on the Down FMJL line on the approaches to Carnforth had the signal oil lamps removed and converted to electric lighting.

From the mid-1970s East Junction signal box was normally switched out as there was no longer any scheduled passenger traffic on the direct line, and the regular goods traffic emanating from Barrow Yard, Millom and Whitehaven to South Yorkshire which had used the direct line had ceased. When East Junction signal box was switched out, the signals controlled by it on the direct line between East Junction signal box and F&M Junction signal box were put into the 'on' position, and the signals controlled by it on the Carnforth Curve and the F&M Joint line were put into the 'off' position. This created a long block section from Carnforth Station Junction to the next signal box at Wennington (9¾ miles), and an even longer one to Settle Junction (24½ miles) if Wennington was switched out. East Junction signal box was occasionally opened when a Boddy

SIGNALLING AND OPERATIONS

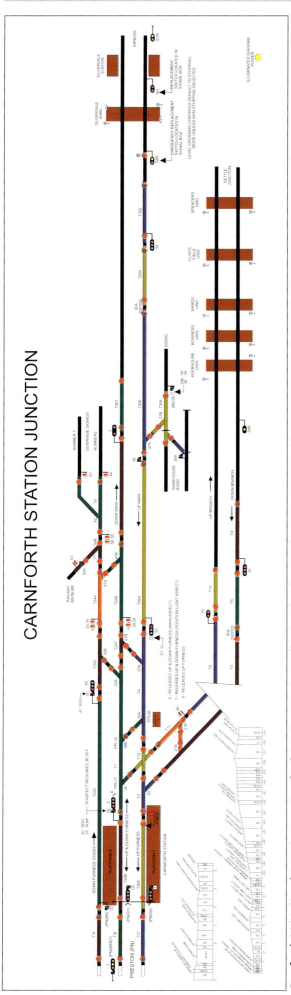

Carnforth 2009. Signal Box Diagram. Carnforth Station Junction. Following the closure of Wennington signal box in early 2009 the Carnforth Station Junction signal box diagram was renewed. It now controls the Yorkshire line as far as Settle Junction and the Furness line as far as Arnside. Note that the two sidings in the permanent way depot are still called Warehouse Road, the goods warehouse having been demolished in 1970. (Drawn by author from the original diagram now in the Carnforth Station Heritage Centre)

Industries limestone train was brought up from the ironworks industrial site to be marshalled and moved to and from the East Junction sidings by BR. In these instances the box was worked by the shunting staff. This traffic ceased in 1980.

As the Cumbrian Coast line was an 'approved route' for steam excursions, Carnforth East signal box was opened if through running to and from West Yorkshire destinations was required, and as late as 24th July 1988, the celebrated A4Pacific 4468 *Mallard* was observed taking the direct line at F&M Junction with a return York-Grange-over-Sands working. However, Carnforth East box was classified as 'only opened as required' from 12th November 1989, following identification of a defective crossing in the Down line East Junction to Station Junction/F&M Junction point-work The crossing was then removed, and the Carnforth East Junction Carnforth F&M Junction section declared 'out of use', although the Up line and its connection remained intact. At some point in the next two years, the Down line was returned to 'operational' status.

On 7th October 1992, in the late morning, a Class 31 locomotive was derailed between F&M Junction and Station Junction, and the District Operating Manager at Regional Railways North West immediately instigated single-line working for DMUs over the Up line between F&M Junction and East Junction, using the trailing crossover at the latter to regain the Down line round the Carnforth Curve to Station Junction. These movements continued on the following day, following which the damaged section was brought back into use. Two days later, on Saturday 10th October 1992, the 'Cumbrian Coast Express', headed by Stanier Pacific 46229 *Duchess of Hamilton*, used the direct Up line between F&M Junction and East Junction, on its return working from Workington to Bradford, train crews being changed at East Junction. This was almost certainly the final through working over this short section of the former FMJR.

On 29th December 1995, the block instruments in Carnforth East box were stolen, and the box was then permanently strapped 'out of circuit'. On 7th November 1998, East Junction signal box was officially closed, and demolished shortly afterwards. New two-aspect colour light signals were installed on the Carnforth Curve Up line and about one mile east on the Down F&M Joint line, all being operated from Carnforth Station Junction signal box. At the same time, the direct F&M Up and Down lines were lifted back to Warton Road bridge and buffer stops erected. They became a head-shunt to the North Sidings, which are now little used by the Permanent Way department. The removal of Warton Road Bridge has been suggested, as this would allow road vehicles higher than 13 feet to access the north end of the town.

At the end of 1971, the Carnforth exchange sidings had been lifted and the Up and Down through goods lines from the exchange sidings to Carnforth F&M Junction were severed at the junction and buffer stops were erected. The Down through goods line was lifted, and the Up through goods line now became the Up and Down Furness goods which connected into the down mainline at F&M junction. Buffer stops were erected, on the remains of the Up and Down through goods lines which became 'North sidings No.1 and No.2', the entrance-exit to 'Steamtown' museum faced north and connected into these sidings. These two sidings were to be used for stabling diesel locomotive, for the changeover of traction from electric to diesel on the Down through Euston-Barrow services; however the change-over took place at Preston (see chapter 9). With the closure of the former exchange sidings the north sidings did for

CHAPTER TWELVE

Carnforth 1952. Carnforth East Junction. The 1903 Midland Railway East Junction signal box and an all wooden two-doll balanced bracket junction signal of MR design. The right hand signals controlled the direct F&M joint line to F&M Junction and left hand the Carnforth Curve to the station junction. The wooden bodied wagons are parked on the Upper Midland Top End sidings. (CRA Collection Ref. BOcln15)

a time fulfil this function as diesel engines were parked there awaiting there next turn of rostered duty.

After the WCML electrification work was completed, all but two of the goods yard sidings at Warton Road had been lifted by the end of 1974. F&M Junction signal box remained in use as a block post for the Furness line from Arnside and for any traffic on the F&M direct line to and from the still-open Midland Bottom End sidings. From the late 1970s Carnforth F&M signal box was switched out for most of the time and the few remaining workings were transferred during 1998 to Carnforth Station Junction signal box. F&M Junction signal box was then permanently strapped 'out of circuit' with the box left in situ. On 7th November 1998, F&M Junction box was officially closed, and demolished shortly afterwards.

The Midland Bottom End Sidings had been taken over by the Permanent Way Department for marshalling and storing ballast and rail wagons and tamping machines and renamed North Sidings. A new permanent way engineering workshop for the maintenance of their equipment was built on the site of the goods yard and was serviced by two 'Coles' mobile road cranes. Colour light ground signals and power operated points controlled from Carnforth Station Junction signal box were installed for working the North Sidings and the workshop line. Network Rail permanent way work is now (in 2011) being centralised at Carlisle and Crewe localised distribution centres (LDCs) and the future of Carnforth as a permanent way facility looks uncertain.

In 1974 a new crossover controlled from Carnforth Station Junction signal box was made for the working of charter train stock from 'Steamtown' directly onto the Furness Down main line and then into the reversible platform 2. When marshalling a twelve coach charter train, the stock is pulled out of 'Steamtown' in a five-coach rake and in three moves, as both the No.1 and No. 2 'North sidings' can only hold a locomotive and five Mk I or Mk 2 coaches each. The train is then marshalled on the Up and Down Furness goods line and, using the new connection, can move directly into bi-directional platform 2 if it is to commence at Carnforth for Furness (Cumbrian Coast) and Yorkshire destinations. Other West Coast Railways charter trains (not starting from Carnforth and departing to the south) traverse the Up and Down Furness goods line, and then pass through one of the southern goods loops, to gain access to the WCML at Crag Bank.

During October 2009 renewal of the Station Junction power operated points was carried out as they had become time expired. Following the closure of Wennington signal box in early 2009 (although it had been locked out for many years), the Carnforth Station Junction signal box diagram was renewed, and the redundant diagram presented to the Carnforth Station Heritage Centre; it is now on display in the Furness & Midland Hall. The signal box has now been fitted with new double-glazed windows and other improvements have been carried out, bringing it up to modern standards. It is now the only signal box at Carnforth, and controls the former Yorkshire line as far as Settle Junction and the Furness line as far as Arnside.

During the LMS and BR era the S&T section based at Carnforth had an office on platform 6 in the 1939 building and a parts store and lamp oil in huts adjacent to the carriage sidings. They were responsible for the maintenance of the signal and telegraph equipment on the West Coast mainline from Garstang to Oxenholme, on the Furness line to Arnside, plus the ex-LNWR branches off the mainline; the Glasson Dock branch, Hest Bank to Bare Lane, and the line between Morecambe South Junction and the resort's Euston Road station; also the F&M line to Wennington and the ex-Midland Railway line from Wennington to Morecambe Promenade, the Heysham Harbour branch and the branch from Lancaster Green Ayre to Lancaster Castle.

The section's areas of responsibility changed gradually owing to track rationalisation and line closure, and in the lead-up to privatisation it became part of Regional Railways – North West within British Railways. With privatisation, responsibility for S&T passed to Railtrack plc on the 1st May 1994, and subsequently on 3rd October 2003 to its successor Network Rail. In 1994 the Midland bay was filled in by Railtrack, and made level with the platform and partitioned off from it with security fencing. A number of portable cabins were placed in the compound for S&T maintenance staff and for the storage of materials. One bay of the retaining wall adjacent to the station building on Warton Road was removed to allow road vehicles access to the area. The area is occupied by Network Rail S&T team and its sub-contractor Carillion Rail.

SIGNALLING AND OPERATIONS

Carnforth 5th August 1992. Carnforth East Junction. The direct F&M joint line is in the fore-ground and a lamp-man is attending to oil lamp on the tubular post signal which protects the junction. The line to Carnforth station curves away behind the signal box and the tubular post signals is in the 'off' position for the Up FMJR line to Yorkshire. (CRA Collection Ref HUG470)

Carnforth 11th August 1956. Looking north east from the FMJL Bridge, the converging lines have descended from East Junction and are the Midland Top end sidings. These sidings and the ex-ironworks loop lines converge beyond Carnforth North Frame to make a headshunt. The tall LMS lattice post Up line co-acting signal is in the 'on' position stopping 6P Jubilee 4-6-0 45719 on the 8.40am Dundee-Liverpool passenger train. On the Down line LMS 4MT 2-6-4T 42544 accelerates the 1.37pm Crewe-Windermere passenger train away from the station. (CRA Collection Ref PEJ541)

CHAPTER TWELVE

Carnforth 11th August 1956. Looking north from the FMJL Bridge, the tall LMS lattice post Up line co-acting signal is in the 'off' position for 6P Jubilee 4-6-0 45563 on the 10.50 am Glasgow-Liverpool (W432) passenger train. The Down northern goods loops converge at the signal gantry in front of Carnforth North Frame. (CRA Collection Ref. PEJ538)

Carnforth circa 1960. The 1939 LMS Carnforth No. 2 signal box controls the Passenger Junction between the WCML and the Furness and Yorkshire lines. The tall two-doll left hand bracket signal at the end of the Down mainline platform No. 3 has a lattice steel main post and has been placed on the right hand side of the mainline for sighting purposes and controls the Up mainline and the Up goods loops. On the right side of the post is a bracket with an underslung signal which controls the exit from platform No. 4 Furness and Yorkshire lines to Down goods loops. In front of this signal is a second shorter tubular post signal which controls the exit from platform No. 4 Furness and Yorkshire lines to the Up mainline. (CRA Collection Ref. BOcln 08)

SIGNALLING AND OPERATIONS

Carnforth No. 1 Junction, circa 1900. This was the second LNWR signal box to be erected at the south end of Carnforth to control the Up and Down LNWR mainline and the goods junction to the LNWR end of the exchange sidings and the entrance – exit for the LNWR engine shed. (CRA Collection Ref. LCR05C-05)

Carnforth Station circa 1900. The LNWR made use of tall posts for sighting purposes and these two examples are at the north end of mainline platforms No. 2 and No. 3. The right hand signal controls the Up mainline and goods loops. The left hand signal has co-acting arms but only the lower arms are visible (CRA Collection Ref. BOcln12)

CHAPTER TWELVE

Carnforth Station Junction circa 1955. The 1903 FR signal box is constructed of red brick with an integral staircase and a five panel base with locking room windows in each. The FR mainline is in the foreground and alongside is an LMS signal lamp and oil store. The Nissen huts remain from the WW2 MoD strategic store. (CRA Collection Ref. BOcln27)

Carnforth F&M Junction circa 1955. The 1898 FR signal box is constructed of red brick with a separate staircase and a five-panel base with locking room windows in alternate panels. The name plate on the front the signal box is made up from cast letters on a wooden board as used by the FR. (CRA Collection Ref. PA0007)

SIGNALLING AND OPERATIONS

Carnforth No. 2 Junction circa 1901. Carnforth No. 2 signal box was the largest LNWR signal box at Carnforth. It was erected at the south end of the Down LNWR platform to control the LNWR-FR passenger junction and the Up and Down LNWR mainline. An array of signals has been positioned on the new tall LNWR gantry to control the Up mainline and the Lancaster bay. (CRA Collection Ref. LCR05A-02a)

Carnforth circa 1935. A wooden FR three-doll balanced bracket signal operated from Station Junction signal box. It controls the Up goods line to the exchange sidings and the Up passenger line to Carnforth Station. (Rear view looking north-west) (CRA Collection Ref. PA0003)

Carnforth circa 1935. These two tall wooden FR signals were operated from F&M Junction signal box; the right-hand signal has co acting arms for the FR Down passenger line and the left-hand for the Down goods line. F&M junction is just beyond the van. (CRA Collection Ref. PA0004)

CHAPTER TWELVE

Carnforth Station, February 1945. At the end of the Lancaster bay is a LNWR wooden post signal; it controls the exit from the Lancaster bay and carriage sidings to the Up mainline. The large water tank was erected by the LMS in 1944 as part of the improvements to the station water supply. (T. Parker collection)

Carnforth Station Junction, June 1967. A two-doll right hand bracket signal with a rolled steel joist main post. This signal at the end of platform No. 6 controlled the exit from the platform to the FR Down mainline to F&M Junction and the Up F&M line to East Junction. (Philip Grosse)

Carnforth No. 1 Junction, June 1967. A four-doll balanced bracket signal with a rolled steel joist main post. This signal controlled the entrance to the LNWR end of the exchange sidings Nos 1 to 4, the Down goods loops and the Down mainline to Carnforth Passenger Junction. (Philip Grosse)

Carnforth Exchange sidings, September 1969. A three-doll balanced bracket signal with a lattice main post. This signal controlled the entrance to Down goods sidings at the LNWR end of the exchange sidings. (Philip Grosse)

SIGNALLING AND OPERATIONS

Carnforth station platform No. 3, June 1967. A two-doll left hand cantilever signal with a tubular steel post. This signal is electrically operated and controls the Down mainline and the entrance to No's 1 and 2 northern goods loops. (Philip Grosse)

Carnforth Station Junction, June 1967. Two short arm signals under slung from the roof on platform No. 4. These controlled the exit from platform No. 4 to the FR Down mainline to F&M Junction and the Up F&M line to East Junction. (Philip Grosse)

Carnforth FR mainline near Thwaite Farm, June 1967. An early LMS designed all-wood construction two-doll right hand bracket signal with 'splitting' distant arms for the diverging routes at F&M Junction. (Carnforth F&M outer distant signal). (Philip Grosse)

CHAPTER TWELVE

Carnforth F&M Junction, June 1967. A three-doll left hand cantilever signal with a lattice main post. This signal controlled the Up F&M direct line to East Junction, the Up FR passenger line to Carnforth station, and the Up goods line to the exchange sidings. (Philip Grosse)

Carnforth station platform No. 5, June 1967. A tubular post signal with a shortened arm and a route indicator box. This signal controlled the exit from the Midland bay to the Up and Down FR mainlines at Station Junction and the Up F&M line to East Junction. (Philip Grosse)

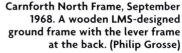

Carnforth North Frame, September 1968. A wooden LMS-designed ground frame with the lever frame at the back. (Philip Grosse)

Carnforth Station Junction August 1985. The 1882 Carnforth Station Junction signal box stands at the end of platform No. 1. The Furness Railway coat of arms can be clearly seen above the large end window. Two 108 class DMUs have been coupled together and are leaving platform No. 2 on a service to Barrow. The colour light junction signal has just been passed and the overhead wires and catenary run beyond platform No. 2 and the 'run-round' line. (CRA Collection Ref. PWR C3813)

CHAPTER THIRTEEN
BRIEF ENCOUNTER AT CARNFORTH

In 1944 Carnforth station was chosen as the setting for the murky and mysterious Milford Junction in the classic British film "Brief Encounter".

Noel Coward and David Lean had started working together in 1939 during the making of the film *In Which We Serve*, in which Lean was chosen to be director's assistant. Noel Coward had become very involved in the theatrical aspects of the film and started letting Lean do more and more of the directing. Recognising that Lean had better knowledge of the technicalities of film production, Coward eventually made him co-director. The film cost £240,000 to make, considerably more than any other film made in 1942; it became the year's most popular film and one of Winston Churchill's favourites. Coward was delighted with the film's success, and suggested to Anthony Havelock Allan that an independent film company should be formed to film his plays. The Cineguild Company was formed in 1942, financially backed by J. Arthur Rank and with David Lean as director, camera man Ronald Neame, and Anthony Havelock Allan as producer. Cineguild's output was not large but it became a respected company among discerning audiences and many of its films became classics of British cinema.

During the early 1930s, Noel Coward had written a series of

A sketch of the Refreshment Room for the film Brief Encounter as it was set up in the London Film Studio at Denham in Buckinghamshire in 1945. I am indebted to Mrs James of Brief Encounter fame who kindly autographed the original sketch, 'Beryl', on the opening of the Heritage Centre in October 2003. (Drawn by Alan Johnstone and based upon a sketch made by Derek J. Kellet, a member of the Friends of Carnforth Station and reproduced here with his permission)

CHAPTER THIRTEEN

Carnforth Feb 1945. The technicians have set up floodlights to test the atmospheric conditions that David Lean wished to capture for the night railway scenes at the opening of the film. Here the engine and crew which were lent by LMS is leaving platform 3, the gantry signal is clear for a mainline train to pass. (Tony Parker collection)

short stage plays, many of which were successfully produced for the theatre by Gladys Calthrop, Noel Coward's Art Supervisor. He also wrote a series of twelve plays specifically to last thirty minutes for the *Tonight at 8.30* programmes, then being broadcast by the BBC. One of the plays, entitled *Still Life*, took place entirely in a station waiting room in which Noel Coward played the part of a doctor and Gertrude Lawrence a house wife named Laura. The twelve plays were bought by MGM who sold them to J Arthur Rank. When Cineguild wanted the rights to *Still Life*, Rank charged them £60 for the rights to the entire twelve plays. With the help of Noel Coward, the 'Cineguild' trio of David Lean, Ronald Neame, and Anthony Havelock-Allan adapted *Still Life* for the cinema, expanding the script (which was ready in October 1944) to provide action beyond the waiting room which became the station tea bar. For cinema release, Gladys Calthrop who had now become a successful designer for Nowell Coward created the title *Brief Encounter*.

Lean directed the film, the soundtrack of which was accompanied by Rachmaninoff's Second Piano Concerto chosen by Noel Coward. The main stars were Celia Johnson, Trevor Howard and Stanley Holloway. The film was about a chaste love affair between a married woman Laura Jesson, played by Celia Johnson, and a general practitioner Alec Harvey, played by Trevor Howard. The wheels of romance were set in motion after he tenderly removed a speck of soot that had lodged in her eye from a passing London-bound express. The film depicts them as very English, highly respected and scrupulously honest. Made in 1945, the film shows no sign of wartime, as *Still Life* was written in 1935 and the film is set in the late 1930s.

Like most films of that time the greater part of the film was

BRIEF ENCOUNTER AT CARNFORTH

Carnforth October 1944. The Cineguild directors visit the station to see how the stations platforms could be adapted for the film. David Lean in the pale coloured coat faces the camera with his producer and art director. The station master in the bowler hat stands with his arms behind him talking to a member of his staff. (Tony Parker collection)

made in the London Film Production studios at Denham in Buckinghamshire, which belonged to J Arthur Rank. The studios had suffered bomb damage during the blitz, and part of them had been taken over by the Ministry of Supply at the time *Brief Encounter* was made. L.P. Williams, the Art Director for the film, had met David Lean when he was a film cutter at the British and Dominion Studios at Elstree. He had recently been invalided out of the Special Operations Executive (SOE), and had called into Denham studios to see what was going on. He was promptly given the job of preparing sketches for the studio sets of the refreshment room, the railway booking office and the Mount Royal apartment which was based upon David Lean's own flat at Mount Royal.

David Lean placed great importance on getting his studio sets right. As the first designs were too 'up-market', they were reworked to give a more provincial and middle class setting. L.P. Williams drew on his own artistic background and on David Lean's impressions of the buffet at Victoria station, to create the *Brief Encounter* refreshment room. In January 1945 the sets for the refreshment room, the railway booking office, together with the Mount Royal apartment and lift, were assembled at Denham studios and filming took place between March and May 1945. During the same months other filming took place outdoors in the nearby town of Beaconsfield, on the lake in Regents Park and outside Mount Royal in London. The walls of the sets were made out of wood, being known in the film business as 'flats'. The flats were individually positioned and could be moved around, so that filming could take place from different positions on the set; the size of the refreshment room set is estimated to have been around 30 feet by 20 feet.

The 'Cineguild' production team had been assigned a London station, possibly Watford Junction, where they could set up cameras and floodlights for filming the night-time railway scenes. The use of a station close to the studio might have seemed obvious, but the Ministry of War and Transport would not give permission for filming as London was still subject to devastating V1 and V2 rocket bomb attacks.

The 'Cineguild' production team now looked elsewhere and according to David Lean chose Carnforth because of the sloping ramps of the subway as David Lean wanted his leading actor and actress to run up and down the slope and not be climbing stairs. Perhaps the murky atmosphere at Carnforth, created by the lingering steam and smoke of passing trains and the ticking of the clock, appealed to David Lean's artistic temperament, along with his fascination for sound and his love of steam engines. The large open concourse of the island platform suited the provincial theme of the film and was definitely an ideal place for setting up cameras, floodlights and stage sets. In October 1944 the directors of the 'Cineguild' company, having selected Carnforth for the film, made arrangements with the LMS Railway to visit the station to make a preliminary assessment.

In a cold January 1945, the 'Cineguild' production team came to Carnforth station to make final arrangements for the film sets. They were accompanied by a stills photographer who took reference photographs for planning the film. There is a good collection of 35mm black-and-white location stills taken by Independent Production Ltd Art Department; these clearly show what the station was like in wartime.

John Huntley, who was acquainted with the work of David Lean during his time at Denham and Pinewood Studios, became

CHAPTER THIRTEEN

Carnforth January 1945. The Cineguild production team at the station in January making final arrangements for the film. The team is stood under the finger board looking towards the clock. It is a cold snowy day and the platform stanchions have been painted white to comply with blackout requirements. (Tony Parker collection)

founder of Huntley Film Archives in 1985. At some point, he recorded an interview with David Lean who made reference to Watford Junction, and based upon this interview the commentary by Huntley in 'Steam in 35mm' states that Watford Junction was used. However David Lean was apparently mistaken with his memories and as there is no record of any stills or filming having taken place at Watford Junction, Carnforth is the correct station, and this has been accepted by Huntley Film Archives.

The London Midland & Scottish Railway had been approached as regards location use. Ever mindful of publicity value, the railway company agreed to the use of the station at no charge to 'Cineguild', also providing a Stanier 4MT 2-6-4, LMS 2540 from Carnforth shed, together with a train crew, guard and two coaches, to create the *Brief Encounter* railway scenes. In addition, the LMS provide two dining-kitchen coaches and staff who served hot meals to the cast and technicians. The coaches were stabled in the 'Lancaster Bay' for the duration of filming. Whilst at Carnforth Celia Johnson wrote to her family, saying that the station was an awful place and the smell of fish permeated the platforms each morning when the fish train was unloaded, and the cast had to sit with the technicians at mealtimes. A copy of her letter is in the 'Brief Encounter Room' in the Carnforth Station Heritage Centre. When they were not filming, the cast and technicians retired to the station refreshment room to drink cups of tea and from which they often rushed out to see the night express trains passing through.

In July 1944, the Ministry of War had reacted to the devastating V2 raids by ordering a mass evacuation of key personnel out of London. When the 'Cineguild' Production Manager E.J. Holding tried to arrange accommodation for the entire *Brief Encounter* cast and crew, he found many of the local hotels had either been requisitioned by the War Department or were full of refugees from southern England. He had to book accommodation in hotels in Carnforth, Ambleside, Lancaster, Morecambe and Bolton-le-Sands. The main stars stayed at the Waterside Hotel at Low Wood near Ambleside, and travelled to and from Carnforth in a chauffeur-driven car to spend ten hours each night on a draughty and cold station platform.

Filming on the station took place between 5th and 16th February 1945, being carried out during the night to minimise disruption to the station activities, with Carnforth becoming the film's murky and mysterious *Milford Junction*. The filming of all the express and local train scenes, the railway carriage scenes, the action around the subway on platforms 5 and 6, and the exterior of the *Brief Encounter* refreshment room were all taken at Carnforth. Filming commenced after the departure of the last local train to Barrow in Furness and finished before the newspaper and fish trains arrived in the early morning.

The sloping ramp of the subway was too far from the real station refreshment room so his art director, L.P. Williams arranged for two wooden 'flats' to be made as replicas of the exterior front and side wall of the set at Denham studios. The 'flats' were taken by lorry to Carnforth, where they were erected along the centre line of the island platform to create a non-exis-

Carnforth January 1945. As well as the Cineguild production team there are a number of service personnel on both platforms 2 and 3. To the right of the picture is the clock and the tall clock cabinet. The winding spindle is just visible at the top of the cabinet together with the 'A' frame portable ladder. (Tony Parker collection)

tent refreshment room for the cast to enter and exit. The south end wall of the refreshment room was about fifteen feet from the head of the subway, and the north end adjoined the book stall. The 'flats' were of lightweight construction and were stored on the station and moved into place for each night's filming.

As the filming took place over several nights, the 1895-built station clock, which played a central role in the film, was fitted with a dummy face and hands to ensure continuity of film-time. The dummy hands and numerals were very different to those on the station clock and Joyce of Whitchurch was missing from the dummy face and it was backlit; another instance of the film-maker's artistic licence.

David Lean, no doubt recalling his childhood memories of steam trains at Paddington, wanted to capture the audience's attention in the opening stages of the film. The LMS Railway issued an official notice to the train crews not to slow down on seeing the floodlights as they approached Carnforth station, but to pass through the station at speed. The crews responded with some fine 'atmospherics' and fast runs, and the opening few minutes of the film captured these effects. David Lean also liked to appear in his own films, a practice he had picked up from Alfred Hitchcock productions. In the first minutes of *Brief Encounter*, as Stanley Holloway (playing a railway porter) crosses the railway lines and climbs on to the platform, David Lean can be seen standing in profile close to the refreshment room.

In his memoirs, David Lean referred to all the night expresses passing through Carnforth as the 'Royal Scot'. Not being a railway enthusiast, his use of the title may be excused, as he was using it generically to describe all express trains passing Carnforth. The station master was described by Celia Johnson as an 'old fashioned gentleman', as he always ensured that the office fire was kept burning so that she could warm herself between filming. The 24th January edition of the *Morecambe Visitor* carried an advertisement asking for applicants to apply for jobs as 'extras' in Noel Coward's new film. A number of local people from Morecambe and Carnforth appeared in the film as supporting cast, and one described Celia Johnson as "a very beautiful woman, only small with delicate features and very sociable".

At the end of filming on the station the production team had to wait two days before the light was suitable in the Lake District to shoot the sequence at 'Middle Fell' bridge near Ambleside.

The film was released in Rochester whilst David Lean was making *'Great Expectations'*. At that time Rochester was a rough town and the audience, comprised mainly of sailors gave the film a derisory response. Upon hearing this David Lean went to Denham to burn the negatives; however when the film reached those audiences it was made for it became a resounding success. The film was released by Eagle-Lion and was shown twice daily for one week beginning Saturday 30th March 1946 at the Tower Cinema, Morecambe, and also in Kendal. Trevor Howard is said to have come to Morecambe on its opening night along with those local people who had appeared in the film as extras. The film reviewer for the *Morecambe Guardian* seemed to have overlooked David Lean's contribution to the film and had this to say:

> *Are you in the film Brief Encounter? There were a few Morecambe people who were accepted as extras when some of the scenes were shot at Carnforth Station. This is another Noel Coward film success staring, Celia Johnson, Trevor Howard and Stanley Holloway.*

For her performance in the film, Celia Johnson (who died in 1982 at the age of 73) gathered both an Oscar nomination and a New York Film Critics Award. In 1946 David Lean received the major prize at the first Cannes Film Festival for best Director and best Original Screenplay, the four hundred journalists and film critics there voting it the best film of the year. David Lean twice received the award of best Director as well as winning twenty eight Academy Awards to become film director *par excellence*. Married six times and knighted in 1984, he helped launch many distinguished cinematic careers. He died in 1991, aged 83.

A TV film adaptation of *Brief Encounter* was made in 1975 by ITC staring Richard Burton and Sophia Loren and directed by Alan Bridges, but this was considered an unqualified disaster.

In 1986, the Lancaster City Council had a number of plaques prepared for heritage sites within the city boundary, and Carnforth station was the obvious site to commemorate the making of *Brief Encounter*. The plaque was mounted on the station building external wall on platform 2 by the door leading to the 'Carnforth Trainmen's Depot'. When the station became unstaffed the plaque was missing, but was later found and put in store in Lancaster City Museum for safe keeping. Originally put up in the foyer of the 'Gateway' building when it opened in 2002 it is now on display in the Carnforth Station Heritage Centre foyer. (The 'Gateway' building was the name given to the main operational ex-LNWR station building following refurbishment, but this is covered more fully in the next chapter.)

To mark the contribution made by Carnforth to cinema history, a second plaque was unveiled on the station by Mrs Margaret James (formerly Barton), of *Brief Encounter* fame, on 6th June 1996. Mrs James had been 19 years old when she auditioned for the film role of 'Beryl', the tea girl working in the station refreshment room. Carnforth station was chosen as the first national venue for a cinema plaque to be presented by Cinema 100, an organisation set up to commemorate the centenary of Cinema. The plaque, in recognition of Sir David Lean and the station's association with *Brief Encounter*, was never put on show until the Carnforth Station Heritage Centre opened in October 2003; it too is now on display in the foyer of the Heritage Centre.

Carnforth 2002. Heritage Plaque. In 1986, the Lancaster City Council had a number of plaques prepared for heritage sites within the city boundary. Carnforth station was the obvious site to commemorate the making of 'Brief Encounter'; it is now on display in the Carnforth Station Heritage Centre foyer. (Alan Johnstone collection and reproduced here with the permission of the Carnforth Station and Railway Trust)

Carnforth 2008. Heritage Plaque. Carnforth station was chosen as the first national venue for a cinema plaque to be presented by Cinema 100. The plaque is in recognition of Sir David Lean and the station's association with *Brief Encounter;* it is now on display in the Carnforth Station Heritage Centre foyer. (Author's collection and reproduced here with the permission of the Carnforth Station and Railway Trust)

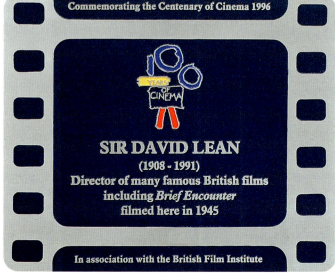

CHAPTER FOURTEEN
STATION REGENERATION

The station is brought back to life through its connections with 'Brief Encounter'. The Carnforth Station Visitors Centre and the Brief Encounter refreshment room soon became established visitor attractions.

When the Carnforth Trainmen's depot closed up in November 1992 the station was closed and the building boarded up. The station fell into disrepair and this view taken in1999 shows what a passenger would have seen whilst waiting for a train on platform No. 1. The large boarded up doorway is now the entrance to the Heritage Centre. (G. Coupe collection/Carnforth Station and Railway Trust Ref A30)

In the 1994, Railtrack North-West advertised the station as being 'To Let'. At the same time the secretary of the Carnforth Chamber of Trade was raising concerns over the future of the station buildings as they were becoming derelict and were giving the township a poor image within the local community. Eventually a Carnforth Station Restoration Project was set up by Peter Yates who was also a member of the Carnforth Chamber of Trade. He obtained from the Chamber of Trade the sum of £100 and this became the starting point for the regeneration of the station, it was recognised that this would require a large amount of capital and the involvement of the local and wider community. It was apparent that to obtain the required amounts of capital Carnforth's connections with the well-known 1945 film *Brief Encounter* would have to be promoted and the station would have to be regenerated as a tourist attraction. This was a positive way forward, and during 1995 articles appeared in the local and national press on Carnforth and its celebrated cinema connections. These mainly commented on how derelict the station had now become, and this heightened public awareness of its plight and its uncertain future.

Fundraising events took place over a period of time and eventually £25,000 was raised, and this was used to prepare a submission to the National Lottery Heritage Fund for funding the project, but they declined, saying it was not their policy to allocate money to community projects. To better represent the project and to be taken as a serious body a small group of Carnforth residents formed the Carnforth Station and Railway Trust Co. Ltd which was constituted at a meeting on 3rd November 1996. Its main aims were: to save the station buildings and bring them back into alternative use: to preserve the site where parts of the film *Brief Encounter* were made and to re-open the now closed ticket office for the benefit of the local community. Arrangements were made to involve the local and national media, and some of the founding members of the Carnforth Station and Railway Trust, together with the fireman of the engine in *Brief Encounter,* went to London to meet the Minister for the Arts. Following this meeting, the profile and aims of the Trust became more widely known, and the local MP for Morecambe and Lonsdale, Geraldine Smith became a keen supporter of the venture both locally and in Whitehall.

Little maintenance had been carried out on the LNWR station building for many years. In 1970 the public rooms had been closed up and with the closure of the ticket office 1988 the whole building was closed up. In 1997 John Pengelly Estate Manager for Railtrack and based at Manchester arranged for a preliminary survey of the building to be carried out to establish the amount of rebuilding that would be needed to bring the building back into use. He provided a great deal of support to the Trust throughout the regeneration process and on behalf of Railtrack saved the station for posterity. During 1998 a feasibility study was carried out at a cost of £30,000, and a planning application submitted to Lancaster City Council. All this attracted local media attention, and throughout 1998 the *Lancaster Guardian*, the *Morecambe Visitor* and the *Lancashire Evening Post* contained a number of articles written by different

CHAPTER FOURTEEN

In 1999 Railtrack placed a restoration notice on the centre bay of the LNWR station building. The wording said: A community-led tourism project based on the original film location for 'Brief Encounter' and Carnforth railway and industrial heritage. (G. Coupe collection/Carnforth Station and Railway Trust Ref. C28)

authors, all having their own 'Brief Encounter at Carnforth station' experience. Even with the heightened media attention, however, the station was still subject to outbreaks of vandalism, and there were instances during 1998 when large areas of reinforced glass in the station awnings and subway screens were badly damaged. Once planning permission was secured, negotiations with Railtrack continued throughout the year, and a project co-ordinator started preparing a number of applications for funding. In an article for a local paper Peter Yates, Chairman of the Carnforth Station and Railway Trust said:

While currently in negotiations with Railtrack, the Trust is finalising several applications for funding including one from the National Lottery Heritage Fund. We have an awful lot of work to do and Railtrack is the only one that can help us. We hope to have the station ready before 2000 but that depends on how soon we get the funding.

In June 1998, the 'Friends of Carnforth Station' (FOCS) was formed to support the Trust, and Railtrack gave 'permission to occupy' the former Station Master's Office in the 1846 Lancaster & Carlisle Railway building. This office was the only habitable room on the station and had been used by British Rail as part of the 'Carnforth Trainmen's Depot', it had been disused and boarded-up since 4th November 1992. It required some renovation before it could be occupied, and on the 12th November restoration work started, and continued over several weeks. The contractors replaced a rotten wooden window lintel, repainted the former office, and replaced the outer door to make the premises secure. A spokesman for Railtrack said:

Railtrack has made space available in the station on the basis that we continue to work together with the Carnforth Station and Railway Trust Co. Ltd.

The FOCS Reception Centre opened to the public just before Christmas 1998, and was manned on most days by two very dedicated local volunteers, Jim Walker and Bill Seddon. The centre acted as a visitors' reception area and as a place where the work and plans of the Trust for the regeneration of the station could be exhibited. It gave the public an opportunity to look at the proposals and to give their opinions, and was visited by both national and international visitors. On 4th January 1999 BBC Television broadcast a ten-minute feature on the Carnforth station clock, as part of a series about famous timepieces. The programme, however, concentrated mainly on the film *Brief Encounter* and the background to 'railway time', with nothing about the clock's history, its workings, or its maker.

The station regeneration project was estimated to cost around £2 million and the first amount of funding came from the Railway Heritage Trust, and this helped the Carnforth Station and Railway Trust to obtain further funding from the North West Development Agency, Lancaster City Council, Lancashire County Council, Lancashire Tourism Partnership, the David Lean Foundation and the Furness Building Society. An application was made to English Heritage but they said that the station was not of historical or architectural importance, nor of listed status.

On 31st May 2000, the Carnforth Station and Railway Trust finalised a contract with Railtrack for a 49-year lease of the station buildings. The Trust's proposals were to refurbish the buildings, and to bring them back into a variety of uses including retail outlets, a ticket office and information centre, together with a 'Brief Encounter' refreshment room and a visitor's centre. The firm Irvine Taylor was appointed to manage the building refurbishment on behalf of the Trust, and a contract given to Leck Construction Ltd of Barrow-in-Furness to carry out the building work.

STATION REGENERATION

June 2001 and restoration work is in progress on the main island platform building. The major work is taking place on of the roof to replace the tiling and gutters so as to make the building weather proof. (Philip Grosse reproduced here with the permission of the Carnforth Station and Railway Trust)

The south bay which contained the Victorian gentlemen's toilet was now surplus to requirements and to maximise their commercial returns the Carnforth Station and Railway Trust decided that a further room for retail let could be made in the bay. The Railway Heritage Trust advised that the south bay should be rebuilt with a gable to match the north end and the

The restored island platform building in September 2005 showing the new doors and windows which were fitted during renovation. In the foreground is the new security railings; the design is similar to that of the railings installed in 1880 around the subway. (Philip Grosse reproduced here with the permission of the Carnforth Station and Railway Trust)

CHAPTER FOURTEEN

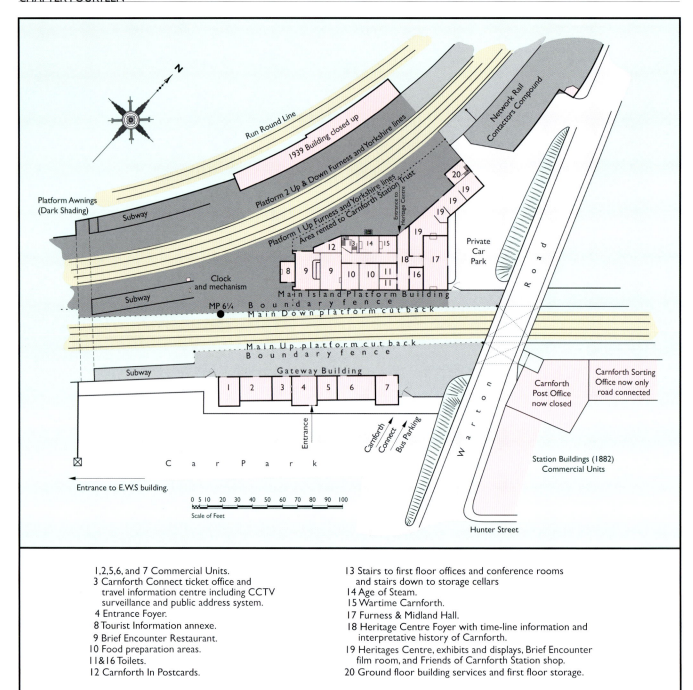

1, 2, 5, 6, and 7 Commercial Units.
3 Carnforth Connect ticket office and travel information centre including CCTV surveillance and public address system.
4 Entrance Foyer.
8 Tourist Information annexe.
9 Brief Encounter Restaurant.
10 Food preparation areas.
11 & 16 Toilets.
12 Carnforth In Postcards.
13 Stairs to first floor offices and conference rooms and stairs down to storage cellars
14 Age of Steam.
15 Wartime Carnforth.
17 Furness & Midland Hall.
18 Heritage Centre Foyer with time-line information and interpretative history of Carnforth.
19 Heritages Centre, exhibits and displays, Brief Encounter film room, and Friends of Carnforth Station shop.
20 Ground floor building services and first floor storage.

Carnforth 2003. Regenerated Station Facilities. A plan of the internal layout of the regenerated station buildings showing the changes made to accommodate commercial units, a refurbished ticket office and the public rooms of the Heritage Centre and Brief Encounter refreshment room. (Drawing prepared by author and reproduced here with the permission of the Carnforth Station and Railway Trust)

opportunity was taken to remove the carriage shed end wall. The first phase of the refurbishment work commenced in June 2001 on the LNWR station building. The whole roof was removed and replaced to make the buildings watertight; the ornate plaster ceiling in the ticket office had suffered extensive water damage and could not be saved, and was completely removed. Internally, the ticket office was completely refurbished, and was equipped with two new service windows and service counters, modern ticket machines, computerised timetables and a CCTV monitoring system which was connected to a camera on the island platform. A train announcement and information system was installed, with speakers on both platforms 1 and 2. A glass screen with sliding doors was erected across the booking-hall, giving access to the platform walkway leading to the subway, and doors were also fitted to the front entrance from the car park. The booking-hall floor was re-laid with heavy-duty Yorkshire stone flagstones. An anonymous donor gave several replica wall lamps, these being hung on brackets on the external building face alongside the walkway. New rooms were created for commercial let, two at the north end and one at the south end of the building, the whole building was fitted out with new double-glazed windows and doors, which were painted externally in dark green. The refurbished LNWR station building was appropriately named the 'Gateway Building' being both the gateway to the station and the whole railway network as well as to the Heritage Centre.

At 10.30 on 14th February 2002, ITV film crews were on location to record the official opening of the 'Gateway Building' by Geraldine Smith, it was broadcast both nationally and locally on the evening Granada TVs 'Look North West' news, also from nine till noon Radio Lancashire's Jim Bowen broadcast live from the Radio Lancashire's bus which was parked in the station forecourt.

July 2003. The Brief Encounter refreshment room replicates the London Film Studios setting. The wooden counter, cash till, tea urns and bottle opener were all individually made. The large mirror on the rear wall is based upon the round top windows of the film set. (Philip Grosse reproduced here with the permission of the Carnforth Station and Railway Trust)

The new 'Carnforth Connect' rural bus service commenced running on the same day. It was subsidised by the Lancashire County Council, and had its own bus and dedicated parking bays in the station car park. It ran to and from Milnthorpe via Warton, Yealand, Silverdale and Beetham. In 2008 LCC stopped funding the service and for the next two and half years it was funded by regeneration, but the service terminated at Yealand. The LCC took it back in 2010 and contracted it to Kirkby Lonsdale Coaches who also terminated the service at Yealand. In 2011 it passed to Stagecoach and it is now included in their daily service to Silverdale.

During March 2002 the operational part of the station was refurbished by Railtrack North-West as part of the Station Regeneration Programme. The railway and public offices in the LMS 1939-built Furness line platform building were closed up and the building face treated and painted, and the roof waterproofed. The subway was refurbished and the station lighting upgraded both in the subway and on platforms 1 and 2. New glass was installed in the island platform awning, and the steel work repainted.

The existing BR platform security fencing on the cut back edges of the closed mainline platform was to be replaced by Railtrack (now Network Rail) as part of the Station Regeneration Programme; however the Trust was able to secure the work with a lower tender. The new security fencing was put up along the entire walkway, parallel with the cut back platform edge. This fencing was much more substantial than its predecessor, having tubular posts and panels based upon the original FR panels enclosing the three sides of the subway on platform 1. It was also painted dark green, with some parts of the panels painted red to match the 'Gateway Building'.

The Carnforth Station and Railway Trust initiated a search in 2001 to find the original 1895 station clock face and the clock mechanism, which had been situated in the tall wooden cabinet still extant on platform 2 but minus its doors. The search was made by Peter Davies a member of the Friends of Carnforth Station, also a local railway historian. He eventually traced the missing parts to a clock and watch collector and repairer who lived in Twickenham; he had purchased the clock faces and mechanism at a railway auction with the intention of renovating it. After careful examination, the Trust bought the mechanism from him and returned it to Carnforth. The wooden cabinet and circular clock case were removed from the station for renovation by local craftsmen at a cost of £25,000. The circular clock case was refitted with the original clock faces and hands and movement mechanism and on its return was re-hung from the station roof. The long case clock operating mechanism was re-assembled in the tall wooden cabinet, which now had doors with glass panes, so that the mechanism could be viewed. Finally the external horizontal operating rod was fitted between the cabinet and the clock case. On Friday 5th July 2002, the clock was officially restarted at 15.00 jointly by the MP for Morecambe and Lonsdale Geraldine Smith and the Mayor of the City of Lancaster Eileen Blamire.

External refurbishment on the island platform buildings continued throughout 2002 with much of the roof being replaced and the fitting of new double-glazed windows and doors. During renovation of the roof, the northernmost chimney stack on the 1857 part of the building collapsed and was not replaced. Some of the floors were replaced and internal walls rearranged to provide a more convenient layout for the new

CHAPTER FOURTEEN

At 15.00hrs on Friday 5th July 2002, the refurbished clock was officially restarted. Standing under the clock with Jim Walker the clock warden are Steve Clarke and Janet Hall who attended as Trevor Howard and Celia Johnston look-a-likes. (Alan Johnstone reproduced here with the permission of the Carnforth Station and Railway Trust)

17th October 2003, the opening of the Heritage Centre. Peter Yates, Chairman of the Carnforth Station and Railway Trust Co. Ltd and MP for Morecambe and Lonsdale Geraldine Smith a great supporter of the project, take a celebratory walk down the subway with a flute of champagne. (G. Coupe collection)

Visitor Centre. Inside the Furness and Midland waiting hall the partitioned walls and ceiling dating back to LMS days were removed to reveal the carved wooden beams of 1880. The beams were cleaned and varnished and the planked roof timbers painted white, the finished restoration gives the room a light and spacious aspect. Public toilets were installed, and as part of an agreement with Railtrack (now Network Rail), they were made available for the travelling public during the Visitors Centre opening hours.

With the regeneration of the island platform building completed, the opening day of the Carnforth station visitors centre took place on 17th October 2003. During the morning the TV film crews had been interviewing Mrs Margaret James (formerly Margaret Barton) who played the part of 'Beryl' in the film *Brief Encounter*, and now the last surviving member of either the cast or crew. With its connections to the film, it was the Brief Encounter refreshment room that was at the centre of media and public interest. At 13.00 the tape was cut by Mrs James, and the Visitors Centre declared open to the public. Surprisingly *Brief Encounter* has many fans and followers and at each of the main events Steve Clarke and Janet Hall has come along to brighten up the days proceeding as look-a-likes for Trevor Howard and Celia Johnston. Peter Yates, Chairman of the Carnforth Station and Railway Trust said:

> It is a great achievement by so many people, that here we are on the eve of the reopening of famous tea room and having Margaret Barton doing the honours, is a real and proud link with Carnforth Station past.

The regeneration project had cost nearly one and half million pounds and for his voluntary work to the community and as the Chairman of the Carnforth Station and Railway Trust Peter Yates was awarded the MBE.

The Brief Encounter refreshment facility is able to seat eighty persons, in the original railway refreshment room and the adjacent railway dining room. The refreshment room has been set out to replicate the London Film Studios film set with its counter, stove, furniture and other fittings, and the refreshment room and dining room tables and chairs replicate the style of the 1930s. The Visitors Centre (renamed the Heritage Centre in 2010) contains photographs, memorabilia and exhibition areas, a railway history room, a memorial room and a shop. The Furness & Midland waiting hall has been set up as a functions room for the local community and as such attracts a variety of events and private functions. The Bateman Gallery (named in memory of Myles Bateman a founding member of the Trust) is used as centre for visiting exhibitions.

The FOCS volunteers are in attendance during the Heritage Centre's opening hours and look after the gift shop and act as guides for individual and party groups. The island platform building is thus once again serving the wider community and continues to be a lasting reminder of the railway age in Carnforth.

On 17th October 2008 an anniversary ceremony took place to mark the first five years of successful opening, over that period of time many visitors both national and international have passed through the Heritage Centre and the visitors book contains many complimentary remarks. Between 2008 and 2012 the centre had attained eight main awards for tourism, community rail partnership and volunteer achievements; by the time this book is published the 10-year anniversary events will also have come to an end.

CHAPTER FIFTEEN

THE MODERN ERA AND RAILWAY PRIVATISATION

With the final BR years and the introduction of rail privatisation (a process taking three years from April 1994), new services, new liveries and new train operators appear at Carnforth, and the station sees a growth in passenger numbers.

Carnforth 25th July 1979. A Derby class 108 DMU stands in platform 1 on a Barrow–Preston working, the unit is in BR corporate blue with full yellow ends. There is still accommodation for 1st class passengers and bars have been fitted across the door windows for operating north of Maryport on the line to Carlisle where there were limited structural clearance. A class 25 diesel locomotive stands in the Midland Bay. (Rock Battye)

Carnforth lost its through daytime service to and from London Euston on 1st May 1977, with the withdrawal of the 07.45 departure from Barrow and the 18.05 departure from Euston, although sleeping car services continued to run, providing Carnforth with overnight services to and from the capital. To compensate for the loss of the direct service, BR introduced the so-called 'Preston shuttle', replacing a number of Barrow-Preston workings with loco-hauled formations, usually handled by Class 47/4 locomotives and modern Mk 2 stock, although other workings were normally diagrammed for Class 108 DMUs.

This service, of five loco-hauled trains daily each way, saw one working extended to Crewe in the 1979/1980 timetable; the first indication of the development of these workings. In May 1980, a further two workings provided Carnforth with departures to Liverpool Lime Street at 08.33 and 11.55, although there were no balancing workings from Merseyside until the May 1982 timetable. Carnforth gained additional destinations in this 1982 timetable, with an early morning DMU diagram at 05.54 to Manchester Victoria, and a loco-hauled working at 08.32 to the same destination.

The May 1983 timetable brought significant changes to Carnforth, with the withdrawal of the Euston sleeping cars to and from Barrow on 10th May; it appeared that this would be the end of the town's direct rail service to the capital. This change coincided with the introduction of new Mk3 sleeping cars, and an associated rationalisation of the UK sleeper network. However, it appears that an overnight service continued for some time after this, in the form of an unadvertised Mk2 air-conditioned carriage. This was attached to the rear of the 02.30 Crewe-Barrow newspaper train after having been detached from the 23.45 Euston – Liverpool Lime Street at Crewe. It is not known when this working finished, but it was certainly observed at Barrow in December 1984.

May 1983 saw Carnforth gain a new direct Inter City service to and from Nottingham, one result of the reorganisation of the former Midland lines Nottingham-Glasgow service the previous year (see later in this chapter). In the Up direction, this working left Barrow at 10.16, called at Carnforth at 11.00, and reached Nottingham, via Manchester Victoria, at 14.52. The train returned from Nottingham at 16.40, calling at Carnforth at 20.22 and arriving in Barrow at 21.21.

May 1985 saw the surprising re-introduction of a Barrow-London Euston through train, running as a complete train throughout; the joining and splitting of portions at Preston now a thing of the past. Leaving Barrow at 07.25 and calling at Carnforth at 08.16, the train arrived at Euston at 12.11, with the buffet-restaurant car open from Barrow and with the southbound traction change from diesel to electric taking place at Lancaster. Northbound the train left London at 18.05, calling at Carnforth at 21.45. The same timetable saw the 05.54 ex-Carnforth DMU to Manchester Victoria extended to York, via Todmorden, Bradford, and Leeds.

Two years later, in May 1987, this day service was withdrawn for the final time (apart from the short-lived retention of a northbound Sunday-only working from Euston), only for BR to replace it with the re-introduction of a sleeping car service from Barrow to London Euston, leaving Carnforth at 22.49 and consisting of the relatively new, air-conditioned Mk 3 sleepers. There was, however, no corresponding northbound working out of the capital. Equally interesting was the introduction, for the first time, of the new Class 150 'Sprinter' DMUs on Lancaster-Barrow workings, but on Sundays only. These units were in the process of replacing life-expired DMUs, some of which dated back to the 1950s. By the following year (1988), Class 150/1s were making weekday appearances at Carnforth on some of the Barrow-Manchester Victoria workings.

The Class 150s, however, were only the first stage in the DMU replacement programme, and with the introduction of the faster Class 156s in 1987, BR began to dispense with loco-hauled stock for longer distance working. In consequence, in May 1989, a two-car unit, complete with refreshment trolley, was diagrammed for the 15.30 Colchester-Barrow, the 327½-mile journey taking nearly 7½ hours, with Carnforth not reached until 22.01. After overnight stabling in Barrow, the Class 156 departed on the 07.04 Barrow-Cambridge, another lengthy trip of 274½ miles; calling at Carnforth at 07.56, Cambridge was reached at 13.21. Such through workings, with no changes involved, appealed to many people, particularly the elderly.

Retrenchment was to come in May 1990, however, with both the final withdrawal of the Euston sleeping cars and the disappearance of the long-distance Class 156 workings, leaving Carnforth with 17 Up and Down Furness line workings daily between Barrow and Preston (although half a dozen continued through to Manchester Victoria). Most of these workings were handled by Class 150/1 DMUs and by the unpopular Class 142 rail-buses, although Class 31/4 locomotives with hauled Mk 2 stock handled some of the Manchester workings. Both locos and carriages carried 'Regional Railways North West' livery, as BR Sectorisation was now firmly in place as a prelude to privatisation.

With the privatisation structure in place by April 1994, creating 'passenger train operating units' (as predecessors to the later Train Operating Companies), the May 1994 timetable reflected

Carnforth 20th April 2002. Three generations of motive power. A steam special with 6233 Duchess of Sutherland in LMS maroon livery waits in the loop for a 'Pathfinder' special hauled by two class 50 diesel engines in BR corporate blue livery to pass on the Down mainline. A Virgin train of Mk 2 stock headed by a class 86 electric locomotive runs past on the Up WCML. (Alan Johnstone)

THE MODERN ERA AND RAILWAY PRIVATISATION

this with Furness line services shown under the business heading of 'North West Services'. Carnforth benefited massively from this change; not only were there twenty workings to Barrow (one less in the reverse direction), but almost half of these started from, or terminated at, the new Manchester Airport station. Carnforth was now within 100 minutes of an international airport. These airport workings were handled by Class 156 DMUs, now with 'Regional Railways North West' branding and offering trolley refreshments throughout their journey. The 'shadow franchise' handling this service was still a subsidiary BR company 'North West Regional Railways Ltd'.

In October 1996, the Train Operating Companies (TOCs) had been established, although 'North West Regional Railways Ltd' was still a BR subsidiary company. By 1997, North Western Trains had been awarded the franchise, this was a partnership between First Group and 3i, but by May 1999, it had been renamed 'First North Western'. Service levels remained virtually unchanged, although some of the non-airport services calling at Carnforth originated from Liverpool Lime Street and Morecambe, one of the latter using the Bare Lane-Hest Bank single line. A number of these services continued to be diagrammed for the unpopular Class 142s, generally considered unsuitable for longer journeys such as those to and from Liverpool.

In 2000, the two-car Class 156 DMUs were replaced on Manchester airport services, by new air-conditioned Class 175 two- and three-car 'Coradia' units: some of these sets received names, one being *Brief Encounter* in 2003, to mark the reopening of the eponymous refreshment room at Carnforth. Other services on the Furness line, however, remained in the hands of the older Class 150/1 and Class 142 diesel units.

On 1st February 2004, a new franchise, 'Trans Pennine Express' (jointly operated by First Group and Keolis) took over several major passenger services in northern England, including the Manchester Airport to Cumbria workings. Initially using the existing Class 175s on a sub-lease from First North Western, TPE replaced these from mid-2006 with new three-car Class 185 DMUs, built in Germany by Siemens. In December 2004, Northern Rail, a consortium of Abellio and Serco, took over other 'First North Western' services; for commercial purposes, the company is known simply as 'Northern'. It continues to operate Furness line services with a mix of Class 156, 153, and 142 DMUs.

On the Yorkshire line to Hellifield, Skipton, and Leeds, most developments during the later BR years were bound up with closure proposals for the Settle-Carlisle route. In May 1978, there were seven Leeds-Morecambe workings, with eight in the reverse direction; all except one of these took the single line between Hest Bank and Bare Lane, thus avoiding reversal at Lancaster. Services were handled by Class 101 Metro-Cammell DMUs (usually of the three-car variety), and also by Class 110 and Class 104 units. From Carnforth, Leeds was reached in just under two hours and Morecambe in a little under ten minutes.

It is unclear whether this relatively low service frequency would have been further reduced by a BR proposal in the late 1970s to single the Carnforth-Settle Junction line, close Wennington signal box, and build a new box at Bentham to control a passing loop there. However, these plans never came to fruition, as, in 1982, BR instigated the run-down of the Settle-Carlisle route, diverting the existing Nottingham-Glasgow InterCity services to run via Manchester, Preston, and the West Coast Main Line.

BR's plan was to provide a fast service over the Leeds-Skipton-

3rd March 2005. In 2000 new air-conditioned Class 175 two and three car 'Coradia' units in new First North Western livery started to operate the Barrow-Manchester airport services. Some of these units received names one being 'Brief Encounter' in 2003 to mark the reopening of the Carnforth refreshment room. Unit 175002 is passing the 1882 signal box on the 12.12 from Barrow. (Alan Johnstone)

CHAPTER FIFTEEN

Carnforth- Lancaster route, in order to allow Yorkshire passengers travelling to Scotland access to frequent WCML services. As a result, a number of the seven return services between Leeds and Morecambe (09.33 and 12.00 ex-Leeds, and 12.39, 14.35, and 19.31 ex-Morecambe) ran non-stop from Skipton to Carnforth, reducing the Leeds-Carnforth journey time to around 90 minutes. Additionally, the quality of the trains themselves was improved, with these fast workings being handled by the more comfortable Class 123 Trans-Pennine and Class 124 Inter-City DMUs, with both first and second-class accommodation.

In May 1984, there was a further service improvement, with the introduction of Class 31/4 locomotives and five Mk1 carriages. There were three return services in each direction which started from Hull, on the west side of the Pennines and terminated at Lancaster, a further four return services to and from Leeds served Morecambe via the direct Hest Bank – Bare Lane route. This loco-hauled service continued into the May 1985 timetable, but reverted to DMU operation (using three-car Class 108s) in September that year, because of track wear on the Wennington line caused by loco-hauled operations. The May 1986 timetable indicated that the service was once more becoming 'self-contained'. Westbound, the only Hull departure was at 07.40, while eastbound only the 06.10 ex-Morecambe ran beyond Leeds, arriving in York at 10.10; this latter working ran non-stop between Carnforth and Leeds. All services once again served Morecambe, although via a reversal at Lancaster rather than taking the direct Hest Bank – Bare Lane route. By 1988, with the reprieve of Settle & Carlisle services, workings to and from Leeds, reverted to 'all stations' and by late summer, uncomfortable three-car Class 144 DMUs were diagrammed for Leeds-Carnforth-Morecambe services.

The service frequency was reduced from seven to five daily return workings in May 1990, and to four the following year, with the 06-36 arrival in Carnforth only originating at Skipton (although with a good connection from Leeds). Once again, all Yorkshire line services terminated at, or started at, Lancaster. Pending privatisation in 1994, as part of the 'Regional Railways North East' shadow franchise, brought no immediate changes in service levels to the route, although 1996 saw a return to five workings each way, using a mixture of Class 142 and Class 156 DMUs. In March 1997, 'Northern Spirit' (a brand-name of transport company MTL) became the Train Operating Company, but retained the name 'Regional Railways North East' until May 1998.

In 2000, MTL ran into financial difficulties, and the franchise was re-let to Arriva and re-named 'Arriva Trains Northern'. Perhaps because of this, the DMUs on this service reverted to the unpopular Class 144s, now reduced to a two-car formation, although the Leeds-Carnforth journey time was once again around the 90-minute mark. In December 2004, the franchise was let to the previously-mentioned Northern Rail. The service retained its five daily workings each way, but has now (in 2012) been reduced to four each way, although since 2009 the more comfortable Class 150/1 DMUs have been used for some of the workings on this route.

With the closure of Carnforth's main-line platforms in 1970, any passengers wishing to travel north or south on the West Coast Main Line have had to catch a Furness or Yorkshire lines train to Lancaster and change there. May 1970 saw Euston-Glasgow trains passing through Carnforth with Mk 2 carriages and double-headed by Class 50 locomotives, in order to maintain accelerated schedules during WCML electrification between Crewe and Glasgow, completed in May 1974. Following completion of electrification, Class 86 and the more powerful Class 87 Bo-Bo locomotives handled Anglo-Scottish workings which, by 1975, saw the allocation of new Mk 3 passenger stock to some services.

Rail privatisation in the 1990s saw the InterCity West Coast franchise allocated to 'Virgin Trains' (51% owned by Virgin Group, with the remainder by Stagecoach Group) in March 1997. It was also allocated the Inter-City Cross-Country franchise, producing the sight of Class 253 HSTs passing through Carnforth on the main line. Having ordered a new fleet of tilting trains for the Euston-Glasgow services over the sinuous WCML, Virgin placed the first Class 390 'Pendolinos' in service in 2001, with delivery completed by 2004. These units have a design speed of 140mph, although the WCML has a maximum line speed of 125mph. For cross-country services, Virgin ordered a fleet of Class 220 and Class 221 'Voyager' DMUs, the latter also equipped with tilting technology, although this franchise, together with most of the diesel units, passed to Arriva Group in November 2007.

By the start of the 1980s, freight over the Cumbrian Coast route was in decline, with many industrial sites and coal mines, once a guaranteed sources of traffic were being closed, although nuclear flask traffic to and from Sellafield remained relatively stable. At the end of the decade, the October 1989 to May 1990 Working Timetable showed a Monday Only flask train to Heysham calling at Carnforth for a crew change at 13.46, with a Monday/Wednesday Only flask train to Bridgwater (Somerset) calling at 19.03; this latter train served Valley (Holyhead) on Tuesday and Thursday Only. Haulage of these trains was in the hands of double-headed Class 31 locomotives, then liveried in 'Coal Sector' grey. Wagonload traffic was catered for by the daily 'Speedlink' working from Workington to Willesden Brent Sidings (London), which changed crews at Carnforth at 20.23. All these trains changed crews in the Up Furness and Yorkshire platform, but the following working, a Maryport to Crewe Basford Hall MGR coal train changed crews in the Carnforth Down and Up Goods Loops at 21-45. Permanent way workings also featured in the WTT, with empty ballast working to Penmaenmawr Quarry in North Wales leaving the sidings at Carnforth F & M Junction at 08.10, and a loaded departmental working for Crewe Basford Hall at 23.00.

The demise of the 'Speedlink' network, in 1991, saw separate freight workings for the Glaxo (Ulverston) tanker trains to Ellesmere Port, and the Albright & Wilson (Whitehaven) bulk powder workings destined for Willesden; these ran on Saturdays Only, and arrived at Carnforth at 08.31 and 11.24 respectively. Both of these services were discontinued in 1994, the Maryport coal workings (which utilised both Class 47 and later Class 60 motive power) having ceased on the 31st March 1993.

The only traffic over the Furness line from Carnforth is now connected with Sellafield and with the British Nuclear Fuels Terminal at Barrow. In 1995, as British Rail privatisation was almost completed, BNFL set up a new company to operate trains from the various UK nuclear power stations and started running them to Sellafield. This company, known as Direct Rail Services (DRS), planned to purchase locomotives made surplus by the February 1996 creation of EWS Railways, (the merger of most of the former BR freight companies). Initially EWS refused to make any sales, forcing DRS to purchase Class 20 locomotives made redundant following completion of the Channel Tunnel construction. It was only after Government intervention that EWS was forced to make redundant traction available on the open market. Today DRS operates a mixed fleet of Class 20, 37, 47, 57, and 66 locomotives, all of which make appearances on flask trains passing through Carnforth.

THE MODERN ERA AND RAILWAY PRIVATISATION

Carnforth 15th August 2008. Class 144 two car-unit 144006 runs into platform No. 2 with the 10.45 Morecambe to Leeds. The overhanging 1939 concrete platform wall and roof are very apparent as is the 25kV catenary which runs above the lines of both platforms No. 1 and No. 2. The unit is in the later Yorkshire Metro livery. (Alan Johnstone)

Carnforth 21st June 2010. A Northern Rail class 156 unit number 156444 runs round the curve of platform No. 1 on the 17.43 Barrow to Preston service. The unit was named 'Councillor Bill Cameron' on the 26th September 2009 at the Community Rail weekend held at Carlisle Station. The regenerated station buildings and the picket fence enclosing the platform area of the Carnforth Station Heritage Centre are forward of the train. (Alan Johnstone)

CHAPTER FIFTEEN

Carnforth 21st June 2010. Class 144 two car unit 144006 now repainted in the livery of Northern Rail comes off the Carnforth Curve into platform No. 2 with the 16.39 Leeds to Morecambe. The fenced off area belongs to Network Rail contractors Carillion and occupies the site of the Midland bay. (Alan Johnstone)

A sad loss to Cumbrian Coast services passing through Carnforth came on 28th September 1991, when the long-standing Whitehaven-Huddersfield Travelling Post Office (TPO) was withdrawn. In its last years of operation, this train left Whitehaven at 18.50, but ran non-stop through Carnforth at 21.04. The train's schedule allowed for the same set to be used for the return working, which left Huddersfield at 01.05. In this direction, it departed from Carnforth at 04.29, seven minutes being allowed for exchanging mails here, with a Whitehaven arrival at 06.46. This train was normally handled by Class 31/4 locomotives in its final years of operation, although Class 47/4s were relatively frequent substitutes.

Goods traffic to and from Yorkshire using the Carnforth-Wennington line also saw a decline in this period. The direct F&M line between Carnforth F&M and Carnforth East Junctions lost its last scheduled traffic with the withdrawal of the 22-56 Wath-Workington coal working and the return 16.20 Barrow-Healey Mills empties in 1976.

Carnforth 17th July 2008. 5690 'Leander' arrives at the north end of platform No. 2 at 18.05 with a train of West Coast Railways stock. Further WCR stock can be seen in the background in front of the wagon repair shop. (Alan Johnstone)

THE MODERN ERA AND RAILWAY PRIVATISATION

Carnforth 24th June 2013. A First Trans Pennine class 185 'Pennine' unit on the 11.00 Manchester Airport to Barrow-in-Furness service enters platform No. 1. (Alan Johnstone)

Freight, via the Carnforth Curve and the Carnforth-Wennington line, still continued to run, notably liquid ammonia rail tank traffic between ICI's Haverton Hill plant and the same company's fertilizer plant at Heysham Moss. The loaded train left Teesside at 03.40, returning with the empty tanks at 11.26, and there was no crew change at Carnforth, Skipton rail men handling the train to Heysham and return. Normal motive power was a pair of Class 31 locomotives. In January 1985, there was a change to this service, the train running from, and returning to, ICI's Immingham plant on Tuesdays and Fridays, and Haverton Hill on other weekdays, as before. Early in 1986, ICI announced that fertilizer production at Heysham was to cease, and the last of the empty tanks was returned to Haverton Hill on 22nd April 1986, the train being worked by a Class 47.

Skipton had facilities for handling bitumen by rail; it was served by a portion of the Stanlow oil refinery-Heysham Harbour working, the bitumen tanks being scheduled as the 19.15 Heysham Harbour – Skipton and 22.25 return working, usually in the hands of a Class 40 locomotive. By 1982, the frequency had reduced, running as the Tuesday/Thursday Only 09.00 Heysham Harbour-Skipton, returning direct to Stanlow refinery at 14.50. The Heysham Harbour oil terminal closed in January 1983, after which the bitumen tanks working became an out-and-back service from Stanlow to Skipton, still running via Carnforth. In September 1986, the service was reduced to Tuesdays Only, and the last bitumen working, behind a Class 37, ran on 23rd February 1990. This marked the end of scheduled freight traffic over the Carnforth-Wennington line, and at the time of writing (2012), the current condition of the track makes it unlikely that scheduled freight traffic could be reintroduced without major expenditure.

Despite worries about the loss of work in the run-up to privatisation, Carnforth was selected as one of the depots retained for working ballast trains, as 'Trainload Freight West' one of BR's freight sectors had decided to reduce the number of other such depots. The problem was the costs associated with maintaining both mainline traction and route knowledge. From 1994, Carnforth men extended their route knowledge to include the following lines: Preston-Colne, Gannow Junction (Burnley) – Hebden Bridge, Hebden Bridge – Manchester Victoria, Manchester Victoria – Guide Bridge and Euxton Junction, Preston-Blackpool North and South, and the Settle-Carlisle line. This guaranteed work for several more years for local train crews, until the closure of Carnforth Train Crew Depot in 1997. Carnforth also provided crew for the short-lived 'Enterprise' freight service, running from Workington to Warrington. A driver travelled from Carnforth to Workington by passenger train, before working the freight service back to Carnforth, handing over there to another Carnforth driver for the rest of the journey to Warrington.

When BR freight sector 'Transrail' was taken over by EWS on 24th November 1997, the administration building at Carnforth was handed over to EWS as a signing-on point for a small number of train crews who were operating the long-distance coal trains to and from the Hunterston terminal in Ayrshire, Scotland, and a number of UK power stations. In early 2006, the few remaining EWS coal trains to run with HAA wagons still stopped in the South loops to change crews, but following the change-over to high capacity wagons, these coal trains ceased to stop at Carnforth. The signing-on point closed and the building was taken over by Network Rail in 2007. Today, on the West Coast Main Line, major operators EWS (now DB Schenker), Freightliner, and DRS operate non-stop through Carnforth station, generally using a mix of Class 66 diesel and Class 90 and 92 electric locomotives.

Despite the regeneration of Carnforth station, and the growing number of rail passengers, it is highly unlikely that Carnforth will regain its main line platforms, as an increase in stopping trains would hinder the large number of 125mph services now using the WCML. Nonetheless, compared with the dismal days of the 1990s, when it seemed that the station would only remain as a basic unstaffed halt, today's restored Carnforth presents a pleasant experience for rail users, and its retention of a traditional station's facilities seems assured.

CHAPTER FIFTEEN

Carnforth 30th September 2011. A DRS flask train runs into the station at 13.23. Heading the train is 37423 'Spirit of the Lakes' in DRS compass livery and at the rear of the train is 37087 'Keighley and Worth Valley Railway' in the earlier DRS livery. (Philip Grosse)

Its 'goodbye' to Carnforth as the sun sets over the south end of the station, a 'Thunderbird' Virgin recovery diesel engine sits in the loco siding alongside the Up and Down goods loops. (Alan Johnstone)

INDEX

INDEX OF PRINCIPAL PERSONAE

Items in **bold type** *indicate a photograph, map or plan*

Ahrons, E.L. iv
Allan, Anthony Havelock 15, 152
Andrews, Eamon 107
Barlow, Peter 5
Barton, Albert Edward 4, 28, 29, 31, 50, 53, 54, 55
Barton, Edward D. 28, 31
Bateman, Myles 162
Bellie, Andrew 65
Bessemer, Henry 28
Bintley, Job 5
Blamire, Eileen 161
Bowen, Jim 107, 161
Brassey, Thomas 6
Bridges, Alan 156
Brindley, James 3
Brogden, Alexander 15
Brogden, John 14, **19**
Brown, Joe 105
Brunlees, James 14
Burton, Richard 156
Cadman, David 107
Calthrop, Gladys 152
Camden, William 2
Carruthers, Elisabeth 17
Clarke, Steven 162, **162**
Clarkson, R. 48, 49
Coward, Noel 151, 152
Cragg, Agness 29, 53
Crossley, J.S. 22
Davies, Peter 161
Duke of Bridgewater 3
Duke of Buccleuch 14
Earl of Burlington 14, 16
Earl of Lonsdale 16
Errington, John 14
Erving, James 4, 31, 54
Garnet, William 14
Gretton, John 105
Hague, John 5
Hall, Janet 162, **162**
Halliwell, Elizabeth 52
Halliwell, John 19
Hartley, John 50
Harty, Russell 105
Hitchcock, Alfred 155
Hodgson, R.O. 33
Holding, E. J. 154
Holloway, Stanley 152
Houghton, W.D. 28
Howard, Trevor 152, 155
Hughes, Christopher 106
Huntly, John 153
James, Margaret (formerly Barton) (Beryl) 156, 162
Johnson, Celia 152, 154, 155, 156

Larmer, George 5
Lawrence, Gertrude 152
Lean, David 151, 152, 153, 155, 156
Locke, Joseph 5, 14
Longsdon, Robert 28
Loren, Sophia 156
Lucas, John 2
Marindin, Francis 60
McAlpine, Sir William 105, 108
McClean & Stileman 14, 22
McClean, Frank 22
Milland, Ray 105
Milner, Martha Dunham 52
Neame, Ronald 151, 152
Orr, H.I. 54
Pasley, Major General 7
Paley, E.G. 60
Pemberton, Robert 28
Pengelly, John 157
Poictevin, Rodger de 1
Preston, William 50
Ramsden, James 15
Rank, J. Arthur 151, 152
Rastrick, John 5
Rennie, John 3
Rigg, John 47
Seddon, Bill 158
Septon 2
Slater, William 27, 51
Smith, David 108
Smith, Geraldine 161, **162**
Smith, Lt Colonel Sir Fredrick 5
Stainton, Robert 50
Steele, George 65
Stelfox, James 47
Stephenson, George 5
Thompson, James 3
Tite, Sir William 7
Walduck, Herbert John 27, 28, 31, 42
Walker, Jim 158, 162
Webb, F.W. 52
Williams, L.P. 153
Wilson, Colonel H.D. 44
Worthington, J.B. 6
Worthington, S.B. 14
Yates, Peter 157, **162**
Yolland, Colonel 14

INDEX OF SALIENT LOCATIONS

*Items in **bold type** indicate a photograph, map or plan*

Albert Street	51
Alexander Road	52
Alma Terrace	49
Annas Bank	52
Bank Terrace	52
Barrow-in-Furness	24, 36, 37, 109, 112, 166
Bessemer Terrace	51
Birmingham, Alabama USA	31
Bodeltone	1
Bolton-le-Sands	5, 14, 42
Booker Terrace	52
Bridge End	22
Burton & Holme	3, 9, 138
Canal Place	50
Carlisle Terrace	49
Carneforth	1
Chellet	1
Chreneforde	2
Cinderbarrow	107
Coate Stones	1, 23
Crag Bank	4, 5, 6, 37, 101, 107, 112
Dalton-in-Furness	13, 27
Denham	153
Dudley	30
Edward Street	48
Egremont	39
Galley Hall	1
Grange-over-Sands	11
Grayrigg	5
Grosvenor Terrace	52, 99
Hagg Lane	26
Hall Gate Farm	9, 14, 47
Hall Street	51
Haws Hill	5, 52
Hazel Mount	42, 52
Heilbronn, Germany	108
Hest Bank	14
Hewthwaite Terrace	52, 99
Heysham Harbour	101, 122, 169
Heysham Moss	112
Heysham	39
Highfield Terrace	52
Hill Street	52
Hodbarrow	39
Hunter Street	52, 53
Hunting Hill	9, 93
Keer Bank	14
Kellet Road	49, 50, 54, 55
Kendal	3, 5
Kirkby-in-Furness	13
Lancaster Road	49, 52, 53, 54, 99
Lancaster	3, 4, 5, 6, 7, 49, 61, 80, 87
Laund House	49
Long Haws Hill	29
Lunds Field	49
Main Street	52
Manchester	27, 103
Market Street	49, 52
Mary Street	51
Midland Terrace	50
Mill Lane	6, 7, 8, 47, 51, 109
Milnthorpe	11
Morecambe Harbour	22, 24
Mount Royal	153
New Street	48, 52
North Road	56
Oxford Road	47
Oxford Street	52
Pedder Pots	55
Pond Street	52
Pond Terrace	52
Preston	4, 5, 105
Ramsden Street	52
Red Court	52
Robin Hill	49
Rose Grove	100
Russell Road	52
Sands Lane	42
Scotland Road	50, 52
Scout Quarry	44
Shore Road	26, 65, 67
Silverdale	14, 27
Skerton Mill	5
Snape Lane	9
Stainton Street	51
Stanley Street	52
Station Buildings	52
Tebay	93
Tewitfield	3, 11
Thwaite Gate	4
Toad Plud	29
Ulverston(e)	13, 15, 19. 109
Warton Crag	44
Warton Grange	**50**, 51
Warton Road	23, 31, 52, 59, 62, 65, 77, 112
Warton Sands	42
Warton	7
Wennington	9, 77, 127, 128
William Street	51
Windermere	22
Yealand	9, 11

Author's Acknowledgements

I have been working on this book for well over ten years and during this time many people and institutions have contributed to the research I have done. In addition I have been fortunate to have had access to the Cumbrian Railways Association's photographic collection as well as a number of individuals who have allowed me to use photographs from their collections. I would, however, like to single out one person who without his help and considerable time in tutoring me the drawings I have done in this book would not be to the standards they are and for this I would like to record my grateful thanks to Alan Johnstone.

I am extremely grateful to Peter Robinson for spending time in selecting photographs and captions from the CRA photographic collection and to Howard Quayle for the careful reading of the original text and for making available historical information – in particular the re-writing of chapter fifteen, and to Leslie R. Gilpin for further historical information.

I am indebted to Mrs Pat Jackson for the use of her grandfather's photographs from the Rathbone collection.

I thank Rock Battye and Alan Postlethwaite for their particular skills in proof-reading the text and making corrections and Clive Holden for reading chapter seven and allowing me access to his own historical information on the township of Carnforth.

I am grateful for the information gathered and the time given by the Carnforth Railway Recollections team: George Nightingale, Pat Woof, Brian Dowthwaite, Alf Butler, Malcolm and Ian Thistlethwaite and Dave Balderson.

Peter Holmes has been very helpful with information on industrial engines also Russell Wear of the Industrial Railway Society and finally Jonathan Wignall for facts and figures on the industrial workings of the ironworks.

Ken Harper has given me valuable assistance when I needed the correct technical terms used in railway signalling and Ron Herbert, also a professional railwayman, for allowing the use of his collection of working timetables and other information on the operational workings of the local railway.

The Staff of the Lancashire Archives Preston and the Lancaster and Morecambe reference libraries and the National Archives at Kew have all been very helpful in giving me access to their archive material.

Alan Gunson has done a wonderful painting for the cover of this book and I appreciate the time he has spent on this work.

I appreciate the help of Alan Johnstone who arranged the first draft and the endeavours of Trevor Preece who exercised the design and production phases of this book. My thanks go to Alan Postlethwaite who has generously given me access to the Barrai Books sales system and offered to help with its distribution.

Finally I acknowledge the unending support I have had from my wife Tina throughout all the years I have been working on this book.

Philip Grosse

Bibliography

Publications consulted in the preparation of this book

Ahrons E.L. *Locomotive and Train workings in the latter part of the 19th Century.*
The Furness Railway (No. 1). *Railway Magazine*. October and November 1921.
Bowtell Harold D. *Over Shap to Carlisle*. 1983.
Brownlow Kevin. *David Lean. A biography*. 1996.
Carter Michael. *The Golden Monarch. A Biography*. 1962.
Charlewood R.E. Notable Railway Stations, No. 23 Carnforth (London & North Western Furness Joint). *Railway Magazine*. February. 1904
Gradon W. McGowan. *Furness Railway Its Rise and Development: 1846-1923*. 1946
Farrer W. The Domesday Survey of North Lancashire and adjacent parts of Cumbria, Westmorland and Yorkshire. *Transactions of the Lancashire and Cheshire Antiquities Society*. 1901
Kelly David. *The Red Earth-The Iron mines of Furness*. 1998
Lean Sandra and Chattington Barry. *David Lean. An Intimate Portrait*. 2001.
Reed Brian. *Crewe to Carlisle*. 1969
Pape T. *The Washington's and the Manor of Warton*. Garner Medalist 1924.
Roger Burt. *Hunts Mineral Statistics*. Published by the University of Exeter. 1983
Railway Magazine. Published monthly. 1897 to present day.
Tee David F. *The Midland Compounds*. Published by the RCTS. 1962.
Steamtown *The first 20 years*. Published by the Museum. 1989
Various records held in the Lancashire Records Office, Preston.
Trade directories and other reference books held in the Lancashire Records Office, Preston, Lancaster Reference Library and Morecambe Reference Library.
Various records held in the Records Office, Barrow-in-Furness.
Various editions of the *Lancaster Guardian*, *Lancaster Gazette* and the *Morecambe Visitor*.

Carnforth Station Standard Bearers

Carnforth Station and Railway Trust Co. Ltd was formed in 1996. It is a Registered Charity (No. 1061179) with a board of volunteer directors. The aim of the Trust is to preserve the station buildings and to ensure their continuing management and maintenance so they can be used both commercially and for the use of the community. To ensure continuity of these aims the Trust has taken a ninety-nine year lease on the buildings and works with other local authorities and the national network owner to make Carnforth station a friendlier and welcoming facility. The Carnforth Station Heritage Centre has four galleries and is '*The Home of Brief Encounter*'. It is situated in the refurbished island platform building along with the 'Brief Encounter' buffet. For further information visit the Carnforth Station Heritage Centre website: www.carnforthstation.co.uk or send email: sdo@carnforth-station.co.uk
or visit facebook.com/CarnforthStationHeritageCentre.

The Friends of Carnforth Station (FOCS) has national membership which supports the aims of the Trust. A dedicated number of Friends attend the Carnforth Station Heritage Centre during opening hours as volunteers. For details of membership send a stamped address envelope to Hon. Membership Secretary: Carnforth Station Heritage Centre, Warton Road, Carnforth, Lancs LA5 9TR.

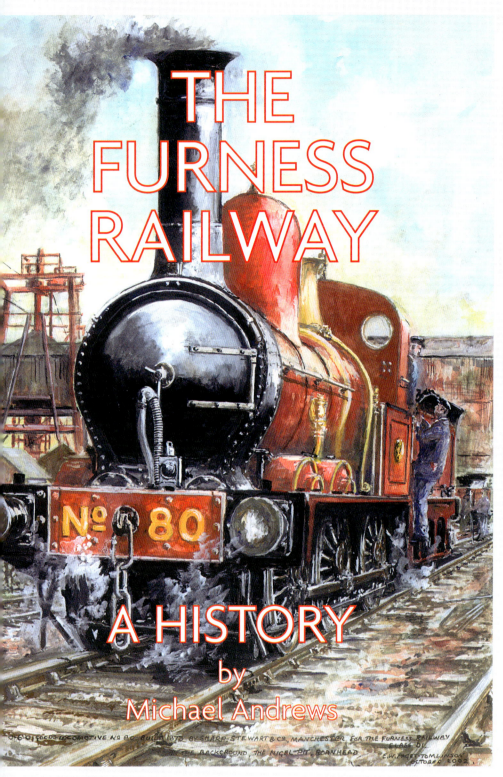

THE FURNESS RAILWAY

A HISTORY
by Michael Andrews

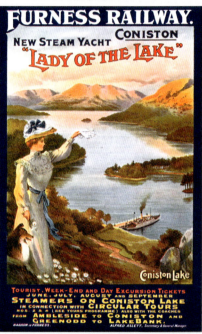

A pair of one of the Furness Railway's series of attractive postcards promoting the merits of visiting the Lake District by the railway. The posters for their Lakeland Tours were so popular that a collector's set of six postcards was produced — two are featured here and the remaining four are on pages 187 and 188 in the book. (Private collection)

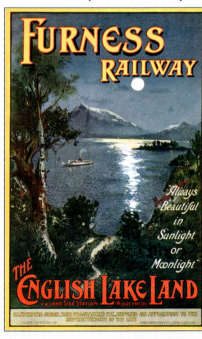

Copies of this earlier publication of ours remain available from booksellers or direct

£25.00

Barrai Books
Barrow in Furness

ISBN 978-0-9569709-0-9

Tel: 01229 468069

Website:
www.barraibooks.co.uk